THE
LONG
GAME

Moving from Failure to Profit

ROD MOORE

Printed in the United States of America
Published by Braughler Books LLC., Springboro, Ohio

First printing, 2020

ISBN: 978-1-970063-58-5

Library of Congress Control Number: 2020905814

Ordering information: Special discounts are available on quantity purchases by bookstores, corporations, associations, and others. For details, contact the publisher at:

sales@braughlerbooks.com

or at 937-58-BOOKS

For questions or comments about this book, please write to:

info@braughlerbooks.com

Braughler™
Books
braughlerbooks.com

Praise for *The Long Game*

The premise of Rod Moore's book is in the title. You may ask, "How might that be?"

The answer is in becoming and applying strategic leadership to very challenging business conditions and opportunities.

Rod takes the reader on a continuous learning and professional development journey. Sharing his experiences begins with developing self-awareness by recognizing your personal strengths and positive attributes, as well as being brutally honest with your shortcomings and the need to move from what we are to who we will become.

Rod's style is straightforward, direct and transparent He is in essence paying his learning and experiences forward. He describes his knowledge in all aspects and facets of leading a business enterprise. His story illuminates many of his strengths, but his uniqueness lies in developing into a strategic thinker and utilizing that competency to lead organizations to success. You will learn how he grew from being an individual contributor and technical expert to become CEO distressed of companies, leading them to profitability.

Rod openly lays out what experiences have allowed him to be a successful business executive. He does not direct or tell you what you must do to achieve success. He doesn't tell you that you must do these five things or ten things to be a great business leader and so on. He respects your intelligence and time by letting you take what may help you from his experience. How refreshing!

Personally, I give *The Long Game* my positive and strong recommendation because of its meaningful content and insightful down-to-earth presentation. If you are open to challenging your current beliefs and mindsets about leadership experiences, I believe after reading this book, you will be encouraged to deeply reflect and possibly change your path forward.

Jerome J. Behne, December 15, 2019

Jerome J. Behne is currently an Executive Coach and Development Consultant with twenty plus years of managing a successful private practice. Prior to coaching and consulting work, Jerome was VP of Human Resources at US Precision Lens Inc., a subsidiary of Corning, Inc. retiring in 1998.

Contents

Introduction

"The Long Game." No doubt you are probably already asking, "What kind of title is that for a business book? It sounds more like a book about sports." You are partly right. The book isn't about sports, although there are times business can seem as dirty as a football game played in the rain at Lambeau Field, as up and down as match play at the FIFA World Cup, or as serene as a smooth water day during the Sydney to Hobart Yacht Race. *The Long Game* is, in this case, a descriptive metaphor for how you can take a failing organization and lead it to success. Bottom line: No long game plan = potential career failure.

I started my career as far away from the corner office as possible with some college and four years of military service in satellite communications. Little did I know that would be to my advantage. At first, I went to work in R& D as the proverbial jack-of-all-trades who could fix or create anything. I also had a huge chip on my shoulder, as I saw promotions going to people who were using my inventions or innovations to further their own careers. This seemed to me an injustice — so many other people were climbing the corporate ladder and I was being left behind. But until I realized I was part of the problem, I would continue to be left behind. Instead, I made the decision to do the required changes needed to make advancement possible, but it took time, mentorships, opportunities, and soul-searching.

Had I fully understood the work I was getting myself into, not to mention the changes required, I am not sure now that I would have taken on rebranding myself. If nothing else though, looking back I will say it was an interesting adventure. What made the ride even more striking was my decision to work with troubled companies rather than established ones. It's also when I realized that my business classes didn't give me much to work with when it came to turning companies around. Come to think of it, neither did the many business books on the market or classroom professors with no real business experience. Hmmm... Time to add author to my hodge-podge of skills.

Over the years, I came to understand that working with stressed companies requires business savvy, human understanding, strategic thinking, and the need to be planning backwards and then forward to five or ten years out. Typically, none of your management team will be doing this, as they tend to focus on the day-to-day. Keeping the *Long Game* in the back of your mind at all times will help you succeed, especially if you are new to corporate management. You also have to constantly think about budgets, equipment maintenance, current/future markets, board-of-directors, unions (if you have one), innovation, customer satisfaction, and employee personality types. The key to success is knowing which type to hire and when. Were you taught some/all/none of these things in business school? I know I wasn't.... They are just some of the many facets needed for success.

There is no magic list of 10 items or habits that makes a successful leader and I make no effort to provide any. This is not a book on short-cuts to being successful like some new fad diet. It is a walkthrough, based on my experiences, of the steps needed to turn around an entire manufacturing company, department by department. The intent is to help you understand what to look for and why certain decisions must be made and when.

If you are taking the time to read this introduction, you are prob-ably looking for ways to improve your business skills, competencies, and understanding. You will find what you are looking for in *The Long Game*. Keep in mind, though, that this is a unique business book loaded with actual experiences that you can learn and benefit from. It is not, however, one-size-fits-all....

My style of communication is direct, straightforward, and even blunt at times. As my staff can tell you, if you don't want the answer, do NOT ask the question. Is that your style? Something to think about since it colors my approach to people and business. That said, I am sharing my approach to leading a business. I am not going to tell you how to do things, but will encourage you to utilize your judgment as to what will work best for you, whether a tried-and-true method, or something unique, but perfect for your success.

Preface

The Long Game Preface — or what you can expect in addition to the unexpected. A business "How-To" book usually provides high-level guidance on what you can do to improve your ability to run or start a business. These often use techniques employed by such notables as Lee Iacocca, Steve Jobs, or Michael Bloomberg. They might even include references to medium or small companies, though usually it's the biggies that get the mention. This is NOT what *The Long Game* is about. Instead, if you have been tasked with turning around a struggling company, regardless of size, or have recognized that your company is on the verge of becoming a struggling company, then this book is for you.

Where do you start first and why? Finance? Human Resources? Manufacturing? Sales? There are valid reasons for picking any one of these departments but, if you don't look beyond the immediate, you might focus on the wrong one. Can you go wrong fixing HR first? Probably not, unless manufacturing is turning out a poor quality product. Having the right staff in place won't solve the immediate problem of unhappy customers and returns, which impacts cash flow and the resources needed to resolve maintenance or sourcing issues which may (or may not) be the cause of poor quality. Confused? Welcome to the "Where do you turn first while keeping your eye on five years down the road club?"

As I've discovered during my career, you must focus long-term even if no one else is. If you know where you want to be, you can work backwards to focus on the immediate fixes that will help you down the road. You can concentrate on hiring the right kinds of people for now, for two years, or for six years down the road. These are real-life examples of where to start, and why — covering every department you will probably have in a manufacturing environment. And if you don't work in manufacturing, the info might still come in handy.

Work in a union shop? The chapter on how to handle unions could be very helpful come contract negotiation time. I mean, how often do you hear about contract negotiations being completed in 16 hours instead of weeks, with the union basically coming away with very little? Read my book for "the rest of the story."

CHAPTER 1

Hard Work Only Gets You Halfway

After working at my present company for about a year, it became obvious to me that we had hired some exceptional people who could have a bright future. Many were straight out of college or had only been working 10 years or less. It seemed to me that this group of people, if trained right, could become leaders sometime in the future. The idea was simple enough: spend a few months working with them as a team and then have them lead some of the future projects I knew were going to be started. In this way, they would get practical individual experience, bring issues back to the group, and then work them out as a group. Not only would this teach them how to manage and lead people, but it would also create a bond with their fellow colleagues, thus making them a formidable team. Even though they would be running individual teams, this would ensure that the biggest issues would be brought back to the main group where I could help guide the decision-making process. This would enable me to manage aspects of the projects behind the scenes while ensuring project managers stayed focused, moved forward, and avoided poor decisions. They gained experience and I kept control, allowing me to slowly release the reins to them as they progressed. Everyone wins: brilliant.

I had never done this before, so I was uncertain as to how to either get started or how the plan would progress. I decided the best way to get things going was to let them take the lead by having them ask questions that would help guide the direction of this training. I clearly recall the first question I was asked by an exceptionally bright individual in the group. She wanted to know how I made it to the top. This shows you not only have to be prepared to be asked personal questions, but also to be ready to answer them honestly. This was a fair question and I asked her what her concern was. She told me that she felt this training I planned to provide was great, but she felt she would never get to a point that she might someday run her own company.

She felt everything was against her. She was an engineer, had not gone to what some consider the best schools, knew no one in a position who could help her, and yes, she was a woman. I told her that we would start from the last concern and move forward. I informed her I had two daughters who were both very successful in their careers, so it is less about being a woman and more about what you bring to the party. Can you manage a project, make good decisions, strategically plan for the future, manage people, get things done with the resources you have, or do you just make excuses for failing?

I can imagine that being a woman does have complexities that being a man simply does not. For example, when a man gets upset, or is upset with someone, he is viewed as hard, tough, and difficult. If a woman exhibits the same behavior, she is called a bitch. There is no denying this, in spite of all the harassment training out there, and it still an attitude society needs to work on. However, for the most part, women who use the excuse that they cannot make it because they are a woman is unacceptable.

How do you then answer her remaining concerns? The questions are valid, the concern is real, and the last thing I wanted to do was to give a superficial answer or blow her off. Since I had never done this before, this was all new for me. I told everyone to wait 10 minutes and I would be back. I then printed my resume for them to read. I told them that they should notice three things on my resume. First, that I had started my career at the bottom as just your average manufacturing guy, nothing special. The second thing was my education. Not only did I not go to the best schools, but I also got my master's degree late in the game. I decided to head for the top late in life and still made it — so it can be done, but you will need help. The third thing I told them is that for most of my life I was an engineer, specifically R&D, and still became very successful.

I was on a roll, so I blazed ahead and told them I thought being an engineer had been an asset to me rather than a hindrance. I explained that there were a number of factors to help you get to the top, if that is where you want to be. Your education, your abilities, drive, and the willingness to recognize open doors, take risks, and a certain amount of luck.

Everyone in life has a certain amount of good and bad luck, and how you deal with this, to a very large degree, will decide how far you will go in life. Let's face it. If you graduated from a big-name school and were lucky enough to meet some important people while there, you have a better chance of climbing the corporate ladder than those without connections, education, charisma, or drive. In fact, the odds of someone without those benefits (all or some) making it to the top are not only slim, but getting slimmer by the minute. Accepting that it takes hard work, some luck, and a willingness to take risks to successfully climb the ladder does help compensate for benefits you don't bring to the table when starting out in the business world.

Those of us just starting out know we must work and fight harder if we want to move up. Those who have made it as presidents of companies succeeded because of the effort they were willing to make along the way and, probably more key, the risks they took. I looked at the group and asked if they thought I came to work every day with an attitude, one that told everyone around me that today we were going to make a difference, and that the day would end with the company being a little closer to our goal than it started out. They all felt I did.

Finally, I wanted to address her concern about having an engineering degree and whether that would hold her back. The short answer is "maybe." If you are a mediocre engineer, then it will not help you at all. In fact, it could hurt your career in the long run. This is because you are going to need other people to believe in you and invest in you and who wants to back a loser? This young woman had an engineering degree, but, really, the degree doesn't matter if people look at your work and don't see anything special. Why would they want to take the risk and waste money investing in you? On the other hand, if you stand out, if people see real promise in your work, and if you are better than the average engineer (lawyer, accountant, scientist, etc.), then they are generally more willing to risk investing in your future. Does the fact that you have an engineering degree hurt you? Well, that frankly will depend on you. If you are any good, you will take responsibility for your mistakes, learn from them, get better, and move forward. Because of my background, I had the ability to knowledgeably participate in technical discussions with those in electrical engineering, mechanical engineering, programming, and a variety of other disciplines. In fact, my weakest subject was chemistry and knew I needed to beef up on this since that is the main thing we did at this company.

The next question asked was "As good as you seem to think you are, why did you leave engineering and move into management?" Again, a personal question, and again, a question that I would normally never answer. Honestly, what business is it of theirs? Months later when reflecting on this conversation, it dawned on me that it was 100% their business because I had formed this group, told them I saw potential in them, and asked them to ask me questions. So, yeah, they had every right.

There are examples that can be verified and googled to show how good I was at my job. I started life out in the Army, where I got my first taste of high technology when I trained in satellite communications/maintenance. I was just your average enlisted person with a mostly unremarkable military career. What I did learn from the military though was how to forge teams and make them function. I also learned that knowledge is where you find it, so pay attention and find something you can learn from in everything you do and become better at what you do. I have never regretted joining the Army because it forged, in many ways, the person who I am.

When I left the military, I started working in the plastics industry and was sent for training for six months. The knowledge gained from this training lead to many great discoveries in my life. After the training was done and we all returned to corporate headquarters, I developed many new techniques and improvements for the company, using my new education, to make our product the best in the industry. I was happy because I knew then that developing new processes was in my blood and I could be good at it, so off I went.

I left the company for a variety of reasons and went to another plastics company where the interesting part of my life really got started. They hired me because I knew how to coat plastic and, like many people, thought all plastics were the same. They are not. Coating this type of plastic made my previous job child's play, but I was determined to develop a coating for this plastic — and did. This got me noticed because we were the only company in the world that could coat this type of plastic and so our market share in the industry skyrocketed. People got promotions, not me, but other people, but at that time other people getting the promotions and pay raises did not bother me.

At this time, I was only interested in impressing myself and what I was paid a lesser concern. It was a strange time in my life where I was discovering how good I might be and the main thing I wanted was to be left alone. Nothing pleased me more than showing off something new I had done, not a small incremental step, but a leap forward, and the other engineering groups had nothing impressive to show.

I developed other things in the company, which I discuss in other parts in the book, but I was good at my job and the company profited from my work. Others around me got the promotions and I got left alone. For a while this was enough but in the end, I grew to resent it. I looked at the group sitting in front of me for mentoring and said, in this case, my engineering background got me noticed and being seen is an absolute must if you want to get ahead because you will need help, just as I did.

An open door

Most of us will always need help on this never ending, winding, potholed road to the top. The help we need varies by individual, but the key is to not be so proud that you do not accept help when it is offered. But it's more important to recognize the help when it is offered.

I recall in the mid '90s when my boss called me into his office for my annual review, which was strange since he normally only did reviews every five or six years. He told me I was a diamond in the rough and that I had potential, but needed help to achieve it. I recall thinking to myself that I was doomed. This assessment was coming from a guy who yelled at people during meetings, who called them every name you can imagine, and who ensured before he was done that everyone in the room knew the person he had yelled at was worthless. He would throw things at people which, somehow, in the '90s he could get away with. I have to say he was the worst supervisor I had ever had and, today, he would be fired for creating a hostile work environment. No kidding. Ugh.

In any event, he believed I might become a good department manager but needed some help. Really? What could he possibly know about me that I didn't and why, given his management style, would I ever believe him? Needless to say, I walked out of his office, tossed my appraisal in the trash, and headed back to my office to design more coatings. Mistake! It would take several years before he approached me again with an offer to help. Years lost because I did not understand he was offering to help and did not recognize the door that had been opened. My ego just would not accept that I did need help if I wanted to move ahead.

I looked at my group, stating that this was a major point each and every one of them needed to understand. He opened a door for me. He presented me with my first bit of luck because he was willing to help. What I said to this group was, "That moment for me is the same one as I am offering you right now — today. Like me, all of you have to decide if you will walk through the door I have opened or walk away."

What I did not understand then, and did not fully understand for years, was that he was being completely sincere. He was not the idiot I believed him to be. Instead he had come to recognize many of the issues he had, putting him in a position to see in me what I could not. He had offered to help someone whom he believed in, someone whose chip was as big as a 2 x 4 but was not still ready to be helped.

In all fairness, people typically do not respond well to others they do not respect, and, at this point in our journey together, I did not respect him. How do you respect someone who goes out of their way to publicly humiliate you, or who throws things at you? That said, I did need help to start a transition from a technical career to one in management but was too blind and too proud to even recognize the help that was being offered. Also, I had not reached the point in my life where I resented other people getting bonuses and promotions from the ideas and developments I was making.

Like so many people, I believed that I should be judged by my ability and the work I had done. A very good friend of mine, one of the smartest people I know, has never been promoted in the 20 years he has been in the workplace. He believes he contributes to the company, has many good ideas, and helps in any way he can. He is not a bad employee, but he is an individual contributor. He works best on projects that require small or no teams. People do not like working with him because he is a poor communicator and people who work with him always feel left out. Could he change? Yes. Will he change? Probably not. Unfortunately, he does not see a need to change, firmly believing that the reason for his lack of promotion is not him but the people around him.

Many times, people see in you the very issues they themselves have. Before you roll your eyes and put this book down, think of the people you have seen screaming at their children for talking too loudly. You walk away and say to yourself "I wonder where they learned that from?" as you smirk and shake your head. The very traits we often hate are the ones we ourselves have. We recognize in others even if we do not see it in ourselves.

My next opportunity for stepping up the career ladder came a year later when I was complaining to my boss (yes, the same one) about all the careers being made from the work I was doing. In the late '80s there weren't any good thin film coatings that could be used on plastics. I set out to develop new techniques that would allow people to coat these plastics with high-quality coatings without damaging the product. This had never been done before and it took me almost a year to develop a methodology still being used today. This, in turn, gave the company the highest quality products on the market, and the company began to grow at a rate which almost killed us trying to keep up.

You might say "OMG, they must have appreciated your work and really took care of you!" You would be wrong on both accounts. They put me in an out-of-the-way office and pretty much left me alone. All the while, I watched other people get big bonuses and promotions based on my development work. Like the friend referenced earlier, I was viewed as an individual contributor who did not work well with others — and saw no need to. Consequently, even though I was doing great work, no one wanted to work with me. What I had to come to terms with was that this was not their problem. It was mine.

I looked around the room and thought many of those sitting in front of me had the same problem. They were good at their specific task and felt this should be all that was needed to advance. I told them this makes you good at what you do, nothing more. It does not mean you will be good at anything else. Just because you excel at what you do now does not mean the world or your company owes you a thing. The company is looking to see if you can become the asset they now need, or if you will just spend your time whining. People are there who will help you, but they need to feel you are worth helping, and it is your job to convince them.

This is how I explain it to people. I am left-handed and the world is set up for right-handed people. Am I owed a left-handed world? No, I need to fit into the world the way it is. I know left-handed people who complain because their company would not buy them a specific left-handed device, like scissors. Per the law in most states, a company must accommodate special needs for the disabled (desks that raise, wheelchair access, etc.), but they don't need to buy random items to accommodate a left-handed employee. This is one of the many challenges to working, regardless of the industry, but it does mean these complainers are often viewed as difficult, pointless complainers. Stop thinking anyone owes you anything because the bottom line is, they don't.

But back to the story. I went to see my boss, who was VP of Operations, and explained to him why I was not happy. To this day I will never forget his response. "Why are you telling me this? I offered to help you and you walked away. Do not complain about the way you are being mistreated when you were too stupid to walk through the door I opened." This is from the same guy who used to throw things. He was right and, because he was a very gracious person, he opened the door again and the work began. I have no doubt he was doing this for several reasons, the primary one being that he did not want me to quit. We made a deal that I would continue to invent new methods and products and he would help me become successful. While I sat in his office, we came up with a plan.

- Step 1: Get the chip off my shoulder.
- Step 2: Take a hard and honest look at myself.
- Step 3: Figure out what needed to change, what I could do, and what I would need help doing.
- Step 4: Be willing to take feedback, both positive and negative.
- Step 5: Stop complaining and start taking responsibility for myself and my actions.

This is important and something I tell people who ask me how to improve their career. If you are unwilling to take an honest look at yourself, to see your flaws, and make the necessary adjustments, you are doomed.

And so it begins...

The first thing the company did when they realized I was serious about improving myself as an employee was to send me to Eckerd College in Florida for a management course. This course forces you to look at and (hopefully) change and improve yourself. That's the first step to becoming not just a manager, but a *good* manager. This course does not teach you better management skills, but focuses on what others see in you and what changes you need to work on if you hope to improve yourself.

Here's why this makes sense. If you are driving along a highway and have no idea where you are, then all the maps in the world will not help you. You need a reference point to mark where you are and who you are if you intend to move forward. Who knows, maybe you are perfect and can skip this step? Initially, I was sure I was. Funny what happens, however, to that perfect, prickly individual if you are openminded enough to not only hear, but also consider how your co-workers perceive you.

Going to Eckerd College for a 7-day class was more involved than just showing up. Prior to the start of the class, questionnaires were sent to six subordinates, six peers, and six senior people in order to provide a 360 snapshot of how co-workers and management saw me. I had to complete testing as well, including questionnaires, etc., prior to the start. Each student is also assigned a group with which all assignments are done. At the end of the week, you take the feedback result you feel the strongest, angriest, or surprised about and ask your team if they agree, or not, and to give you specific examples.

For example, one of the issues that showed up in my testing was that if I did not get my way, I withdraw from the group. I asked my team how this could be, given that I work within a company where there was no real way to withdraw. Obviously, I was looking at this situation from a literal perspective and not from an attitude perspective.

Almost every team member provided an example of something that happened during the week where the team had decided something was not what I wanted and I withdrew for hours. Basically, I was there physically, but was no longer actively participating. I am not sure if I was sulking or if I felt unappreciated, and really it makes no difference. If I was not participating, then I served no purpose. In fact it is even worse, as I was taking up space and getting in the way.

It is one thing to see a score on a piece of paper but quite another to hear it from people you've known only for a week who could show you evidence corroborating what your co-workers said. They had no reason to lie to me, nothing to gain by lying, and they would never see me again, , so you must assume they were telling the truth. This hit me like a bombshell and I was crushed.

I still struggle with this trait on a daily basis, but the point is, I know it's an issue and I deal with it rather than give in to it. Once you know you have this tendency, you look for it, and when you see yourself beginning to act this way, you force yourself to engage.

Step 2 — Take a hard look at yourself
The big lie

It does not matter what you have to say, what you think of yourself, or how good you think you are. The only thing that matters is who everyone else thinks you are. Always remember this, what others think matters, and yes, I know that is not what you are told, but people have lied to you. If people think you are a snob, they will treat you like a snob regardless of how you think of yourself.

I believe the biggest lie people tell is that one should be honest with oneself and not worry about what other people think. A bigger pile of horse crap could never be told. How other people see you is incredibly important and to a very large degree will determine how far you go in life! If you meet someone and they have the impression you are not very bright, do you honestly think they will come to you for advice? If people feel you are always stealing their ideas to impress the boss, do you think they will want you on their team or will even talk to you? In every case, you might feel they are wrong, that you are honest, that you never steal people's ideas, but do you really think how you see yourself will matter how they treat you when you interact?

Let's say you went to work in a bad mood. For whatever reason, this day you had a new hire starting and you snapped at them. You can be the nicest person in the world 99% of the time, but you just set the stage for how this new person will work around you. In the eyes of this new employee, you are not a nice person and people need to tread lightly around you. While you may apologize the next day, and be forgiven, the workplace experience for the new hire may even be copacetic now. While that might be true in time, over the next several weeks, he or she would be deciding who is the real you.

I have often read that people get hired because of their ability, while 70% get fired because they cannot get along or don't fit into the culture. This fact is so vital, so overlooked, and even worse, too often ignored by both employees and employers. The problem is you have been told your entire life not to worry about what other people think.

The point of all this is that perception is reality and people will treat you how they perceive you. Not what you are or think you are, but the way you have been perceived. Bottom line is that employees who cannot get along, who do not or will not fit in, are not wanted.

Step 3 — What you need to change and who can help
Going it alone guarantees failure

It does little good to find out you are a complete ass if you will not change. Change can come in many forms, even though most people will tell you that by the time you are 30, you are pretty set in your ways. I would say you are set in your ways earlier even than 30, but, regardless of your age, there might be things you could do better. The question is how?

The test results I received from Eckerd showed that not only am I an introvert (which I had suspected), but that I had maxed out the chart for introversion. I am the guy you see having a conversation with a plant during parties or the guy who stays on the back porch in order to discourage people from talking to him. During meetings I would be the guy who would sit behind the largest person in the room, hoping not to be seen.

Conversely, if you talk to people I work with, they will tell you I am an extrovert, giving numerous examples to prove their point. The point is that while you cannot escape from who you are, in my case an introvert, you **can** play the role of an extrovert for periods of time. Think of it as the acting career you never knew you wanted or needed.

Any introvert will tell you that we have no idea how to make small talk, which is why we talk to plants at social gatherings or nurse our drinks hunched over at the bar. We're great at smiling and nodding, but not so much with conversation.

When I started on this journey, I got the help from my wife, and your help could come from a spouse, partner, relative, or friend — someone who has your best interest at heart. She would write conversation starters on 3 x 5 cards that I could use for small talk, starting with a generic "How are you?" Based on the response, I would use either side one of the next card: "Good to hear." or "I am sorry to hear this." Sounds simplistic, but sometimes you need to go back to the beginning in order to get comfortable talking to people about topics you don't know or care about, but that they do.

Think about it. Small talk is having a conversation with someone about something insignificant that will be quickly forgotten by both of you. What will not be forgotten is that you had the conversation which, if an opening conversation, will be used to determine if both parties like/can tolerate each other. Thus, this conversation is both insignificant and important all at the same time.

I worked with these "cue cards" for months before I felt comfortable enough to step out on my own to attempt acting as an extrovert. My wife and I went to bars, clubs, dancing, house parties, etc. Anything that put me in a social setting where I had to interact with people. Again, my wife was vital in this since she would keep an eye on me, and when I struggled, she would come and help me out. This is true even today.

Over time I became more at ease in social gatherings, and, if you saw me now, you would never know this was a learned trait.

You might say small talk is unimportant because you both are discussing something insignificant, but at the same time both of you are trying to figure out who the other person is. If the other party decides they do not like you, then your business opportunities with them are now gone. A door shut because you had no idea how to make the other person feel comfortable around you. Again, not their problem, but yours.

The point I am making here is clear. I figured out some way to work on or around these undesirable traits so that I would demonstrate a manner that people would view as positive. This did not happen overnight and was not easy, but I wanted to move up the management ladder and this was the price tag. Remember, everything in life has a price tag — everything — and if you are not willing to pay it, then do not expect the results you are hoping for.

I should clarify that all the changes I made boiled down to creating a superficial persona. The introverted "me" is still there. The extrovert "me" is nothing more than what I want the world to see. I have what I call a 95% rule, meaning that if I can maintain this facade 95% of the time, it was a good day. The other 5% of time people need to overlook, and will, or attribute it to me having a bad day.

Why this rule? Simple. When you get really stressed, feel boxed in, or believe everything is going poorly, you will revert to the real you. For me, that means becoming authoritarian, pushing back, and upsetting people. This is because introverts typically tend to lash out inappropriately rather than quietly fading into the background, as you would expect them to. As a result, I will not ask for advice. I will tell you what I want, when I want it, and you had best not contradict me. Hence, the need to present the extrovert "me" to the world.

This change did not happen overnight, but over time with practice and feedback. It is no different than learning to play the piano. You practice, you get better, and your teacher helps guide you. To expect this type of change to be easy or immediate is to be unrealistic.

Step 4 — Willing to take feedback
Feedback and *more* feedback

You are not going to get better at anything unless you have some sort of feedback. If you are on a diet, the feedback is the dreaded scale. Feedback is needed to identify the traits, or subconscious things you do, that could negatively impact moving up in management — anything from swearing to biting your nails in public, to constantly interrupting at meetings, etc. If you have no one giving you feedback, you will not change because you have no idea that you exhibit habits or traits that are annoying, inappropriate, or out of place.

I had an employee who I believed could be extremely vital to the company from a business perspective. Unfortunately, however, this employee was disliked by co-workers because of two bad habits: refusing to listen and being argumentative. I sent them to Eckerd because I saw potential. This employee returned saying they wanted to change. I said that when I found this resolve wavering, I would mention it in order to get things back on track. The response to this was a resounding "no" unless the discussion took place in private after meetings in order to avoid embarrassment. I agreed even though I was pretty sure this would not work.

When it comes to feedback, people really are no different than training a house pet. If your dog misbehaves today, but gets punished tomorrow, do you really think they understand why they are being punished? Do you really think they will change their behavior? If you are trying to quit smoking and the only feedback you get is how often you buy a pack, do you really think you will change? Some might, but most will not. What you need is someone who mentions your promise every time you take the pack out of your shirt pocket.

After several weeks, this employee no longer wanted the discussions after the meetings because people were beginning to talk. They believed, right or wrong, that people knowing about their efforts to change attitude/performance/interactions was reducing their level of respect. The next request was to only have follow-up discussions once a week in my office — and that it was either once a week in my office or nothing. As I predicted, the feedback was so after-the-fact that it did no good at all, resulting in termination rather than the personal growth I had hoped for.

What was not understood was people did not think less of them because they were trying to change, having someone to help them, and adjusting their attitude on the spot when they reacted inappropriately in conversations, people actually respected them more.

When a door is open, you must commit to it. Not only does the door need to be open, but the person needs to be ready to walk through it. Keep in mind you cannot force some things, but must allow them to happen organically. This employee only wanted to look through the door, maybe adjust the mat on the floor inside, but not commit to walking through it.

Step 5 — Stop whining and take responsibility for yourself

In short, this is the summation of everything already said. People avoid complainers or whiners because, frankly, the conversation gets old really fast. Decide what you want, what it will take, what price you will have to pay, and get started. No one is going to beg you to improve yourself, and honestly no one will care.

We can all be replaced, me, you, and anyone, so either be happy with where you are, or make a conscious decision to change it.

The 5 steps in a nutshell
You need to take an honest look at yourself

The Eckerd College management class was an eye-opening experience for me. In fact, I went twice to judge if what I had been doing was working. This, too, would have never happened except for the people who believed in me enough that they were willing to spend money to help me improve myself. If you want to move up in the corporate ladder, you will need to have people believe in you. Most of us cannot make this climb by ourselves.

I had worked on myself for several years between these two visits but was not moving up the ladder in any way. In fact, my working experience had gotten worse. People questioned why I did things that they never had to do in the past. There seemed to be a growing animosity that had never been there, and it was harder for me to get things done. That's when the company decided to send me back to try and understand what was happening. You might think I worked for an unusual company in that they would pay twice to send me to an expensive course. Fortunately for me at the time, senior management really wanted to change the culture of the company, so understanding why things were not working for me was important to them.

The first time I went, my testing showed I was extremely honest, trustworthy, sincere, and someone you could count on. The testing I did the second time, however, showed almost the exact opposite. People viewed me as dishonest, untrustworthy, and a person you could not depend on. The second set of tests also showed that I manipulated people, which was a big change from my first visit.

As you might imagine, I was devastated, but the real question was: why such a change? Fortunately for me, I was assigned the same psychologist the second time around. She pulled me aside and explained why the testing made sense.

I had changed, but the people who I worked for were still the same. They remember the old me — the me who was blunt, standoffish, often rude, and generally said what was on my mind no matter who it hurt. The new me was more diplomatic, tried hard to work with people, would come and talk to you, and tried to be part of a team. Co-workers saw the difference as well and the only way they could reconcile it was to label the new me as a fake. They were not wrong one bit, as the new 'me" was a fake (at least my exterior persona was fake), but it was a "me" I needed to become in order to get where I wanted to go. So, I took my first real risk; I left the company and took a job as a department manager in another company.

The people there did not know me, allowing me to start fresh with the "new" me. Since they did not know my past, they could only judge what they saw. While I was not at the new company as long as at my former job, I did begin to see that my efforts to evolve could pay off. They just needed to be smoothed out.

Learn to repackage yourself

One of the funniest things about climbing the ladder is that the very attributes that got people to look at you, consider you for promotion, and that your superiors thought positive, are the very traits that become your Achilles heel. People love the fact that you are honest, a straight shooter, call it the way you see it, and get results. They love these attributes because you used them on someone else and not them, or took care in meetings to not embarrass your new manager.

I worked with an accountant who everyone loved because his numbers were always perfect and not just with accounting. If he said the closest gas station was 3.35 miles away, you could rely on it being exactly that distance. The decision was made to promote him based on the following: his team could close the month and do budgets, and with him checking their accuracy, we would never have to worry about errors being made. This guy just never made mistakes, so what could be better than him running the department and making sure all mistakes were eliminated?

My entire senior team agreed this was perfect and that he was the right person. Everyone liked and respected him, and he was the go-to accounting guy for pretty much everyone in the company.

He was promoted. Unfortunately, within six months, the entire accounting department came into my office and informed me that either he had to go or they would. I asked them to clearly define the problem since there had been not one accounting error since he took over. Things had never been better. They told me that he expected the entire department to be as focused on perfection as he was, and they simply could not take it. He would make them work late at night anytime the books did not balance, rather than having staff work normal hours and pick up on resolving the balance issue the next day.

The very thing that most impressed everyone and got him promoted was tearing the department apart. There was nothing wrong with this individual other than unrealistic expectations. He needed to learn that not everyone was or needed to be just like him and he should instead have focused on helping his staff improve on what they already knew, and not just judge them. In the end he was put back in his old position, and the department settled down. We came to find out the staff was driving him as crazy as he was driving them. He was happy to return to his old position.

As we move up, we need to look at ourselves, view ourselves as other people do, and consider what we would expect from someone in the position we are about to occupy. Here again, you need to understand how other people see you and view life from their perspective to ensure you fill their needs, not just your own.

Another good example of the need to do this comes during a department meeting regarding a 10% layoff. This meeting was early on before my Eckerd training. We were talking about different people within the department and the attributes of each. I was running R&D at the time and, as an individual contributor, had no sense of being politically correct about anything.

I methodically went person by person, discussing each with about as much concern as I would put into judging ice cream flavors at the store. How caramel was overly sweet but the caramel with sea salt was great. Johnny talks too much and is dumb and will never amount to anything. Shelly is distracting because all she does is flirt and serves no purpose on the planet. You get the picture.

The department manager at the time thought it was great. I could give him the best and worst attributes of each person with absolute accuracy and absolutely no emotion about the individuals being discussed. At the end, the decision was made to terminate most of the people I felt were poor performers. I walked away thinking that being brutally honest was the best way to go. Why was it so hard for everyone else to do the same or see the benefit?

It was not that the accountant's perfectionism or my dispassionate approach were attributes, particularly if those traits got you promoted; it's that they don't take you far enough. What worked "before" now has no place in your new role in management. I can promise you, though, that before long you will be told you can no longer behave, speak, or act the way you used to because you are now part of management. They make it sound like it is some sacred society that requires a sort of secret handshake or Friday night bloodletting.

The trick is not to change who you are, but instead to package it slightly differently. Get used to this because as you move up the ladder you will repackage things, and yourself, many times.

When I had decided to give classes at my present company, I thought of it as my way of giving back to help young people prepare to move up the ladder. I am a very hands-on president, so as I go around the company, I look for people with potential. These people were then invited to join a group I call "the company's next managers." I feel that even if they quit and move on, they will be a stronger manager. Not only have I done them a favor, I have done their next company a favor.

Think of a time when you were promoted. Did anyone help you, send you out for classes, give you a mentor, or help you in anyway? I bet not. Most people are promoted and sent out to fend for themselves. People with some natural abilities do well and the rest of us stall out or get dismissed with HR saying, "It just didn't work out," "That was a mistake," "The fit isn't right," etc.

So, when I say you need to package things differently, what am I really talking about? Let's go back to my discussion about the layoff and my ability to review each person based on what I saw as their flaws. Everyone thought it was great when I said one of the guys was dumb and would never be a good operator. Same was true when I mentioned that one woman was disruptive to the entire department. Both observations were accurate, in my opinion, but both needed to be presented in a different manner once I became a supervisor. In the first place, how do I know the guy was dumb? Maybe my ability to teach him how to run the machine needs to be improved? Maybe I was making wrong basic assumptions about his education or experience? Phrasing his potential lack of education as being dumb are, in reality, two different things. It might even be that the guy was having issues learning because he simply did not like me.

Now let's assume the guy really was dumb. It was minimally acceptable to say this when I was the R&D guy in casual conversation, but absolutely not acceptable when I was a supervisor making decisions about an individual's job. Let's say he was fired because of his inability to learn the tasks needed and word gets out that his department manager did this because he had been labeled as dumb? What stops this person from getting an attorney and suing the company? All the attorney has to do is prove he has normal intelligence, no learning disabilities, and that there was the slightest dislike between me and this person. Clearly, this is not the way to handle things!

All that needed to be said was that this individual struggled to learn to run the machine and he might need to be moved to another department or be dismissed. Same assessment as before, but in such a way that neither HR nor senior management cringe. Remember, you need them to think of you as promotable when the time comes. The last thing you want to be known for is as an embarrassment when you would be speaking to the president of the company, a board member, or a major customer. Keep in mind you are trying to move up in the company, so when people judge you, they ask themselves if they can trust you in front of their manager or their customer. Would you embarrass them, the company, lose a sale, or put the company at risk?

How about the woman whom I said was disruptive and useless? Same issues with terminology when I get promoted, and in fact even worse because maybe I fired her because she refused to flirt with me. Did I discuss this behavior with HR? Did we have a conversation with the employee? How hard would it be for her attorney to prove she was fired not for being disruptive, but because she did not pay enough attention to me?

If she really was a disruptive influence, then that is what needs to be addressed through proper channels and the whole flirting thing needs to be canned. It should be tackled without the flirt attachment at all because that leads you down a path you will never win, even if you are a woman talking about another woman.

When I mention this exact example to people, the first thing I hear is "You sold out" and I respond to them, "Grow up!" As you move up the food chain, you need to see people differently. They are not just a can of beans you can take off the shelf, but are the very thing that makes your company function. They came to the company with a certain amount of dignity and self-respect and should leave with the same.

Your past is who you are, but as you progress, you need to look at this and make sure you fit into the new chair you will be given. This is similar to learning the new traits I spoke of previously where you need to take an honest look at yourself.

It's important to emphasize I have never said you need to abandon who and what you are. Simply improve the skills you have. Learn to use them differently to achieve the same result. You can think someone is dumb, a flirt, useless, and any other adjective you want, but what comes out of your mouth needs to be well thought out and respectful. This shows maturity and will also keep your company from being sued.

One of the hardest things for people to grasp is that there are two ways to get things done in any company. The first way is dictatorial: "I am the boss and you will do as you are told." The second is to have people do things because they believe in you, respect you, and trust that you can make things better. You will see both have a place and that the trick is to understand when to use one or the other.

A Bold move and a bigger risk

My slow rise in management started eight years after my boss first offered to help me. I never stopped honing my skills, improving my leadership qualities, and, yes, I did make small upward moves, but things really changed when my old boss called me one Sunday.

The person who called me was a former boss who felt that I could invent a process where a very thin layer of glass is coated in the inside of a plastic bottle to increase its shelf life. Yes, I was lucky that my previous boss was hired by a company that needed someone with my talents. However, if I had not been successful for him in the past, he would have never called.

The role would not only be R&D, but I would also have to manage a team of people, interface with the board, and give regular updates to senior staff. If he did not see that I had improved these skills, would he have called me, risked his own reputation, put himself into a position where I might embarrass him? No, he would have found someone else.

I not only had to invent something, but then I had to also help build a market for a nonexistent product. While I had helped other people do this before, it was always in a secondary role. Now I would be leading an entire project where everything depended on my ability to perform.

Luck does not just happen

Even though we've all heard people coming out of a casino saying how lucky they were, this is only partially true. You can be the luckiest person on the planet, but if you are bad at cards, you will still lose. Luck only gets you part of the way. You still need to know what you are doing. In fact, in my experience, luck tends to happen more often to people who know what they are doing rather than to people who are clueless.

For most things in life, I rely on luck to get me over the finish line. If there was no such thing as "luck," then casinos would not change the dealer at blackjack tables when someone has a winning streak. However, sometimes luck is nothing more than being in the right place at the right time for someone willing to take a risk. My brother has told me many times that I have been successful because I am a lucky person, but is that really true?

Did I know how to make this coating? Not initially. In fact, the group working on this had tried for over five years, spent $12 million, and had still failed. I am a bright guy and understand how to coat plastics, so that expertise was to my advantage before I even started. Also, when I was in the U.S. Army, I worked in satellite communications and had learned all about microwave energy. This was a unique and totally unrelated benefit that I brought to the table. Partnering my new expertise with the work previously done could have been luck, a wise decision by my former boss, or a combination of the two. My team and I were only given six months to make this project work. Not five years, but six months. At that point, I counted on a certain amount of luck to get us successfully to the finish line.

I believe that 'luck' is simply having enough knowledge so that you understand what you are doing even if you do not have data to back up your belief. Oft times your gut feel is just as accurate as any data you might review. There were a couple of things I did while testing just because I got frustrated, and fortunately, they worked. Was I lucky or did some part of me know this is what needed to be done? Probably a little of both.

With all that being said, it should not seem far-fetched that at some point you will have to take some risks rather than relying on education, experience, self-improvement, and luck. It's at this point when your career seems to have stalled that you need to be willing to identify, evaluate, and take risks.

This book is called *The Long Game* because we are looking at ways to make a long-term difference to a company. As we move through this book, we will focus less on you personally and more on how to turn around a company, but if you are not ready, if you have not put the time into making yourself a better manager, then all the advice in the world will not help you. We will go into this in much more detail later, but I wanted to mention communications in this chapter because it is one more hurdle you have to get over.

As you move ahead, assuming you stay at the same company, the biggest issue you will have is being taken seriously. People will tell you that you are now the boss and your subordinates have to do what you say. However, is this really how you want to run your department or company? Do you really want people to do as you ask only because they have no choice?

You will see as you move through this book that at first it is true, but as time progresses you need to move away from this. You want people to want to do as you ask because they believe in you. Final point is, if you have to remind people you are the boss to get things done, then you are not in charge. You need to think of the discussion from their point of view. You are now management, making you the new enemy or, at the very least, someone to be careful of. A topic we will cover later is fear and how it can work against you. For now, understand that fear is a very short-term motivator and will, in many cases, actually be counterproductive to your goal of long-term success.

When having a discussion, think about why people are arguing their point, why they are resisting your advice, and where the gap between you both really is. Subordinates frequently do not care what you want, what you think, or what your needs are because you are not one of them. This is not unusual. However, if you never enter into a conversation without considering things from their point of view your advancement opportunities will be limited.

This does not mean you should give in to their issues, but rather to look at it from their point of view. You may lead the conversation in a different direction. This not only goes for employees, but also for customers. In the end, you need them to perform a specific task, and if you think about your conversation from their point of view, you might get this done quicker and with less drama.

I had a customer once who demanded to see the president of the company (me) because he believed the sales department had been dishonest with their company and was charging them too much. Since our pricing can vary depending on usage level and product complexity, they were probably charged correctly. Of course, this really does not matter since they were refusing to pay their bill and said they would not buy from us any longer.

They explained how a competitor came to them and offered exactly the same product at 20% less. They felt this proved that I must have cheated them by at least 20%, right? I sat and listened to them until they had completely exhausted their points which, believe me, took quite some time.

I understood they believed they had been overcharged because they were a small company and felt we could get away with it. While some of that is true, they also charge more for their end (?) product than a large store because they offer individual service which a large store does not.

It would have been easy to simply tell them they had been quoted a price, accepted the price, used the product, and so now they had to pay. In the long run though, what would my company have gained? Probably nothing. I would have gotten my money, but lost a customer. Even worse than that, due to social media, I might have lost several customers. Instead I asked them:

- Did our competitors offer technical service that they could use to optimize their product line? Well, no.

- Do they offer the same specialty codes that we do which enables you to change your product slightly to stand out from your competitors? Well, no.
- If they wanted to test a different meat product, does the competitor offer an USDA-approved kitchen they can use? Again, no.

Because we offer all of this, our product is slightly higher priced than our competition.

I explained that I would not apologize for our prices because clearly , we offer many extras our competition does not. This is all shown on our website, and had they taken time to go over or it, the information could have been explained by their salesperson.

They, once again, became defensive and asked me why I was attacking them.

I explained I was not attacking them. I tried to clarify that I did not understand where we went wrong when we have so many services designed to help small and medium companies such as theirs to compete with much larger companies. I asked where they felt we had failed them and what we could have done better so that instead of them being upset, they would be thanking us for all the support we offer and how that has helped. The discussion went on for another hour but in the end, they paid their bill, ordered more material, and thanked us for taking the time to speak with them.

The exact same result was achieved by repackaging my blunt honesty with just a teaspoon of positive temperament while attacking the problem. It was not from my point of view that they should just shut up and pay, but from their perspective that they felt they had been cheated.

As your responsibility increases, you will be required to negotiate contracts with customers if in sales, suppliers if in purchasing, and with the union if you are working with HR. If the only thing you think about is what *you* want, what *your* needs are, and how you can beat your opponent down, you will lose more negotiations than those you win. If on the other hand, you understand what your perceived opponent needs from this, it gives you the advantage because you will understand the approach you will need to take. Consider most people only think of how they can win from their perspective opponent, never considering the person on the other side of the table. If you think of yourself on the other side, understanding what your adversary needs, you can make sure you concede some things, things he might consider a win, and you'll ultimately get more than you ever thought possible.

In the end, I told the people in the conference room I had no interest teaching them quick fixes or how be impressive. I had no time to just find the quickest way, leave, and let the next person clean up my mess. This did not interest me because I had done this before in my life, and there is nothing less satisfying than knowing you did a half-ass job.

So many people claim they can turn around a company going in, make the numbers look better, take their bonus, and get out as fast as possible. But typically a few months after they have left, the company begins to fall apart and is in worse shape than ever. It will now take much more work to repair the damage than if it had been done right the first time.

I was opening a door for this group, and if they should choose, they could enter and begin a journey, one only they could complete, but I could help guide. I could teach them how to play and win the long game!

CHAPTER 2

Motivation

Okay, you have worked on yourself and are beginning to see a new you. Still working on perfecting the new you, but you have gotten far enough that you are promoted. Good for you!

Remember what I said in Chapter 1, that this takes time, practice, and feedback. You need to work on this self-evolution every day so that it will become a natural part of you. Keep this in mind though: *you* are who you are. That means that if you are a person who carries emotion on your shoulder, then find an outlet — someone you can go to when you need to scream, rant, or to just tell the world to piss off. Tell this person from the start that their only job is to listen, grunt once in a while, and let you say whatever you need to say.

There are times when I really get mad because company politics are tough for me. As a result, I often need to blow off some steam. I use the company VP of HR for this — an individual who understands that I am only there so I can let it out. After just listening, and when it seems like I am done, the only question asked is "all done?" I will say "yes" followed by their response, "Glad I could help and now I need to get back to work."

This HR person knows I am not looking for either advice or sympathy, so none is offered. In fact, when I ask for advice during these emotional outlets, I am normally told "I have none to give. Your problem, and you will figure it out." They are right. I will figure it out, and often, the solution occurs while I am there. Just hearing myself say the issues out loud changes how I see them. I am sure we have all had great ideas in our head, but after we said them out loud, as when discussing with someone, they don't seem quite so great. Same thing here. Once I hear them come out of my own mouth, either they are not as big as I made them out to be or the solution is obvious.

This person and I have an understanding that I do not mean anything by my ranting. I simply need an outlet — someone who will not hold it against me and who also knows they are doing me a great favor. I am not alone in this need. Many people have the same issues I do but are afraid to ask someone to help. Believe it or not, most people understand and are willing to be your listener, especially if you agree to reciprocate in kind. All it takes is the courage to explain what you need, why you need it, and ask if they are willing to help.

The bottom line is that the real you won't disappear, so you have to find some way to take care of the little devil inside you. I know some of you are saying this is the dumbest thing you have ever heard. For those people, I say enjoy your life because you have peaked.

Now that you have taken care of yourself, which must come first if you want to help everyone else, let's move on to the topic of motivation. Whether you are now a supervisor, plant manager, or the president of a company, you all have the same problem: motivating your new team. If you just inherited the perfect team, then we are done, and you can turn to the last page where it says "the end" because you will have a wonderful life. This book is about fixing something. This is true no matter if what needs fixing is a team or a company — turning things around takes work and strategic planning.

Anticipate a problem

How do you know if you are about to inherit something that is broken, is going to take work to fix, restructure, or recreate, and it's something no one else wants? It's easy really. Just listen for phrases like "They are a pretty good group, but they just need to be managed" or "They are a good bunch, but seem to lack motivation," or my personal favorite "The company overall is in pretty good shape, but we seem to be struggling to significantly increase sales."

Any phrase like the ones above tell you some very important facts about what you really are about to inherit. What you are going to get is a mess; the person who just told you this is part of the problem if they are currently in a position of authority. But how do you know this to be true?

When you get promoted or hired into a position, people will normally congratulate you. They might say you are getting a good group of people, or talk to you about sales, but there will not be a conditional part. People will not normally add the "but they need," or "but seem to lack," or "but sales is struggling." It is the conditional part that you need to listen for.

Does this mean you should run away or feel you were somehow not given all the facts before signing on? No, it just means you have work to do and need to start thinking in a different direction, that this will not be a 9 to 5 job for a long time, and that it will put lots of pressure on you. Anticipate from the start that you will bust your butt and work hard.

When I took over a manufacturing facility in New Jersey, I recall my interview vividly. I was picked up at the airport and we found an open diner, not hard in New Jersey, and talked. In the course of two hours, he used all three of the phrases mentioned when describing the overall status of the company.

The manufacturing group was described as a great group of guys who needed to be better managed. They worked very hard but, it seemed, they did not accomplish as much during a day as they should. It was felt just some simple tweaks should get things resolved. I sat very patiently and listened as the person interviewing me described what they felt should be done.

I asked if the fix was so simple why had no one already taken care of this issue? Why had no one ensured the work was organized, schedules were adhered too, operational areas kept clean, and people held accountable? I was told that the supervisor in charge was pretty laid back. I did not, at that point, ask the next obvious question which would have been why is he still in charge?

Then the discussion moved onto the engineering department,

where I was told they really lacked motivation and did everything at their own pace regardless of project deadlines. They really needed a fire lit under them, in his opinion. Again, I sat and listened because, who knows, they might be right.

I did ask what he thought of his company overall and its prospects for growth. The response was a textbook red alert:

Well, as I explained there are some minor things which needed to be addressed, and I do consider them minor, but the main issue is sales. Sales is not closing, and this is stopping the company from growing. If people saw equipment backed up on the floor, the other problems might take care of themselves, but sales is the big issue.

It was also mentioned that an in-house consultant, who also happened to be a board member, had been working directly with the existing president, but with few positive results.

This was a company in serious trouble, for a variety of reasons, not the least of which was the in-house consultant/board member. During a two-hour interview, I was told how well things had begone when he was president. What was not said while reminiscing was whether or not the company had been profitable, if inventory was under control, if he had brought in any new technology to the company, or used measurements/data/audits which would show the company was stronger under his control than when the next president took over? Remember, it's just as important to hear what's *not said*, especially if you know what you are doing.

Culture

I am sure you are thinking why I would have culture in a chapter about motivation? Culture is everything and your actions will influence the culture of the company and this will either be a demotivating or motivating factor.

When you rejuvenate a company, you get to make the culture anything you want. You do not have to fit into the old value system, especially if it was a failure or not adaptable to current business practices. You get to create one from scratch, which can be crucial to moving the company forward.

After the company is functioning, manufacturing is producing a high quality product, and quality assurance is in place it is time to focus on sales. I will say with some pride that during the great recession of the mid-2000s, we doubled sales in the company and showed a profit every year while other companies were struggling just to survive. That was the result of operational fixes, cultural changes, and new technology that provided sales with a solid base from which to increase sales.

I recall once during an ISO audit, the auditor came to my office and asked if we could talk for a few minutes. I assumed the worst, of course, that the audit had found something wrong. Surprisingly, the topic of discussion was not the audit, but the change witnessed in the company over the past five years. This auditor had worked on our company audits for years, and even though we had always passed the ISO audits, for some reason it was obvious the company was different. People were proud of the company, of the work they did, and there seemed to be purpose, almost a passion, to the company. My answer was short — culture.

Each president develops their own culture within their company. No one is right and no one is wrong. They are all unique, clearly reflecting the personality of the person in charge. The one thing they all have in common, however, is passion.

Define the problem

How can you motivate people if you don't understand the problem?

Instead of coming in like an old-time Wild West sheriff to just sweep all the bad guys out, as I was advised to do, you need to walk through the swinging doors and then sit back. This is when you take time to realize that defining the problem is the first strategic decision you have to make. Questions to ask yourself:

1) Is the team bad because they do not care?

2) Has the team suffered from poor management?

3) Has the team received poor training, or no training?

4) Has the team been saddled with unobtainable objectives?

You need to get this assessment right because there will be no second chance. You also probably need to erase the term "bad" as well. "Poor performers" or "underperforming" might be better, given that "bad" implies a course of action made by choice. Food for thought as you work through this.

If they are doing poorly because they do not have what they need to do the job, then you can skip over some of what comes next. If they are underperforming because of poor management, then you will need the following. Let's start with not having the tools to do the job that has been assigned.

Once I was given the engineering group to manage and our task was to build a new factory, move equipment from factory to factory, and optimize poorly running factories. The company was in the middle of building a factory and it was going poorly when I was hired. Who am I kidding? It was going to hell in a handbasket and the president of the company was livid about it. The company was honest during the interview process, so I knew what I was getting into before I accepted the job. After all, who doesn't like a good challenge?

I called everyone together on the first day, and after we got through with introductions, I started to discuss the new factory. It became obvious within the first 30 minutes that not a single person in the room had ever built or even helped to build a factory. They had also not been allowed to hire an outside consultant to help because corporate did not budget for one. The fact that they were failing was clearly not their fault. For starters, they had no having on-site expertise working the project. This was compounded when the company consistently sent engineers in to shelp but only sent engineers who could not help due to lack of expertise or who refused to help because the project was beneath them. Pouring bad after bad with no recognition of why this process did not generate positive outcomes helped nothing. The team had been set up to fail and they were doing just that. The problem was threefold: (1) Expertise was required. (2) Get company politics away from the team. (3) The board needed to understand that hiring the expertise needed would save money.

Naturally, this needs to be done in reverse order because if I did not have the board on my side, then the politics issue would not go away and the money needed to get expertise would not come. Later in the book, I describe what was done in detail, but for now know that in the end the project was completed, slightly above budget, but well below what the board had projected when I was hired.

Now let's look at people who have been poorly managed. This could be the result of weak managers, people who really don't know how to manage, people burnt out to the point of not caring, people who just don't care, or even people who have risen to a point of incompetence. There are more in this latter group than any other.

It does not really matter why a team has been mismanaged. What does matter is recognizing poor mismanagement led to the problem and, more particularly, with one or more members of the group. The adage that the universe abhors a vacuum is also true of people. If there is no real leader at the top, someone else will fill the void and it is never one of the good guys. Ever!

Both groups described above know that they are thought of as the worst in the company. They are not stupid, even if functioning poorly. The group building the factory needs what I call a biblical revival where you give them something to believe in, give them back their respect, and like Moses, lead them to the Promised Land.

Let's look at a revival first. This team had no spirit and was emotionally broken. They knew they were not good at what they did, and they also knew that they had been shoved aside. Frankly, everyone on the team was waiting to be fired. I am sure every one of you has seen a dog that hangs its head with its tail between its legs because of owner abuse. This was my team. What they needed was their pride back and some respect.

Look for the things they have done correctly, things they tried to do, how small changes would make it better. Most of all, though, you need to sell yourself to them just as the minister does in the tent. I covered the building projects I had done, how I would work with each person to correct the mistakes, and get the project back on track. How I understood they needed some help and that I would go to the board to get it.

Express how amazed you are with what they have accomplished with the resources they had. Remind them where in the project they had done very well. Avoid stating the big mistakes, as there is plenty of time for that. The goal is when you are done, the group believes, honestly believes, that in this battle they have been in they have just been thrown a lifeline. They now can and will survive.

After this, I went into proper project management mode, which should have been step one of the project design phase, breaking the project down into manageable pieces. You are also probably thinking to yourself right now that there is no way a company would just hand a group of people $20 million and turn them loose. Sorry to say but, yes, it happens more often than you would believe. In this case there was a reason, which we will get to later.

Did the project come in over budget? Yes, it did. We found ways to save some money so that, while it did not come in on budget, it didn't come anywhere close to the disaster the financial department anticipated.

Was the project late? Yes, it was, and it was an issue we did not even try to fix because it was already too far into the timeline when I took over. Here is the most important part though: that as the project moved forward, you could see the group working more like a team every day. They now had someone who honestly cared about them and helping them be successful.

Their decision-making got better, they were more self-confident, and really tried to help each other succeed. At first, they came to me for everything, not sure if the decision they were about to make was a good one. I would sit with them and we would work through the problem, look at different approaches, until they understood and could make a good decision. As the project moved forward, they came to me fewer times and made fewer mistakes.

The second group is where a different motivation comes in. It always seems that people who have been managed poorly develop an attitude, and not a good one. There are a number of reasons why this happens, maybe because it helped them survive, or maybe they felt it was either me or them and it sure is not going to be me. Maybe their manager was extremely weak so they could bully people around.

Now before I start, be very clear that I am not a psychologist and do not pretend to be. I am, rather, an individual who has worked hard at learning social skills. Thus, the more I study people and pay attention to what they say and do, the easier it is for me to move through life. Being an introvert, I do not have the charm many managers have and which I envy. I must study people because I really struggle to understand why people act the way they do. What I am talking about here are things I have come to understand after years of observation.

I am sure you or someone you know has worked for a person who was always threatening termination if what they wanted was not done when and how they wanted. I have never met a single person who has not had a story about "that ass" who was their boss, using fear as a motivator. Fear is an extremely strong motivator that will move mountains if used correctly. However, it is also a short-term motivator. If used often, it will, in fact, have the opposite effect and will demotivate people. Once your crew no longer reacts to fear in a way you expect, then you have most likely lost them for good. The next obvious question is if fear is so bad, then why use it? Well, it works — for starters.

For this group of people fear is, in fact, what you are going to use because you need to get their attention and you need to get it fast. If they had no respect for their previous manager, they certainly will not have any for you, and if they do, it will take time, time you do not have.

Earlier in this chapter, I said that people are not stupid and generally they know their reputation within a given company. To know it and to hear it spoken out loud are two completely different things. People who are obese know they are obese, whether due to overeating or a medical condition. However, go up to one, tell them they are obese without knowing why, and see the reaction.

Filling the void

It is said that the universe hates a void and, in order to fill that void, will take whatever solution is at hand — good or bad. Unfortunately, it in poorly managed groups the leadership void is often filled by three types of people: the bully, the shadow, and the ever-helpful.

The first is the bully with a big mouth — the person who has something negative to say no matter what the topic is. It does not matter to them if what they say is true, sort of true, or a complete lie. Say it loud, say it often, and always make sure there is a crowd around to see how you stand up and tell off management. Every person alive can name someone who fits this description. This person makes sure everyone knows the company is bad, management is the worst ever, and that no one other than he/she cares.

Fortunately, bullies are the simple ones because it is usually easy to find some way to fire them (based on documented facts of infractions, of course). Believe me, doing so will send a very clear message. Never wait or debate about finding and firing the bullies in your group as fast as HR will let you. These people destroy everything they touch and will prevent your team from ever improving as long as they are employed.

Bullies need to become someone else's problem, and as soon as possible. Next "to-do" after you fire them is to not say a word about them and I mean NOT a word. If someone asks just say "Oh, him? He's gone," as you turn and leave. This clearly tells the rest of the team/department that this person is not even worth your time to talk about, that they were nothing other than an inconvenience you took care of and have already forgotten about.

It also shows the group that bullies are no match for you, and that you took care of the problem with no more effort than cleaning the mud off the bottom of your shoes. Obviously, you're making a power play here and the best to way to obtain power is to appear to everyone as though you already have it, which you do. Remember you are changing a culture, and this drives motivation.

More difficult is the saboteur in the shadows. They are not obvious, do not have a big mouth, do not stand out in the crowd, and are difficult to find. These people are dangerous for several reasons. They quietly sow discord among the team, and they are generally very smart. They make casual comments to their fellow workers over lunch, when they go out after work, or even on little things during the day. They are like the bad smell in your refrigerator. You have no idea where it is coming from or what it is, but everything in the refrigerator is going bad just the same.

Shadow individuals are master manipulators and will make everything they say seem like a good idea. Your ideas, your thoughts, something you need to inform your friends about because somehow you have the insight they do not. Think Grima Wormtongue from Lord of the Rings.... (This reference might be a little obscure for this reader?) They are not the person everyone is sitting with during break, or the person everyone hopes to meet at the bar after work to have a drink with. They are more likely to be the nobody, the person who never seems to be anywhere specific, not the center of attention, and not part of any group for any length of time. Have you ever been to a party and a few days later someone asks if you recall seeing a specific person at the party? You stop and think — did I see them? After giving it some thought, you are still not entirely sure. There are people who go through life without leaving much of an imprint. This does not mean there is anything wrong with them, it is just who they are.

But there are also some people who understand that their retiring personality can be an advantage. Most of us have come across this type of person at some point or other. Have you ever said, "Why does everyone hate me?" "Why is everyone always against my ideas?" Why does everyone ignore what I have to say?" Why? Because you have someone working in the shadows who takes great pleasure in watching you fail.

Even if you know this is happening and who is doing it, the dumbest thing you can say is "What did I ever do to them?" No one cares. Most people will tell you to find this person, sit them down, have a discussion with them, find out where the conflict is, and resolve it. The logic behind this approach is simple; if they were able to get large numbers of people working against you, think what they could do for you. Unfortunately, logic doesn't stack up against reality, and 9 times out of 10 that approach will fail. When you read this type of advice in a book toss the book into your charity pile.

I cannot count the number of seminars I have gone to that this was their advice. Turn your biggest problem into your biggest victory. There is no wonder why these people have seminars because they sure as hell have no idea what they are talking about other than to be very good at getting your $100.

Feel free to give your $100 guru's advice a shot. However, if you fail with these people you then will have caused even bigger issues. For starters, the shadow will view you as weak because you came and kissed their behind. They will make you jump through all sorts of hoops, always telling you that they are helping you to win the hearts of the people. That when, in fact, they will be laughing at how you have become their puppet. And believe me, everyone will know since they are so good at sneakily dispensing bad information.

Just remember that person you paid to go and listen to most likely has probably never actually managed anyone or anything. They may have managed Alexa from Amazon but, other than that, have never done anything remotely like what they are teaching you. Most of these people have read a paper or a study someone else did for their graduate degree and then promoted it as their own.

Next point. When the time comes that you finally decide you have wasted enough time and energy and decide to fire the shadow, they will scream you fired them out of retaliation, which is illegal. Always document, no matter how trivial or long it takes, because that documentation becomes your best friend when terminations and/or unemployment benefit payments are challenged.

If you find your shadow saboteur and eventually fire them, people will accept it, and even welcome it. In fact, most will fill in the void with something like "I knew they would get fired someday." Not because they have any idea what "they" did, but they must have done something, or they would not have been fired. People always fill in a void with something negative and right now that works in your favor.

With the bully, you were presenting the image of being tougher than the bully. With the shadow, you want people to know you see all, that nothing gets by you. No one is sneaky enough to escape your observation.

If you ever have to say "I am the boss," you have lost because if people viewed you this way then they would not need to be reminded. At the same time, getting rid of this person sets a standard for the group. Work with me or work somewhere else.

The final group I call the "ever helpful" and they are the worst group of all. The reason I say this is because some people honestly want to help and have no bad intentions at all. They like the company, the group they work for and really want, almost long for, things to get better. These are great people and you want to take care of them.

That said, some people act like they want to work but they really want to undermine you from the inside. You have had your meeting and they will come up and introduce themselves, even shake your hand, and tell you how they want to help. They have been there a long time and know most of the people and they are a pretty good group, but there are a few who are bringing the group down. The first discussion with this type of person always goes this way.

The question I hope you are all asking at this point is how do you differentiate between the person who is attempting to undermine you and the person who honestly wants to help.

I find people remember the end of a conversation far better than what was in the middle. Does the conversation end with something negative or end with something positive? The ending really tells the story. If the conversation ended on a negative note, even though 90% of the conversation's middle was positive, then you are being manipulated.

If the conversation was balanced, but ended on a positive note, then the person really wants to help. They see the positive and negative in the situation, but want you to walk away feeling there is hope.

I am sure your mother told you it is not what you say, but how you say it. She was right and if you listen to how you are told information you can often read between the lines as to what the intent was.

You want to make good decisions, so pay less attention to what people say and a great deal of attention to how they say it. Listen to how they present things and, most importantly, to how they end the discussion.

Respect the best motivator

Now you have scared the hell out them, or at least have them talking, wondering who you are, and what you are planning. Good. The troublemakers are gone and now you need to get the department or company moving again. This is more complicated then presented here and I will cover it later, but for now we want to move from fear to respect.

Begin by sharing information with everyone about the department or company. This information can include things such as financials, costs of goods sold, yields, efficiency, turnover, scrap, and cost per element. You would be surprised to know most people working there have never seen these numbers and had no idea how bad they might be.

You need a baseline. Everyone needs to know where things stand, how problems will be measured, and what is considered good. If you cannot define the problem, you cannot fix it. The first step of defining a problem is to understand it.

Your people need to be taught what the numbers mean and how things will be measured. It's important to keep things relative. If you are a department manager, do not compare your numbers to unrelated departments, because people will become overwhelmed. Focus them on relating only to acceptable numbers that they can impact.

I took over a company once where there was 25% internal scrap in raw material manufacturing and another 14% scrap in finishing. For those of you not good with math, this means that 39% of everything made went into the trash. During my introduction meeting with the entire company, I informed the group that these losses needed to decrease because the company could not sustain itself with this much material going to scrap. Many people spoke up, informing me that they made a product from a natural source which resulted in variations from batch to batch that could not be helped. What they said was true, which both they and I knew. However, that did not change the fact that things needed to improve.

In their defense, they had never been told what the goal was so they believed they were doing the best they could. How would you react if your scrap rate was 39% and then someone told you that the goal was 5%? I don't know about you, but many people would just give up at that point.

Throughout this book I have said several times that it's important to ensure you do not overwhelm people. It should be obvious, but I will say it again. If your people do not believe you and you cannot convince them to believe, or if they see no light at the end of the tunnel, then they, and you, will fail. This does not mean everything must be taken in little chunks because then everything will take forever, but they must believe in something or someone in order to get the ball rolling. Overwhelming them would be to portray only the end goal with no clear vision of how to get there. Providing details and timelines on the steps that will be needed to achieve the goal is not only easier for employees to grasp, but also to buy into.

Maybe they know that your proposed changes will make things better, or that the new equipment will improve things. They might also just believe in you because they have learned that you tend to win and people who are around you tend to win. Even if they themselves do not see how this project will succeed or a long-term goal reached, they believe that with you at the helm, they stand a good chance. For them that is enough.

The ultimate outcome of respect

Remember the worst manager I had at one of my companies? Over time he changed and changed for the better. He hired me many years later to work on the process of coating the inside of a bottle to improve content shelf life. I told you I had no idea how I would accomplish this at the time.

I remember the night he and his wife took me out to dinner. He looked at me and said he knew I had no idea how to make this work.

He told me that people had been trying to do this since the late 1980s and even though the process had been developed it was a process that no one had ever been able to scale for use in manufacturing. He then said "Rod, there is one thing I do know. If there is anyone who can make this happen, it is you. I have no idea how, and neither do you, but at some point, the answer will come to you. It always does and you will succeed."

That was enough to motivate me to take on this challenge. Not because I believed I could accomplish this task, but because I believed in him, and if he thought it could be done, I could do it. Then that was good enough for me. By the way, we did accomplish upscaling this process for large manufacturing and I did figure out how to put a thin layer of glass inside a plastic bottle. It is still used in Europe today.

The last thing to keep in mind is that everyone is going to feed off you. People above you, the board or owner, are all going to be looking to see if you are making a mistake. And one way they do this is by judging your confidence. If you appear unsure or your confidence level drops, they will view this as you are losing and what you promised is not going to happen. Conversely, people below you will be looking for any mistake they can throw in your face to show that you have no idea what you are doing. They do not care what the mistake is, maybe you said something they can prove is wrong, or you changed something that made things worse, or quality deteriorate, or customers start to complain. Anything they can use they *will* use, so be ready. Fact: You will have to manage the people above you and the people below you, and it will have an emotional drain on your life.

CHAPTER 3

Begin With The Right Senior Team

Okay, you have worked on improving yourself and any other factors that may keep you from attaining success. Don't think you need to work on everything that seems negative about yourself. If you do, you will be overwhelmed and will fail. Just take the biggest items that you think will hold you back. For example, do you have an issue listening to people, taking suggestions, or anger issues? Work on these and let the little things go. They will work themselves out over time.

You must get a new team in place fairly quickly. As you might recall, most of the time you inherit a company that needs to be fixed. Courts of law know that when a new president takes over, they will typically clean house or do a reorganization and give you a little time to get this done. That timeframe varies from place to place, but it is never very long. During this time, you can pretty much dismiss anyone under the guise of reorganization, and it will hold up in court. Always work with your company attorney, though, to ensure you are in compliance with the laws in your state. The other reason you want to get this done quickly is because six months after you start, you will have begun to get to know the people in the organization and will find reasons why they should stay.

At almost every company I have ever worked for, at some point, someone senior would decide things were not going well. In other words, the company itself needed to improve performance, not just one team or department. They would get all the top management people in a room where, inevitably, the discussion would lead them to review employees: which ones are good and which ones should be replaced. However, what should really happen is that the company president, along with HR, should review the senior people first and determine who should stay and who should go.

Your employees are only as good as top management, so if you are discussing "getting rid of dead weight" then you need to ask the same for your senior team. First, if you have so much dead weight that you need to have a formal discussion about it, then why have your VPs not taken care of this long ago? Why would your senior team leave poor performers to continue to work for you?

One excuse I always hear is that it is so difficult to find good employees that these are better than nothing. Think about how ridiculous that statement really is. How much overtime are you using because this poor performer is not contributing? How much rework is the company doing because of this person, and how much poor product are you sending to customers because of this person? Start at the top rather than at the bottom....

I have been in meetings where it was decided that a particular department was weak and that 20%—30% of the employees should be replaced. The reasons why these individuals should be replaced ranged from alleged low productivity to bad attitude. In this situation, the first person who should actually be out the door is the person who heads up the department in question. I am not talking about the department manager, but someone even more senior. Who is the director or VP that oversees the entire organization this department is part of? This person is where I would start the replacement process. After all, how could the department be that bad for so long with no one working to improve it? This tells me one of two things: 1) either the director/VP has ignored the department, or 2) they know themselves to be the problem but are looking for someone to take the blame for their incompetence.

You will keep hearing me talk about the top and the importance of a quality senior management team. This is because good teams are built from the top down, NOT from the bottom up. A good team at the top is vital when changing culture because it is their responsibility to ensure your new message trickles down to everyone in the company. They are not just managers. They are also vital messengers. Because of this, picking your senior team is vitally important. Doing it right sets the groundwork for everything that comes afterward.

I used to say that once people have achieved a certain level (director or VP) you really do not need to focus on their ability any longer. My thought was that no one can rise to the level of director or VP and still be incompetent. Unfortunately, my thinking was wrong. Many incompetent people do rise up the ranks, often having done so on the backs of better individuals.

Look for passion first

It goes without saying that most hiring managers are looking for competent and qualified people: the brightest they can find. Normally we would as well. However, competent and qualified are not the most important traits we are looking for. The number one attribute we want is passion. And when I say passion, I mean it needs to be equal to your own. Earlier I mentioned that your company is a reflection of you. Thus, if you view this as just another job, I promise you everyone else will view this as just a job. Your passion needs to drive this company and inspire people to do more than they thought they could. Your passion needs to encourage them to take risks and drive the company into the future. Without passion, you just have another company and it will be the same as the company down the street.

In a way it is kind of funny that as I write this book, I am looking for a new opportunity myself. So many times I've talked to recruiters who told me "you are not a good fit because you do not have the right background." I recall telling one recruiter if this is his top priority, then the company will continue to fail. The president the board just fired had the right background or they would not have hired in the first place. So now you are working on replacing one loser with quite possible another. The company is supposed to be full of experts, so another expert is not what the company needs. What they need is a competent leader who can move the company forward. I have no idea how to make cars, but I do, in fact, know how to manage people who do.

The recruiter disagreed and we both moved on. However, the reason why so many companies fail is because they have the wrong people at the top, and when they do look to replace them, they go looking for nearly a duplicate of the person they want to get rid of. When you go to hire your new senior management group, break the paradigm. Look for people who know how to manage people and projects, but most of all hire people who are passionate about what they do. If they have no fire in their gut and cannot manage people, who cares what kind of expert they are. They are of no value.

If you look at all the great companies such as Microsoft, Apple, Amazon, or Google, the one thing they all have in common is passion at the top. They also have great employees, but talent can be bought, passion cannot. You are either passionate about something or you are not. It really is that simple, yet, finding people with this passion during an interview is really difficult.

Don't get me wrong. What I am saying is look for the passion first. These people will often be overlooked at other companies for the simple reason that less capable people view them as competition, and the one thing there is plenty of is incompetent people.

Don't always view longevity as a plus

In many cases, I will fire most of the senior people in the first 30 days. That sounds drastic, but on the other hand, if the senior staff was so good why is the company failing? That gets back to starting team-building from the top down. And now let's look at why I could do this and know that I was doing the right thing.

I ran a company which had been sold three times when they had hired me. When the first firm sold the company, do you honestly believe the best managers, scientists, accountants, maintenance people, and everyone else who was instrumental in making this company work stayed? Does it make any sense that they would just sell off the company and not retain their best people? Don't get me wrong, it is possible, but the odds are not in favor of it. In this case they kept the best for themselves and let the mediocre staff go as a condition of sale. They not only let them go, but probably laughed while signing the selling documents since they were getting rid of the people they did not want while saving the cost of severance packages.

I always ask to see the seniority list of everyone at director level and above when I take over a new company. What I found was that most of these people had worked at the company long before for an average of 25 years. Think about what I just said. Given that I had to ask myself how good could they really be? I will then interview each individual at director level and above to see if they could say something that would change my mind, and, in fact, once and a while someone will — but most will not.

The next thing to keep in mind is that the best people know when a company is in trouble and they will be the first to leave. From top to bottom, the people you need most, the people who could turn the company around, left long before you ever got there. They are now happy and working for someone else. So, when you walk into a company that is struggling never, ever, forget that you are not getting the best. You are probably getting the very best of the worst that is available. You will find that many remaining managers, if not most, will be close to retirement and more interested in what they can get out of the company for themselves than helping the company to be profitable. They will justify why the company should pay for the fees to their favorite golf club or why they should have a company car, even if not in a sales position.

The worst employees know they have a good thing and will stick it out for as long as they can. Just because they are poor employees does not mean they are dumb. They simply know that at some point they will be forced to go and whatever job they get next will not be anywhere near as good as what they have.

The final reason you want to make this change is because of culture, plain and simple. As you might recall, I have mentioned before that to turn a company around you need to create a new culture. Keeping the original staff would most likely be an impediment to that.

Don't get me wrong. Every now and then you will find a gem worth keeping. Someone who really believed they had been making a difference as part of the few who were keeping a finger in the dam. These really are gems and, when you find them, treat them well because what they wanted most just showed up. You. Someone to fix the very thing they loved. They have been waiting for you.

The biggest mistake I normally see is hiring managers thinking how lucky they are because they hired someone from P&G, Apple, Google, or some other firm in the top 100. Sadly, most of the time it will turn out to not be a good hire — not because the individual is not competent or qualified, but because of cultural differences. These Fortune 100 companies have very strong cultures and whatever the culture is where they came from, it is not what you have right now.

Now, if you wish to hire everyone from a specific company and copy its culture you might stand a chance, but generally speaking most people within a year or so, will tell you they made a mistake. Actually, it might even set you back in turning things around.

If you are honestly interested in righting the course of a company then it needs its own culture, not someone else's. A culture that works for you and your people, one that you can all identify with and call your own with pride. When I interview someone as a potential employee for a stressed company, I tell them they need to think of this company as a startup that failed, found a little money, and decided to give it another try. Most people fully understand what this means but, if they don't then thank them for coming in and ask HR to walk them out.

I say this because if they had no idea what you were talking about, then within six months they will accuse you of not having been honest during the interview process. They will explain they never planned to work 60-80 hour weeks or juggle five different things at once. When you remind them they were told this was like a startup that failed, they will give you a blank look and ask you what that even means.

Not that many people have worked at a startup, but they have read about them, heard about them, know someone who has worked at one, or can at least imagine what it is like. Now, if they look at you with glee because they know they will be creating something new, then you have found a person of interest. If at the end of the interview you sit back and wonder if this is the right person, then by default it is not the right person. If you are thinking to yourself that they "might" work out, then move on and interview the next candidate.

Picking the right senior staff is vitally import. The two primary things you are looking for are passion and attitude. As I have mentioned before, your staff is going to be one level down from where you are so if you have no enthusiasm, then they will not either. Their staff is going to be one level below them and so forth. So, as I said earlier, if you see this job as "just a job" then your staff is going to view their employment as just a way to pay the bills while their staff will just show up. On the other hand, if your staff comes in every day pumped up and ready to "dig in," their staff will also feel this is a good job, and those below them will view this as a good place to work.

Employees must believe three things: that things can get better, that the company can be turned around, and that no matter how bad things get, you and your senior staff can conquer these issues. A big part of fixing an ailing company is having the ability to sell yourself and getting people to follow you.

Pay attention to body language

When you interview people, watch to see if they are sitting back in their chair or leaning forward. If leaning forward, they are paying attention, interested in what you are saying, and engaged. Leaning back says they do not want the job, really are not qualified, or conversely, that they feel they are so qualified that you would be an idiot not to hire them.

One of the main things I look for when interviewing is to see if the candidate is engaged. Are we having a discussion or are they just answering questions? If we are having a discussion then they are engaged. However, if all they do is answer questions and perhaps ask a few at the end, then they are just interviewing. They are simply supplying rehearsed, memorized answers to the questions you are asking.

Remember back when you interviewed? You were interviewing the company at the same time they were interviewing you. You should be expecting the same from people you are interviewing. Are they just answering questions or are they talking to you? If all they will do is answer questions, I have very little use for them because in the end, I really do not know who they are or what they think. I do know they would make a great parrot because they recite what they have been taught. This should be a red flag when you interview someone.

You should have no interest in people who cannot ask anything beyond a canned question. I am intrigued by people who want to know how much authority they will have in the department they will run. If they feel someone is not working out, do they have to have my permission to replace them? Will they have the authority to change procedures in the department? How does interfacing with the other department work and how easy it to work between departments? These are questions from a person who is really engaged.

A mistake created by pride

I once had on opening for a VP of Finance. There had been very little meaningful capital spending until I talked the board into a $6 million project which would reduce our costs and make the company more competitive. This becomes relevant to the opening because, with no VP of Finance, there was no one really managing the finances of the project other than myself. The project also was not going well, as we had to adapt a different technology to work with our product. On top of this, the city had changed their mind about permits and had decided that we would not be grandfathered if we extended the building. They would make us bring the entire factory up to code. The factory was built in the late 60s and virtually everything had been grandfathered, so nothing was at 2018 code. It would have been cheaper to tear the place down rather than rewire, replumb, etc., basically replacing 70% of everything in the building. The bottom line is that I was spending most of my time trying to work too many issues and needed someone at the helm in finance so that I did not need to worry about it. HR had found someone they felt was a good fit and asked me to interview him.

I came away from the interview thinking that he felt he was doing me a favor if I hired him. Yes, alarms should have gone off. However, I was so deeply mired in quicksand with the city, actual project issues, and a union contract negotiation that I overlooked every red flag, did not trust my gut, and hired him.

After about six months, the union contract was signed, I had worked out a deal with the city, and the new design for the system looked good. On the other hand, the CFO was not doing so well and making a great deal of mistakes. So instead of admitting I should not have hired him, I then made mistake number two by deciding to "fix" him. After your new VP of Finance has been on the job for six months, you would expect he/she to understand the books better than you do, given that this was his/her full-time job. However, every time I had a question, they needed to go speak to their team to get the answer. More red flags, but I dug the hole even deeper because, hey, he is smart so I just need to light a fire under his butt. I began to devote more and more time to him trying to get him to engage in the company, but the harder I pushed, the more he pushed his team, and the less engaged he became.

Everything finally came to a head when it was time for the yearly review, which was at the same time all managers were reviewing their subordinates. I was curious what he would say about his team, so I asked HR to forward them to me. On a side , I feel it imperative that HR reviews all reviews before they are given to ensure there are no serious issues not already raised and that nothing is going to be said that could be construed as racist, sexist, demeaning, or otherwise wrong.

In this VP's review I had said they did not have a firm grasp of the financials, was not reviewing the end of month reports completely, and was sending incorrect reports to corporate. All of which had been documented, by the way. Instead of taking responsibility for functions and activities that were part of their job, the team was blamed. In their appraisals, he told several of them they made him look bad because they had not adequately reviewed the financials with him so he could answer my questions. He also told others he rated them as unsatisfactory performers because they were sending mistakes to corporate. In short, he expected his team to do all the work and make him look good, and, because he looked bad, it was their fault.

A bad hire, my refusal to take responsibility and replace this VP sooner rather than later, and thinking I could fix their work ethic almost cost me the entire financial team who, frankly, had had enough. Remember the good ones leave, the bad ones stay.

Being enthusiastic/passionate is much more than just running around telling everyone how happy you are working there. People who are enthused about working at your company roll up their sleeves, learn their job, even learn about the work done around them. The CFO ran finance so they should know why we do inventory twice per month, why scrap on some products is higher than other products, and why union negotiations took longer than expected, almost ending in a strike. If you really care about doing your job and are honestly engaged, then you would seek out these answers.

Finance has everything in the company feeding into this department, so I would expect a person holding this position to have at least a basic understanding of the different departments. What do they do, what materials does each department use, why are shift schedules different in various departments? The expectation is not to become an expert, but at least have some basic understanding. How can you help other departments improve if you have no idea what they do?

What are you looking for?
Pick each person for a reason

You are looking for a person who will contribute as a player on the field, not someone who sits in the stands. The issue is people's perception of what it means to be a player on the field and not just the latter.

Many people feel if they have completed their reports on time, met deadlines, etc. then they have done their job and I should have nothing to complain about. In my view, these employees are just doing the bare minimum and are not people I would consider valued employees.

When I take over a new company, this is one of the first things I discuss with everyone in the company. I want people who are active, engaged, and working on finding solutions instead of just reporting them. What is really meant by this?

Therefore, when you are interviewing someone for a key senior position, ask them about a project they are most proud of and then ask for fine details that only someone who was actually participating on the team would know. It is the only question you need to ask to find out if you have found the right someone. Be alert for phrases like "give you a bird's-eye view" or "from a 10,000-foot view" or "high level" as these are all phrases used by people who have no idea what they are talking about. You asked them to tell you about a project they are most proud of. If they are truly proud, are honestly active, and are not just taking credit, they will care less how long it takes to explain the project. They don't want to discuss this from a "high level," they want to get into the nitty gritty with you.

I understand everything was done as part of a team, but if the person sitting in front of you had really participated there will be excitement in their eyes because they are being given the chance to brag about something. Everyone wants to pat themselves on the back over something they did. You don't have to care about the project or even understand what they did, just watch them and see if they stirred any excitement in you.

None of us are perfect. However, we all have things that we are good at and we all have areas where we need help. I happen to be very good at strategic thinking and I can see what is needed for a company to grow. A company I was once president of had received no funding from its corporate office for 20 years. Whether deliberate or due to an out-of-sight, out-of-mind mentality by failing to update technology and equipment corporate contributed to the company's decline. By telling my predecessors that corporate would not spend money until the company could turn a profit, they contributed to the company's decline. Basically, the company could not turn a profit because it needed an infusion of capital to drive costs down, improve machinery, upgrade technology, and train staff and sales in order to restore production to the level of its competition.

After coming on board, I said many times at corporate board meetings that there was a race to the bottom, and we were losing because of the neglect the company had faced for so long. Of course, stating the obvious did not win me many friends. Our competition was focused exclusively on price, where we would never be able to compete. This meant that if we wanted to stay in the game, we had to change the rules so we could become the leader and not the follower.

In addition to fixing the factory, what if you added some sort of value to your product that competition did not have? What can you do to change the game that allows you to compete in a market you normally could not? I travel quite a bit and one day bought a fold-up hairbrush. After 14 hours in plane, it is nice to at least comb your hair. My wife used it once and mentioned a mirror would be a good addition so, of course, I googled the request to see if anyone sold this. Not only did another company sell a brush, but now being curious, I found out they sold four times as many as the brush without a mirror. A small metal mirror increased sales by four times.

Fill in the gaps

I know what is needed to propel the company, but what do I need to make it happen? I am not a detail-oriented person when it comes to running manufacturing or a finance guru even after spending days reviewing the P&L. I can tell you what is needed and what to expect when we get there, but I need someone else to figure out all the details needed to achieve the desired results. I know you need to say "thank you" to people, to recognize their hard work when it is done. Being an A-type personality, though, it simply never dawns on me to actually say "thanks." Something I need is for someone to remind me to say it from time to time. My problems start once something is solved because, at that point, I have already started thinking about the next problem. Focusing on what already happened is important, both to let your staff know you appreciated what they have done and to keep momentum going for future projects.

When you take an honest look at yourself, you will find you are lacking certain traits that would make you an even better manager. There is absolutely nothing wrong with this if you are willing to be honest and admit to these shortcomings. The bigger question is how to fix this? When you start looking for your staff, look for people who have the traits you are lacking. My VP has absolutely no idea how to decide which products will make money in the future, but they are exceptionally good at getting the company where it needs to go. They are very detailed-oriented, and understand how to take a concept and turn it into reality.

The same would go for finance at my previous job. After working with me for a period of months, my finance director would generate the reports I wanted that would explain the details of the company without me needing to take days/weeks on-end reviewing an entire P&L statement. Based on these reports, I knew exactly what sections I needed to review so I could spend my time working on other issues.

HR handles my caring side and when I need to say "thank you," they will drop me an email reminding me of such. In this way people who have worked hard are, in fact, recognized when they should be.

Different people have different ways to balance or enhance the faults they might have. You recall the guy I said was the worst manager I ever had, but in the end turned out to be one of the best? He kept fresh flowers on his desk to remind himself that you cannot beat flowers into submission. He kept them there as a cue that if you water them, nourish them, they will bloom.

Everyone knew why the flowers were on his desk. Most people also know HR reminds me to express gratitude to people. Some people say this lowers people's respect for me, and I am here to tell you this is not true. The fact I know I have this issue and have asked for help has earned me a great deal of respect in the organization, not less.

The firefighter

I would remiss if I did not include something about firefighter mentality in this section. This is not someone you hired to fill in a weakness you have in yourself or even a drawback in your team. This is a person you have brought in to tear something down and rebuild.

First let's define what that is and if having them is good or bad for a company you are turning around. I have a consultant working on team-building with the senior team. The consultant was the VP of HR at the optics company when I started my career. He once asked me if there was anything he had ever told me I had not forgotten or viewed as good advice, maybe wisdom. I said there was. He had told me it is my job to get things done, and that people were tools to be used to accomplish the task. He said he was so embarrassed to have given me this advice and hoped he had matured beyond this since then. No, I said, it is great advice and I use it all the time. Let me explain to all of you what I told him. By the way, he is the same person who is recommending this book.

Firefighters are exactly as the word is defined. They are good at putting out fires, no matter when or where they might be located. For a firefighter, the world is always on the edge of total collapse, and only by will alone are things holding together. In their mind, had you not hired them, the entire company would have failed, but because of them, and only them, the company stands a chance of success. In fact, they will tell you your only hope is to follow every direction they give, support every policy they propose, and get everyone out of their way. The worse things are, the happier a firefighter is. There is no heat hot enough to scare them off. They can shut off anything around them, focusing only on the house burning in front of them. I recall a Star Trek movie where Captain Kirk is telling Spock he, Kirk, races in where angels fear to tread. Firefighting....

Sounds great, doesn't it? I will admit there are times when this is exactly the type of hire that is needed and no one else will do. I took over a company that paid vendors with nothing more than a phone call. Someone would call and say they were owed $5,000 and the finance department would issue payment. No invoice, no PO, no statement of work. Nothing but a phone call. Only 20% of all payments made had documentation associated with them. I also knew there was fraud happening in the finance department. Not with the CFO, but with the director. To this day, I do not understand how they managed to get through their year-end audits, but somehow they did, which is really saying something about the auditors used.

So, I have a company that, from top to bottom, did not believe or even know they needed to get quotes, issue PO's, or justify spending. The finance department was just an open checkbook with no accountability whatsoever. There were no internal procedures or policies, no tracking of any kind. I would love to tell you that only the CFO could issue as large a check as he felt like, but so could his controller. In all my years, I have never seen a more dysfunctional department.

I needed someone able to step in to not only fix the finance department, but also to get corporate actually working in partnership as well. In short, I needed someone with an ego so large that nothing, no one, and no problem could stop them. These people are called firefighters for good reason. When a fire truck pulls up in front of a house and the firefighter can hear a baby screaming in the burning house, they do not sit and wonder if they should take the risk of entering the building. They do not call a meeting or consult a committee; they put their coat on and run as fast as they can into the house to save the baby. They have no fear, no doubt, and not the least bit of hesitation. They see what needs to get done and they jump in and do it. Got to love these men and women.

There are people just like this you can find to help resolve issues in a company. No matter how big the task, how big the problem, how deep the hole, they will jump in and get it fixed. So, I was at a company that needed the finance department torn down, issues resolved, and restored from the ground up. I needed a firefighter and set out to find one. The nice thing about them is that they are always enthused. For them it is not about the win, but more about the battle to get to the win.

I explained to HR what I was looking for. Someone who was practically jumping out of their chair, someone who was drooling at the problems you describe, a person who when asked if they could fix this, simply said "yes" or "when do I start?" with very little explanation. These are people who don't walk, but run to their assignment, want to be left to themselves and their team, and do not take crap from anyone. To say they have an A personality would be the understatement of the year. They don't care whose feelings they hurt, whose toes they step on, or what people think of them. They are singly focused, and nothing had better get in their way.

When HR thought they found this person, we set up an interview. I asked a few questions about past employment and why the desire to come to a company that was obviously a complete mess. The answer was simple: "I can fix this and, in the end, create the best department, not only in this company, but one that will set the standards for all the subsidiaries in the group." There was only one stipulation and that was I had to hire the team she had worked with in the past, the only people who could be trusted. This was better than good; this was the best you could ever ask for. I had my firefighter! Sort of.

What I had was a firefighter who only worked on level 5 fires even if the entire city was burning down around them. My job was simple: keep the body count as low as possible and ensure people knew things were rough, going to get rougher, but in the end we would be better off. It was not that people would come to my office and threaten to quit over a flaming directive from finance, but *how many per day* would come.

The firefighter was a project in and of itself, but things got fixed and at a pretty quick pace. We originally had a department of five people, all of whom were fired on her first week. We got some temp help, but worked 100-hour weeks to make sure everything got done until the agreed upon team arrived. I never saw anyone as happy in my whole life as this person was during those years. Meanwhile, I worked 16 hours a day, eight hours mopping the blood off the floor caused by finance and eight hours of my own work, but things got done. It took 18 months for everything to get fixed, but we had a finance department every president dreams of.

Before you go out and hire your firefighter, just understand they will leave no stone unturned, no document unviewed, and no one is safe from their prying eyes. People often ask me how I found this person so easily. It is not that hard. Look for people who have changed jobs often, and when asked why they changed jobs, they use the "for personal reasons" excuse a great deal. When references are called, their previous employer simply says the company had a change of direction. If you are honestly looking for a firefighter, then you are looking for people with vague pasts.

When I tell people firefighters have vague pasts, I always get this strange look of puzzlement. If you look at most people's resumé, things follow a sequence in one of two directions. Either they have worked for a single company for 10-25 years and have now, for some reason, decided to make a change, or they have changed job every three to five years. If they have changed jobs this frequently, you can assume they are working their way up the ladder and have decided the best way to achieve this to make a move into a new company at a higher position. There is good and bad with either of these two scenarios and it is really is not the topic of discussion here.

Firefighters, however, have a resumé that looks different. They will have changed jobs every ,often but no longer are progressing up the ladder. They seem to be stuck at one level — often at a director level — and no matter what they do, they never seem to move beyond this. Most HR people will look at this and conclude these people are damaged in some way. Otherwise they would not keep moving around and not getting anywhere.

When I explained to my HR what I was looking for, they were really very hesitant. After a few weeks, I was given a resumé and told this seemed to fit the bill, but normally it would be one I'd toss in the trash. I would not even consider keeping it on file, but would literally throw it away. The person they had found moved from a controller to director in the same company, but then quit to take care of a sick spouse.

Very noble, but also most likely not true, or at least a big part of it not true. If you have a family member who is ill, would you honestly give up your health insurance at a time when you will need it the most? Even with insurance, if your family member is ill and you are the only person brining in an income, would you give this up? Perhaps, as everyone's situation is unique. However, 99% of the time people realize taking care of an individual who is terminally ill will be very expensive, even with insurance, and will hang on to their job to pay the bills. In most cases, people will work out a deal with their employer to work from home part-time or some other agreement. Most people will go out of their way to help an employee like this.

I am not saying they were lying when asked for a reason; I am just saying there is more to the story than they were willing to talk about. The giveaway was they had in fact moved to different companies, but never able to achieve any position beyond controller. Then as soon as they got a master's degree, they quit their company. We were told the company had asked them to take the VP slot, which was open at the time, but they had declined. When the company was called, they did confirm the VP position was open and several people were being considered. They did not say who was on the short list.

A firefighter always wins. If they don't, it is because you did not do your job correctly and got in the way or let politics of the company get in the way. If you hired a firefighter and they are not winning, then go find a mirror and find out what YOU are doing wrong.

There is a downside to hiring a firefighter in the business world because when the fires are all out, they will start one just so they have something to do. Think about it, if you are hooked on the adrenaline rush and every day is an emergency, a fight, or you are moving 100 miles per hour just to catch up, what do you do when the battle is won? You find something to break so that you have a purpose again. For them, the battle is never done, the fight never over, a victory never declared. Firefighters need the battle to justify their own purpose and if there is no fire, they have no use.

As you might imagine, this mindset can create a great deal of animosity in a company because if their department is perfect, and it pretty much is, then where do they have to go? They go to other people's departments to tell them everything that is wrong and how to fix it. The thing to remember is that a firefighter is not interested in working with other departments to improve things. They are hell-bent on taking over and telling people what to do.

One year we were in union negotiations when my firefighter came in and began telling our attorney how best to run the negotiations. This attorney was from a law firm that specialized in unions and was known in the Northeast as among the best. The firefighter, on the other hand, had no law background, had never worked with unions, and had never done any negotiations, but right then declared they were the best. At this moment, the person you had hired to fix one problem began creating a whole set of new problems.

You might think I had made a bad hire, but let's look what would happen had I hired a different type of person. Let's say I had not hired this firefighter but, instead, hired someone who was a team player, who wanted to work with people, not ruffle feathers, and who would ask people to please follow the policies they were putting into place? A person who under normal circumstances would be considered a good hire, or at least, the type of person which most companies consider a good hire. What if I had hired a person who would sit down, put together a list of problems, and tackle them one at a time until everything got done? This is the person you want long-term, but would it have been the right person for the issues I had at the time? The odds of this typical, non-firefighter, being successful are slim, very slim. The inmates had run the prison for so long that they would not listen to this person. They would not care what policies were put into place. They would just continue working the way they always had. Nothing would change or your new employee would try hard, fail, and within six months would quit out of frustration. You hired the wrong person, so their departure is your fault, not theirs.

Remember you have a company culture which is always the hardest thing in the world to change. You can replace everyone you want, but the culture will survive. Not only do people within the company enforce this culture, but so does everyone you've done business with for 20 years. Your perfect employee would have left, happy that they had jumped off a sinking ship before it was too late. You will lose ground because now everyone knows if they kick hard enough, they can win this battle.

Before I hired my firefighter, I had hired another person who quit after only one day. He could not understand how he was expected to fix a department everyone used like toilet paper and who would yell at him, on his first day, that he better get on board. If you had hired this perfect employee, you would have done them and the company a disservice, and put the company in a worse position than it was in the first place. No, you had to have this firefighter, even knowing that in the end, they would have to be dismissed.

Yes, the firefighter was a tool that was used to fix a problem, but it was what was needed at that time — a short-term, and not a long-term solution. Come to terms with this because firefighters almost never work out as long-term senior people. Just keep in mind they came to you with dignity and pride and should leave that way as well. They did something very few could ever do, so be good to them on their departure. So yes, when all this was done and finance "fixed," I let my firefighter go because it was the best thing for them and the company.

This is one place where I think many people get it wrong. They have a department they know is a complete mess, but when a firefighter does interview with them, they sit back and say, "No, I cannot see this person as a long-term hire." No kidding! So, they go on interviewing, trying to find a person with a strong enough personality to fix the problem, but who will also fit into the company and work out long-term. You are trying to find both a fighter and a enduring team player and they just are not in the same package. In the meantime, you have done both your employee and the company a disservice. There are times when you cannot accomplish something in one step, but must take a couple of steps to achieve the results you are looking for. (This is an important aspect of hiring/problem-solving, but I think you extend it too long. Try tightening up and keeping the main point — hire/let them do their thing/they have to go.)

Work one level at a time

Moving on from the 'firefighter' candidate, when you hire a senior person discuss what it is that both of you feel is important to the company and that department. Make a list, with the most important at the top and least important at the bottom. On the positive side every employee is being given a fresh look to see if they are right for the company. On the negative side, seniority means nothing, everyone gets the same look, those that cut it, stay and those that don't, leave. This needs to unemotional, which is why you have lists, either they are what is needed, or they are not.

Don't let your senior staff evaluate the entire department. Instead have them focus only the people who work directly for them. You are building a team from the top down. Once your VP has evaluated his direct reports,then this review process is pushed down to the next level. All the directors will evaluate everyone who works for them. This must be accomplished in 60 days or less and then it will move to supervisors.

Think about this. If you replace the people at the bottom of the ladder while still employing poor supervisors, what do you think will happen? Either the new employees will give up, become problems, or they will leave. Build the company one rung at a time, starting at the top, and finishing with the people who empty the trash. Always work your way down one step at a time. Never work from the bottom up and never skip around. Picking and choosing out of order and saying you will get back to the rest of the department later is a big mistake. The only thing you will do is ensure you have to clean up that group twice.

Not only do you want to do this to ensure you are fixing problems rather than just putting Band-Aids on problems, but people need to see and understand what you are doing. Cleaning up a company always creates a great deal of uncertainty and stress. To help reduce some of this, people need to understand how things will work. If you skip around and today decide to work on directors, but not all of them, and next week finish this, then people are always nervous they might be next. When people are uncertain or nervous, then they are not doing their best and make a great deal of mistakes. If you take care of all VPs, move on to directors. When you have finished with directors, the senior staff will know they are done and can get on with their work. At my present job, it took about 18 months to get through all of this. There was some secondary cleanup, but it was minimal.

You cannot replace an entire company at once, even if you start at the top and review/clean house there as soon as possible. After you have replaced the first two levels then you must decide which departments are the worst. Again, make a list and rank all departments from worst to best in order to determine the direction you will go. Obviously, the criteria for ranking will then expand depending on the type of department. For example, HR would be measured on different outputs than would QA.

It is important that your new senior teamwork is with you on this because you need to make sure they own it. If they help with the list, assist with the order, and have input on all the explanations as to why a department is where it is, then they cannot come back later and say, "I told you so." They now need to begin taking ownership for the decisions being made and begin to view the company as "their company."

Work in order

HR is normally the first group I review and then decide to either replace or maintain. This should be pretty obvious because they are going to be fundamental to everything you do until the day you leave. If you have a weak HR group, you will struggle to get the rest of the company straightened out.

Finance would normally be the next group because you must have accurate accounting to ensure you are in compliance with all laws, and be kept current on the financial situation for all the departments. How do you know if things are getting better if you cannot trust the numbers coming from the finance department? If you have a situation where a non-functioning department is impacting everything, then, of course, that is where you would start.

The thing that typically throws everyone off is why salespeople are last on the list. It can take a year before you might even start on the sales group and the issues with sales. If you do not have a good product, then what exactly is sales going to sell? Even worse is if your company has a product which is not consistent/in development. Today the product is okay, but by Friday the product is being tossed in the trash. If you do not have a quality, predictable product, then you have nothing to even sell.

Think about this from the salesperson's perceptive. They have worked six months to close a deal unique to a specific customer but then are stymied because Operations cannot produce a consistent product. The customer complains about it and, within three months, drops you for quality reasons and starts buying from someone else. You now have a salesperson who feels they have wasted six months of their time working this account for nothing. While this obviously upsets them, the thing that really bothers them, and what will convince them to quit, is they feel their reputation has been tarnished.

Just as bad? You now have a customer who believes they were lied to and cheated. It will be very difficult to ever convince them to buy from you again. Remember it typically takes much longer to get a customer back as it did to win them over the first time, because they feel they were treated poorly.

Many people feel sales is a collaboration between everyone in the company and, to some extent, this is true. However, from the customer's perspective the transaction is between them and their salesperson only. It was not between the customer, the operations manager, logistical crew, or packaging team. Only. Their. Salesperson. When you go to a restaurant and get a bad meal, do you demand to speak to the cook? No, you get upset at the person who delivered the meal even though they had nothing to do with preparing a single item on your plate. All they did was deliver it to you and hope you liked it. (Good analogy, but most folks know the serving staff are "just the messenger.")

Sales is the last department on the list because, but before you start addressing salespeople, you need a product that you know is going to function the way it is advertised. While salespeople are a dime a dozen, good salespeople are rare, and, typically, it doesn't take much for them to get discouraged and move on. The nice thing about sales is that as the product improves, the good salespeople will begin to shine and the questionable ones will start to complain.

When quality is bad your salespeople will fall into one of three camps: complaining, quiet, or comprehending. This really makes sense if you think about it. If quality is bad, like the waitress, the salesperson is taking the heat and does not like it. They want things fixed and will apply as much pressure to the organization as they can to get it fixed. The quiet ones are just keeping their head down and hoping to survive the entire mess. It is the in-the-know ones who are the interesting group.

These people are sympathetic and understanding, always saying they know everyone is doing their best and they are in the field fighting for the company, telling customers things are improving and buying the company a little more time. People in the organization are so thankful they work there and are holding things together. You will hear people say, "Man, I don't know what we would do without Bob!" Then things begin to change. The quality goes up, the product becomes consistent, manufacturing costs begin to drop, and sales begins to improve, but not Bob's sales. You sit and wonder why Bob cannot sell, never could sell, and you begin to find out that all Bob ever did was take the purchaser out to lunch, play golf with customers, or other fun things to keep people happy. Unfortunately, the bottom line is Bob cannot, never could, and never will be any good at sales. So, Bob now is extremely quiet and hoping no one notices that even though company sales are moving up, his are flat. This awareness definitely helps with your decision making.

Boards

As you get started on this reorganizing/fixing adventure you will find board members will become very nervous. I have always found it a bit ironic that I was hired to run a company and the very people who hired me were the first to scare. Seriously, what did they think was going to happen? That you were going to come in, make a speech, and everything would just get fixed?

I would love to tell you how best to handle this but in all honesty, the best advice is to have open communications with them. I have run companies where I would start discussions with each board member a few weeks before the board meeting.

The biggest issue with boards when you are turning around a company is to find the information balance. If you give too much, they feel you are doing so because you are unsure of your own success and looking for their approval. Too little, and they feel you are keeping something from them. If you wait until you are at the board meeting to share information, then the questions will become far more severe and pointed. They need to ensure the other board members do not view them as weak or not performing the oversight they are supposed to perform. So, they will tend to attack more and discuss less. This does no one any good.

Manage your board just like any other department in the company. Within one board meeting you should know who your harshest critic will be and who needs to be coddled the most. You must manage this group carefully, especially if board members change frequently, and it is where I still struggle. You need to think of board members as low-key investors. They should be given enough information so that they will keep investing in your organization, but not so much that they want to make decisions for you. No one knows the problems you are facing better than you do and even though you are always open to a discussion, in the end you need to keep all the decision-making in your office, not with a board member. At the end of a board meeting, they will admit they suggested "X" but will backpedal from taking any responsibility for the outcome of said suggestion unless it happens to work.

CHAPTER 4

Define Roles

Roles are defined, according to Merriam-Webster, as "a function or part performed especially in a particular operation process." From the minute you take control of a company you need to make very clear not only your role, but also the roles of everyone who works for you. Communication, especially in the early stages, will make or break the entire effort of turning a company around. Unfortunately, many people in companies are unclear as to what the role of their boss is, or even what their own roles are, regardless of titles.

Most of the people reading this book are employed. Regardless of your level in a company could you sit down and make a list of the goals your immediate supervisor has? Would you be able to write down the goals of his supervisor? Do you really know what their expectations are of you? Could you write down a list of the 10 things you know they are looking for and, even more importantly, their criteria for a great employee? I am not talking about the ridiculous responses people always give to this question. Such as:

They expect me to do my best.

They expect me to make good decisions.

They expect me not waste money.

Think about these answers. "They expect me to do my best." What does that mean? How do they actually know you are doing your best? How would you be able to prove to them you are doing your best? "They expect me to make good decisions." Define what a good decision is. Is a good decision from you identical to the one your supervisor would make? "They don't want me to waste money." Again, how do you know if you are wasting money? How would you measure this? If you cut spending by 10% in your department, what impact will that have on the product the company manufactures? Would the quality go down? How does your supervisor define your role in the company? How does your supervisor feel you are making a difference? Are you actually making a difference, or do you just make life easier? If you left tomorrow would anyone know or would anyone care?

The reason you, as an employee, have such a difficult time with this is because the people above you assume you know all this information. If you don't, have you ever asked for clarity, either from your supervisor or HR? More challenging is that without role clarity on both sides of the fence your supervisor may have no idea what he/she should expect from you, never mind if you do it well or not.

When you begin the process of breathing new life into a company there are some absolutes that make things even more difficult and stressful. I have never been hired into a company requiring turnaround that did not have a cash issue. In fact, most of the time lack of cash and the bank not being interested in increasing loans is how the board decided they had an issue and the company needed to be fixed.

If you have decided to take this plunge and make the effort to turn a company around, you need to understand the reason things got as bad as they are is because the board probably refused to see it.

Your role needs to be defined from the very beginning even at the stage of interviewing so that both interviewer and candidate are on the same page. Explaining your turn-around plan, when in place, and keeping them up to speed on the progress you're making should never be an issue. However, you and the board need to be very clear that the freedom to do your job is a must. I would strongly suggest this to be done during the interview process because the board is the one group you will have virtually no control over once you start. Do you need to interview with the entire board? Of course not, but meeting with the chairman of the board would be nice, if not a couple of board members.

Take a wrecking ball to silos

Now let's talk about defining roles with your staff and why this is important. One of the big issues with many companies, big, small, functional, or falling apart, are silos. People try to protect their turf at the expense of everyone else. The Operations department does not care if QA is functional as long as the Operations department is working. Departments will throw each other under the bus just to make sure everyone knows a problem, issue, or failure was not their fault.

The more stressed a company has become, the more you will see this happen and the harder it will be to tear down the silos. Everyone knows that at some point someone will show up to clean up the company and they want to be able to demonstrate how well they have been doing. Everyone else is a mess, but not them. Survival is just human nature, but what they do not understand is the very thing they think is helping is a big reason the company is in bad shape.

People will often times tell you need to protect their area to the betterment of the company, while promoting the idea that the other departments were dysfunctional because of the person running it. They also tell the board they would be more than happy to take these people because they are good people, knowing it will never happen but also knowing it makes them look very gracious with the company's future in mind.

Silos are often the number one complaint in many companies, but they are even worse in companies that are failing. When a company is failing, people know it and these people have a single thought: save my job. They don't see it as "save the company," but rather — "save everyone's job." But how do they save themselves?

I can assure you that in the first week you start, every single senior manager will want to just say "hi." During this hello they will tell you, "Let me know if you need anything." They will then go into how they have really worked to optimize their department and how they have tried to help others. This part of the discussion is why they are really in your office in the first place.

Let them come and let them say hello, but the minute they start on what they are doing, shut them down. Let them know you will be interviewing the entire staff and you would love to hear all about what they have done then, but you simply do not have the time now. If you let them go into the entire story when they came to say "hi," they are in control, get to tell the story the way they want, spin things in their favor, and dictate how the story unfolds. You want to be in control and ensure the story they will tell unfolds in the manner you want, to answer the questions you have, and ensure the spin is kept to a minimum.

As you hire your new staff you need to make it quite clear that you do not allow silos. Tell them their department has the worst silo, and while they are evaluating staff, they need to look at how to tear down the silo walls. They will all get the same message because, with a little creative thinking, you can justify why each department is bad.

Nothing kills stressed companies faster than silos. The best way to begin dismantling is to get your senior staff looking at departments that they either support or that support them. Let's take a very simple example and one which is very fresh in my mind.

I took over a company which had no buyer. Everyone in the company did their own buying, which is an issue by itself, but let's just focus on hiring a buyer. How do you think this went over? To say there was yelling and strong negative feelings would be the understatement of the year. My Operations manager explained to me how technical the equipment was and if the buyer failed to deliver the correct equipment, we could suffer downtime, poor yields, and even customer returns. Operations went into great lengths to explain how it took an engineer to make these decisions, and even they made mistakes. So, to hand this off to a buyer would be the biggest mistake I could ever make.

I looked at the VP of Finance and asked if they understood the concerns presented. They assured me they fully understood. I then asked how they proposed to address these concerns and continue to support Operations. Notice I never even considered allowing anyone in finance to have their way; I only tasked them to find some way to make things work. In the end, they agreed that criteria for a buyer included some engineering education and previous technical experience. In addition, a process change was needed to ensure sign off from Engineering before changes to a request were made just to save money. For example, if the buyer found a pump for 30% less, he had to convince Operations that the pump would work, and Operations had to sign off on the less expensive pump.

Did this get rid of the silo between the two departments? Of course not. What it did do was force two people to work together, trust each other, and opened a door for future discussion/cooperation that had previously not existed. Now here is the funny part. Operations felt he did the Finance group a favor by allowing the buyer to help with the purchasing of equipment. Strange, right? That the buyer would be helping Operations do a better job of finding good equipment at good prices actually means finance is helping Operations, but I can assure you this is not how it will be viewed. This is perfect because it now gives you an opening you might not otherwise have. Operations may now feel that finance is sticking their head into Operations, but I can assure you that Operations folks are chomping at the bit to do the same with finance.

As I have said many times, the biggest shortage you have in a company you are turning around is cash. Operations uses more cash than anyone in the company so now you can use this process change and new position to your advantage. You inform finance that they will invite Operations to the weekly meetings they have in the department when they discuss cash flow. The Operations person is smiling from ear to ear at this point because they will get to inject themselves into the finance department. Boy, is he going to teach finance a thing or two! The truth is, you have opened another door and taken down another brick in the silo between these two departments. Operations is now going to see that they are one of the big reasons why the company has no cash, why no one can have raises, why all bonus were cancelled. You have Operations now working with finance to improve the cash flow.

Yes, there will be battles between these two organizations. And yes, you are going to have to help this relationship along, but think of what you get in the end. Two department heads who now understand each other's problems, have a better idea of how they each contribute to the company's cash challenges, and are working to help each other succeed. Why? Because they will quickly see that for either of them to succeed, they have to help each other. And people inherently like to win.

Set expectations from the start
Learn how your employees think

In the first couple of days after your new person starts, they will be completing HR paperwork, meeting and greeting with people, and just getting to know their surroundings. Give them this time so they begin to see where they fit in and to meet their subordinates. I normally give a new person a week before I sit down for my first heart-to-heart discussion with them. You will have a great deal to convey and you want the attention that you will not get if they are concerned with and distracted by what insurance plan they should choose.

Normally when I sit them down for the first time, beyond "hello and welcome aboard," I discuss five things I want them to focus on in the first two months:

1) Evaluate all their direct reports and then be prepared to tell me each individual's strengths, weaknesses, if you plan to keep them and why.

2) What are the three biggest issues in their department?

3) Their thoughts on the culture of their department.

4) What areas do they feel they can help other departments with?

5) What quality issues do they have in their department?

I cover the five points I am interested in very thoroughly with my new employee so they know why I want their department review discussion within the first 60 days. I also make it very clear that they were hired to make decisions and I need to understand how they accomplish this.

Let's discuss why you want them to evaluate each person's strengths, weaknesses, and if they are worthy of remaining at the company. This has to do with both their ability to evaluate their staff and evaluating your new hire. You need to begin to understand how your new hire thinks, what they find important, and what drives their attention. Frankly, you need to understand them and how they think. I am less interested in the decisions they make than I am in how they made them. If they can think through a problem, understand the results of all the decisions they might make, how their decisions will affect not only your customers, but also the company, then you don't need to worry about their decisions because they will probably be good ones.

You need to cover this with them so they understand you will be looking more at the process than the results because with a good process the results will follow.

I can promise you this will make people very nervous and they will accuse you of not trusting them. Well, they are new and so, no, you don't trust them. But this also is a check for yourself. If they are making bad decisions, then one of two things are happening. Either they are not thoroughly thinking through a problem before making a decision or you are not giving them the information they need.

Different people need different amounts and types of information to be able to make sound decisions. You need to understand what this new person needs from you to ensure you are delivering. I have known people who could make wise decisions with virtually little information and I have known other people who need every scrap of information available to stand any chance of making a good decision.

I worked at a facility where the VP of Manufacturing needed to know every detail, no matter how small, to make a decision. It could take them weeks to get all the information they felt they needed in order to write a report on what is required to complete a project.

On the other hand, I have people who need just a few key points in order to tell you what they will need for a project to get done. The best part is they will be right more often then they will be wrong.

This does not mean one is any better at decision-making than the other, no it does not. They simply have different ways of working through a problem. The real key is what the results were/are and, fortunately, they typically were/are good. I have always found it interesting how some people need a few pieces of information where others need a great deal more but, in the end, I would rank the success of both the same. Different people process information differently not correctly or incorrectly — just differently.

Having this discussion in the first week brings out interesting responses. For example, I once hired an individual and detailed my expectations with them during their first week. At the end I was informed I was treating them like a child, that they could make good decisions, and had no plans to have this discussion with me at any time. I thanked them for their time and let them know they could perform this way at their next job because they were not needed at this one. I let them go after the discussion.

If you have hired a capable person, they should be able to tell you some of the biggest issues in their department within 60 days. They most likely will not have details but they should have some idea of what they face and what needs to be turned around.

Remember you are building a team where at some point they will manage their departments with little input from you. They need to understand the urgency of what you need and at the same time trust between you is needed.

Many people go wrong at this stage in thinking that they can just order people around, which they can. They believe that because they are higher in the food chain their direct reports should do as they are told and not whine about it. Technically this is true, and you might win in the short run, but when the time comes that you need them to will they come and stand with you or will they smile as you fall?

You are being paid to get things done, to accomplish a task, and to do this you need the people around you. Maybe not right now but, at some point, to turn a project or company around you will need support from not only all your staff but also from other departments.

Something else you need to understand is that you are not the only one talking to the board. There are people in the company the board will be speaking with to confirm if what you are saying is true or just a line of crap. If they are hearing good things about you from different people in the company, they will be talking with other board members, giving you support you might not normally have had. Even if the information to the board is not totally positive, they will be hearing that things are moving and changing.

Properly define your problem

All of this can be done if you now understand the problems you have in your company or if your senior staff can recognize the problems they have in their departments. I always tell people that 80% of solving a problem is being able to accurately define it. Believe it or not this is where most people go wrong. They will start working on a problem before they can accurately articulate what the problem is.

So many times people will jump in and start working on a problem and later find out they wasted their time. I have done it and I am sure you have as well. A few weeks ago, I saw a water bill for the company which we pay once per year. It was 40% higher than the previous year and I was livid. Cash is tight and now I need to find and extra $100,000 to pay the water bill.

Like all good presidents, I call all my department heads in and ask what they have been doing which required so much extra water. They replied business as usual and they could not understand why we had such a large bill. I decided if this was true then obviously either they were lying or some piece of equipment was not working correctly. They spent weeks looking at everything in the plant and in the end could not find anything wrong, and there in fact was nothing wrong.

Had I taken the time and really looked at the problem completely, I could have saved everyone a great deal of time. At this facility they get two bills, one for incoming water, and one for water discharge, and they come from two different agencies. If I had reviewed both of these bills, I would have seen that many times our water discharge was higher than our water intake. This, of course, is not possible and so I had people working on the wrong item.

The problem was that the water discharge meter was no longer working correctly and needed replaced. The problem was wrongly defined from the beginning and so people were wasting time. Had I reviewed all the information the problem would have been defined differently and people would have been focused on the real issue.

Yes, quality throughout the company is a role

Quality issues are the last topic you have planned for the discussion with your new senior employee. You spend more time explaining this and getting departments to take ownership than almost anything else. Operations understands quality issues, but other departments like Human Resources or sales do not. You will get pushback from Operations when it comes to QA, but you will get arguments from other departments when you talk to them about it.

Human Resources will not understand how they have any issues with QA because they will view it as an operational issue rather than a potential problem for every department. HR will not only struggle with how to measure their own performance, but will also grapple with understanding why it is so important. Let's look at HR and how they could be measured from a QA point of view. Actions that could be tracked for improvement include:

- How many people do they retain beyond the probation: six months to 1 year?
- How much do they spend on each new hire?
- What is the turnover in the company?
- How long does it take them to find people and are they finding the right people?

If people leave or must be let go in the first six months, then you have a real problem not only in HR, but also in the company as a whole. How can people be interviewed by three to six people, be hired, and in a short amount of time be the wrong person? Many people will say it is not HR because other people interviewed this person. My argument is that it is 100% an HR issue. It is HR's responsibility to ensure there is a proper interviewing process and have people trained to get the best out of the interview.

Do not let people off the hook. Recruiting is the responsibility of HR and if you are hiring the wrong people or they are quitting shortly after they are hired, then it is HR's responsibility to find out why and correct it. All of this can be measured as a means to tell you the quality of your Human Resource department. Getting HR to understand this will also take time and patience, especially if they have never been measured in this manner before.

Now let's look at the sales department: the second most difficult group to understand that quality in their department can, and should be, measured. You can measure what the hit rate of each salesperson is (how many projects each salesperson quotes versus how many accounts they close). You can also measure the gross margins each salesperson achieves which by the way, directly relates to cash flow. You can measure how many accounts a salesperson sees in any given month.

You must always remember if you cannot measure something, you are not working on it. If you are not working on it, then it will never get better. This ties back to why you want to know what the biggest issues are with each department. You need to find a way to measure these issues to ensure they are improving. This connects into quality assurance of the department.

I hope you are beginning to see how all of the points covered relate to each other and why you want your new senior hire to bring back to you not only the information they uncover in the first 60 days, but also how everything interconnects with each other. I can assure you most people you speak with will not understand this until it is explained. And if no one has ever explained it to you, then this book has put you one step of head of everyone else.

Always ask for real examples, not a "feeling"

When speaking to your staff, make sure they can give you examples of what they are talking about. "Jim" is a poor supervisor because I observed the following over the past 60 days:

- He loses his temper easily and did so on these (documented) occasions.
- He cannot explain what is needed in a way his people understand and here are some examples.

The same goes with issues within the department itself, not just employees:

- We have quality issues because the extruders are not being maintained correctly.
- The preventive maintenance program was abandoned because of cash issues.

In neither case did I ask for ways to solve the problem or for extreme details because in 60 days there was not time to fully understand all of the issues. What they can, and should give you are the basics.

What you want to make sure of is that they are not giving you a "gut" feel or, even worse, reiterating something they were told. Remember, people are trying to salvage their jobs so they will toss other people off a cliff if they need to. You need to ask enough questions to know that your staff is telling the truth and not just something they heard. In many cases what they heard they now believe is the truth, but this may not be the case and it is up to you to have enough knowledge of your company to set them straight.

The most overused excuse of them all

Training is the most overused example of poor performance I hear. Everyone always lists lack of training of why someone is a poor performer. The problem is if you have told your staff for examples of why someone is a poor performer you cannot allow them to decide what information they give you that you will believe and what you won't.

I ran a company where I was told the issue with most of the operational people in the company was poor training. Most of the people were being ask to perform tasks they were not really trained to do. I knew that training was not going to fix the problem. The product they made was very low tech and required very little training. But if you tell your team they must develop a plan to solve a problem, you cannot turn around and shoot down their idea. What you can do is measure the performance of the group getting extra training and see if the training has any real effect.

Since operations was going to go through an intense training process, I informed my team I would go through all the training myself. This would not only teach me how to make our product, but I would also be able to see how good the training we were doing was. So, for several weeks I went out on the floor at night for several hours and went through the same training that every new hire went through.

After several weeks of training, we got back together and, after looking at the data, recognized that training was not the main issue after all. The team then felt that maybe the current yields were simply the best the company would ever have, and I needed to just get used to it. Wrong! But now they are ready for you to help move things along.

One of the first things people ask me when I tell them that at times I let my senior team work on something I know will yield little to no results is why do I do this, given that it's probably a waste of time. The answer is simple If they only do things I agree with, then they will stop thinking on their own and simply wait for me to tell them what to do. Why should they think on their own if they will only be allowed to do what I want? They will view thinking as a waste of time, and long term, these people need to be thinking and making decisions on their own.

Even though you are certain that what they are about try will not be effective, you must demand that the results be measured. This gets them used to you monitoring them from afar and that they will be expected to deliver results. Letting them do this then opens a conversation on how the results will be measured, the timeframe for completion, and the expected results. Measuring results also keeps them focused on what they are after and ensures the plan's definition does not change halfway through the process.

I let people work on training because it is inevitably the first solution raised. I'm often also told training would be a success because employees understand their job better than before. Who cares…did it really make a difference?

- Did yield improve?
- Did overall plant utilization improve?
- Did overtime go down?
- Did the cost per element go down?

If the answer is "no," then all they really proved is that more training was not the solution. Time to move on to identifying the real root cause/causes.

Conversely, don't ignore that you might be surprised and things do improve as the result of training. Be very careful of this, though, because you might find that short-term, during the initial training period, things do improve. The key is whether or not improvements last long-term. When employees know they are being looked at, have people working with them, and understand that they are being evaluated, things will improve. As soon as this effort stops, however, too many revert right back to the way they used to be.

When I was a department manager at a company, we had a very large scrap issue, which management believed was the result of poor training. As I said, this is always the very first thing people go after. I set up a detailed training for all the key operators, technicians, and supervisors. We took two months and reviewed every aspect of the system, process, and Operations. I had put together written documents, cheat sheets and testing, all to ensure the best training possible would be given.

One of the first things we noticed was that as the training went on, yields began to get worse. By the time we got to the end of the training scrap had gone up by 5%. When you are producing 1 million parts per month this is really a big deal. What we found was that the more people learned, the more they tried to outguess the system. They now had knowledge and felt they could do their job better than the computer could. They were wrong, of course, so we then had to lock them out of the controls to stop them from overriding the system.

Turning a company around is not a sprint. It takes thinking ahead and figuring out what you need long-term and then backing that into what it takes to achieve it. You want your team to think, to hold themselves accountable, to recognize when they have gone in the wrong direction and do a self-correction.

I hope you are beginning to see that your goal is to NOT have your staff make the same decisions you would make. Your goal is to have them understand you expect them to make good decisions which can be supported by the data they have. You are not their babysitter. Your role is to understand what needs to get done from a strategic point of view. Their role is to figure out the details on how to get it accomplished. This is the point you need to make clear from the very beginning so there is no confusion as to what is expected from them.

They need to understand that if you work on day-to-day issues, then you are not working on longer-term issues. If you are working on those at that level, then the company has no future. This is why it is worth your time at the start to work with your staff, train them to be what you need, and make sure they understand their roles and, most importantly, they understand yours.

CHAPTER 5

Human Resources

I once walked into work and an employee was in HR with a complaint. The department manager had written him up for being late to work, but he had an email from HR stating that he would not be written up for this infraction. Ask yourself — if this went to court or arbitration who would win?

I understand the outcome is not as simple as I am making it; maybe he lied to HR and the decision to not write him up was based on this lie, but not knowing whether it was a lie or not HR cannot reverse, explain, or change the email. Let's keep it simple and say no one was lied to and there are simply two people who came up with two different decisions, both having heard exactly the same story. I can tell you that at arbitration the HR decision will overrule the department manager every time. I know this because I have been to arbitration over this very issue.

My point is, in this case HR and the company were not working together, and each was doing whatever they wanted, regardless of policy (if in place). If HR was seen by employees as a viable and active participant in the company, then managers/supervisors would have a discussion with HR before making decisions on their own.

In many companies the HR department reports to finance. If this is the case with the company you just took over, split them apart. At the beginning, you want everything to be reporting directly to you since you have no idea if any of your senior staff will be kept. You have to assume at the beginning that you are completely on your own and that no one at the company can fully be trusted. I realize this is a very negative attitude, but you are new, the company is failing, and people are fighting for survival.

When you start, you want no middlemen between you and all the main department heads until you have had an opportunity to begin making changes. Even if both HR and finance want to remain combined, resist and keep them apart for at least one year. People need to hear the intensity in your voice, see the urgency in your face, and hear the words you are using.

The day you start, you will conveniently land in HR, like everyone else. You have forms to fill out, benefits to enroll in, tax forms to complete, and any number of other New Hire tasks to do. You are no different than anyone else as you must process into the company before you can get started. Since you first land in HR, use this to your advantage. Have a discussion with the HR person and find out a few things by just having an easy conversation. How HR is run will give you a very good feel as to how the rest of the company has been operating and what to be looking for.

These first days, there is nothing more important than getting your senior staff into place as quickly as possible. Remember you are working from the top down. For example, if you have no one running Engineering then you, by default, are running Engineering. If you have no one running sales, again, you are running that department.

How many departments do you think you can run efficiently by yourself? Personally, I can run manufacturing, engineering, and sales all with no issue because I am proficient in all these areas. I have run manufacturing for many years, spent a great deal of my life in Engineering and R&D so no issue there, and was blessed to work with some great salespeople, but no one is great at everything and you will not have time to spend days or weeks working on a single problem.

I would be the worst person in the world to run HR and would never even attempt it. If I had no HR people, I would hire a temp from the outside to get me by until I could hire a person to fill the position. In fact, I would possibly even hire an outside company to run my HR department until I could hire the right person to lead it.

I can read a P&L exceptionally well and understand what every-thing means, but do I have the time to drill down and chase every number down? For example, if the gross margin dropped dramatically, then someone needs to drill down and find out why. Maybe costs went up for a month or two, maybe sales dropped for a couple of months, maybe there were equipment issues, or any number of other possibilities, but someone, other than I, must figure out the details and be able to explain it efficiently. This needs to be done and if you are working on this then you are not working on other issues. (Should you mention finance dept. here or is that understood?)

The longer it takes you to get your senior staff into place, the deeper the hole you are digging, simply because you cannot effectively run everything yourself. You are not a superhero, so getting your senior team in place needs to get done quickly. This means spending money on good recruiters.

Once you have decided which departments you can run yourself, you can be confident in removing the existing lead person before find-ing their replacement. If you are not confident in running a specific department, find the replacement before removing the lead. For example, if you are like me, your weakness may be running HR so you decide to go to a temp agency until you find a full-time replacement. Do not delay replacing someone just because you do not have someone in place already or you do not feel competent to do it yourself. Find a work-around. There are plenty of temp agencies out there that can put someone in place the next day if you need them to. Are they the best, no, but will they get you by until you have found a permanent solution? Yes.

If you wait until you have a replacement for everyone you plan to dismiss, it will never get done or, if it does, it will take much longer than necessary. Do not let yourself off the hook, stick to the plan, and get creative. For Pete's sake, that is why you were hired!

Since I have spent much of my life in R&D, along with running operations and assisting sales, running these departments was a natural for me. This is a major benefit for people like me who have worked their way up the ladder rather than starting a management role straight from college.

If you use a recruiter, you will pay 20%—30% of the position's base salary in fees. Most finance people view this as a waste of money. Thus, they feel it might take longer but you can get the same recruitment done if you just use the free boards available. For example, at the time of this writing LinkedIn charges about $450 to post job openings for six months. This is nothing compared to $20-40k you will pay for a headhunter. On the other hand, it takes a good HR department to not only conduct online searches but to also weed through the resumes generated by board postings. If you go the free board posting route, your HR needs to be strong from the onset, and overstaffed. If you plan to use a recruiter for staffing a number of positions, they may be willing to give you reduced rates, so don't be afraid to negotiate. In this case, you have the power because you need to find three or four people and can go anywhere. If they want this business, then they can reduce the fee they charge to get it. Another key factor is to look for a guarantee from the recruiting firm that they will do background checks on the resumes of interest. Unfortunately, people will put false information on their resumes or web pages because they know without it, they will not land a job. They also count on potential employers doing minimal background checks.

I once ran a company where we were looking for a senior engineer and, after looking on our own for six months, decided to use a recruiter. We had a job description written, so explaining what we needed was easy. We also used a recruiter who specialized in this field and felt we should be able to find someone within a few weeks.

Sure enough, within 30 days we were presented with a candidate who sounded perfect on the phone, so he was brought in for an interview. This person knew all the right words and sounded extremely intelligent, so we made an offer that was accepted. Within a few weeks it became obvious that he had no real knowledge about process engineering, even if he knew all the right words. This shows we were not doing a good job of interviewing, but depended far too much on the recruiter.

We called the recruiter, explained the problem, and he assured us that a full background check had been conducted and there should be no issues. I asked if his school had ever been contacted to ensure he had a degree and was shocked when I was told they only did background checks of items recorded in the state. His college was out of state, so no check was ever made.

Think about this for just one minute. People in the USA are extremely mobile and the odds of a person getting a degree out of state are extremely high. Still, this recruiter did not feel it was important to send the school an email. What if this person had shot someone in Texas and was now living in NJ? We would have never known because the recruiter checked nothing out of state. Recruiters are not cheap, and I think companies deserve better than what some of these people provide.

Truth is, the recruiter was paid a good fee but did not do his job and we hired an individual who was not qualified. I have worked with many recruiters over the years. Most are very good at their jobs and are honest people.

By the way, make sure your contracts with recruiters cover bad hires. This means that if you fire someone within 30, 60, or 90 days from their start date, the recruiter should give you either a refund or find another employee for you at no cost. Any recruiter that will not agree to this is not worth working with. If they were good, they would have no issue guaranteeing their work.

I still work with recruiters to find new employees, but now have my HR department do the background checks prior to making an offer. They are not very expensive, and you can do various levels of checks depending on your needs. You can find if they have a degree from any college, ever been in trouble with the law, what companies they have worked for, and what type of security level they may have had. You need to have them sign a release, which is often available from the background check company you are using, or you can use one written by your attorney, to ensure nothing ever comes back to haunt you. Don't rely on other people to do your work for you. Take the time and make sure.

Now, you might say I am putting a great deal of responsibility on HR. And what about the hiring manager? Don't they get some of the blame because they also let these poor performers through?

Yes, of course they do. Here is the ugly truth though. Most people are incredibly poor at interviewing, and I would include myself in this list. They have no idea what questions they should be asking initially, what follow up questions to use, or examples to substantiate what is being asked. I have never actually met a person who ever received training on how to interview people, but one day found themselves promoted to a position where they were expected to interview someone and help decide if this person should be hired. They give it their best but really have no idea what they are doing and will make a final decision on whether they like the person in front of them or not.

If you think about this, the amount of money it costs to recruit and train someone that you will fire in 90 days makes no sense. The only thing more expensive than keeping a poor performing employee is hiring a worse one. This is the main reason why I put so much on HR's shoulders because they should be the best interviewer in the company. They do more of it, should be learning better interviewing techniques, and should be good at reading people. In short, they should be the best you have for identifying a potential employee, and if they are letting everyone through then you have an issue.

While one of the things I am trying to do in this book is to provide you with ideas on how to solve problems but for this I really do not have one. I have read a couple of books and gone to a couple of seminars but, rather than give me good advice, they often try to get clever.

HR could sit and listen to people interview and then, when the interview is done, review and critique the interviewer on what went well and what did not. HR should help the interviewer improve his/her skills because interviewing is like any other skill. You get better at it with training and practice.

Is HR really functioning?
Let's find out and look at job descriptions

Let's move on to job descriptions; every single position in the company should have current job description. At a company I once ran there were job descriptions for everyone in the company, but they were last updated in 1986. I recall asking the director of HR how this was possible because it implies that not a single job had changed in 32 years. If this were true then it would help explain why the company was failing. But, of course, it was not true.

Job descriptions are actually a great indicator of the health of the entire company and aid in identifying what needs looking into. If neither HR nor managers could do something as simple as keeping job descriptions current, nor saw the need to do so, it makes you wonder what else has not been updated in 32 years. Believe it or not, HR and how well HR is running can give you a window into how the company was run prior to your arrival.

HR is almost completely an administrative function, in that they do not need to schedule production, work with external customers, or ensure the product is correct. Don't get me wrong, HR is very important and is the front end of the company, but if they are unable to keep job descriptions up to date, how are they doing with more difficult tasks like harassment claims, theft, abuse of sick time, and all the other issues HR handles on a daily basis.

Accidents

Time lost due to accidents is something you need to take a long hard look at. I approach this from a monetary point of view, whereas other presidents may approach this as a safe work issue. Both get to the same point but for different reasons. Consider the cost of worker's compensation insurance, which goes together with accidents. If you reduce accidents, the insurance premiums will be reduced. Since you are now leading a stressed company, cash is vital. Fewer accidents = lower premiums = improved cash flow.

You are not looking to hide accidents or not report them. You simply want the accidents to be less frequent in order to get lower rates. One of the worst companies I took over was having one to two accidents per month and the worker's comp rates were close to $1 million annually. This is cash going out the door — cash you vitally need to make payroll, pay suppliers, and a million other things.

I have spoken to many people who say worker's comp is the best money they have ever spent. I say it is the biggest waste of money on the planet. Every dime you spend on worker's comp is money that could have been spent on equipment, safety, or any number of other items to improve the company.

Other presidents who want to reduce accidents to ensure a safe working environment also achieve the same results. They want to reduce the number of accidents in the workplace so that employees are at work and not at home recovering. Bottom line is, we both want the same thing, just for different reasons. In both cases, the uninjured employee is the winner. (Why introduce "other presidents" here? You've established your argument.)

Time lost to accidents will also clarify how safe the company is in general. If you have one to two accidents per month, then the company is not a safe place to work. It is only a matter of time before you will have an extremely serious accident resulting in either death or permanent disability. You also risk OSHA coming into your plant, finding the environment unsafe, and fining the company heavily. Can you afford to have a $100,000 fine from OSHA when you are struggling to even meet payroll?

There are also many ways to reduce worker's comp claims. The insurance agency you work with should be willing to visit your company and, after touring the entire facility, give you a list of items to correct before you even get a visit by OSHA. Their input can save you thousands of dollars and time lost.

Now if you noticed I said IF you have one to two accidents per month? Just because this is what is being reported does not mean it's an accurate number of accidents. People fake accidents all the time to get free time off.

Installing cameras throughout the company oftentimes can help. At one particular company, as the number of cameras increased, the amount of accidents went down. This quickly told me that many of the accidents were faked. Without the cameras there would have been no way to prove this, but now we had evidence. We also made sure that we made a big deal about installing the cameras so that people not only knew we were installing them, but also knew where they were.

If your company has a high number of accidents and cameras are not working, the next step is to have HR hire a private investigator. This is especially important if you have multiple employees receiving worker's comp for accidents that may have been faked.

To find a private investigator, tell HR to get in touch with your worker's comp insurance company. They will know where to find someone and, oftentimes, will be willing to split the costs with you. They want to find people filing false claims just as much as you do, so do not be afraid to ask about splitting the bill. Also, don't be the least bit surprised if someone on your senior team comes to you and asks why you are doing this. I think your senior team should know that, when you have egregious worker's comp issues, hiring a PI is not out of order!

You have also just made your first statement to HR; false claims will not be tolerated, period. Once the first employee fraudulently receiving worker's comp is discovered and dealt with appropriately, you will have made it quite clear to the entire company that insurance fraud will not be tolerated. Along with this, do not be surprised if the agency handling your worker's comp wants to investigate other claims. Work with them. They are on your side, and now that they have discovered there may be an issue, they will want to get the entire mess addressed/resolved as quickly as possible.

Cleaning up a company is more than just turning a profit. It also includes taking care of the employees, make sure they are working in a safe environment, and ensuring people are working towards always reducing the accidents that do occur. It is also about finding those employees who are abusing the system and firing them. During the interviewing process with HR, this is one of the topics you will want to get into. What type of accidents happen, how often, and what is being done to reduce them?

Reviews

The next area you need to review in HR are yearly appraisals. Were they ever done? When were they last done? Are managers just checking a box? Is there any written dialogue, positive, negative, or constructive? I am not a big believer in yearly appraisals and only do them every few years, believing that ongoing reviews of performance are not only timelier, but also help provide continuous feedback that contributes to employee development. However, the key for formal written reviews is every few years, not **never**. If there are no appraisals, the obvious question is, why?

You personally are just interested in reviewing directors and above who have been with the company a while, again working from the top down. Therefore, you should be very interested in reading their past reviews. Never assume they are meaningless or a waste of your time. Why can I say this with such assurance?

If the appraisals are accurate and show you have a problem employee, then why are they still here? If this is a stressed company and your predecessors were not getting rid of poor performers, then what were they doing to get the company moving forward again?

If you do not need to read them, then why ask for them? For one thing, they are good for legal reasons. If you fire someone and they take you to court and you can show they received yearly appraisals which were always bad, you will have a decent case. Another reason is because people both hate reviews and need them. Sounds contradictory but both statements are true.

People who do not get regular reviews will often say their manager must not care about them because otherwise they would have yearly appraisals. They will say: "How do I know how I am doing without feedback?" "How do I know that my manager knows what I do if I do not get an annual review?" "How can I get a decent raise if I'm not getting a review?" On the other hand, most people who get an unfavorable review will say their manager is biased against them, does not really know what they do, is never around to see their contribution, etc. The onus for a poor review tends to fall on the appraiser, not the employee, at least in the employee's opinion.

The issue I have with appraisals is that most people who give them fall into one of two camps. Some will keep track of every negative thing you did that year, never acknowledge the positive, and put only the negative into your appraisal at the end of the year. They seem to focus on every mistake you have made— even if you have a list showing your contributions, successes, and accomplishments.

The other camp is the entire review is based on what you have done over the last three to four months. No one recalls what you did 10 or 11 months ago, so they focus on the most recent events which is why the entire review is based on recent behavior.

The obvious question at this point is, if I do not believe in annual appraisals, why would I care to see them? Simple. People want to feel recognized in written form, but if you are relying on appraisals to determine employee problems, then you really do have issues because they will not address or resolve them. (We will cover this in the next section of the book.)

Reviews serve one other purpose as well. A review can tell you how the manager of a specific department is both performing and thinking. For example, if all white people get better reviews than people of color then you and HR have a diversity issue with the manager. If all men get better reviews than women, then you and HR have a gender-biased issue. If someone used to get great reviews and, after changing departments, is now getting poor reviews, this is an issue to be looked into. Maybe they cannot do the new job due to lack of experience/training/education/incompetence. Perhaps their previous manager was a friend who gave them better reviews than they should have received. Or maybe their new manager does not like them and is setting up a reason to fire them. All of this is why HR should read every review before it is issued. If the previous administration did not do them, the question then becomes, why not?

Did the previous administration just not want to do them or were appraisals simply something that was overlooked? If you are told that the previous administration simply did not believe in doing one every year, like myself, then when was the last one done? If, on the other hand, you are told it was just something that fell through the cracks, then HR was not doing their job.

No more chit chat; let's get to work

Initially, all of this has been casual conversation with HR. Now, however, you want some real information in order to begin making the first assignment in your new company. Tell your HR person that you want a list of all employees who have been late to work in the past year, along with details on what actions were taken with these people. If written warnings were issued, then you want to read them and if people were dismissed, you want to understand why. There are other items you want to know as well, including:

- Lost time   When and how long
- Accidents   When and for what
- Worker's comp   Who and for how long
- Who has been out on disability in the past five years and when?
- Pay rates and increases every year for the past five years
- Who has been released in the past year and for what?
- List each position each employee has held in the company since hired. For example:
  - John Doe
  - QA director three years
  - Manufacturing manager five years
  - EHS manager for two years
- If you have a union, then ask for a copy of the contract, current and past, as well as all agreements outside of the contract with the union. There may be many.
- Who are the officers of the union?
- Who has been promoted in the company, when, and from what to what?
- What is the policy on unused vacation at the end of the year? Policies for accrued and unused vacation?

All of this information tells you a great deal about how well HR is functioning. Many people will comment that HR is not in control of who is dismissed, nor does HR have any control over many items in the list above, but I disagree. Let's look at the list so that you can better understand why HR has some control over more than people think.

1. Lost time: when and how long?

You are not so much looking for individual people who are chronically causing lost production time due to lateness, accidents, or other reasons. But you are looking for problem areas in the company. Does one department have more accidents than other departments? I can assure you that you will find issues everywhere but normally, one or two departments will stick out as being worse than the others. In the problem department (s), what type of accidents seem to be most common?

My involvement aside, HR should normally do the accident report. If you have an environmental health and safety (EHS) person and they report to HR, they should be demanding department managers address the accidents happening in their departments. These issues should then be reported back to EHS and resolutions discussed. If no EHS, then HR should be overseeing accountability and resolution from the department managers. If not, you need to know why not?

2. Who is out on disability and for how long?

I have worked in both union/non-union shops and have learned that union shops not only have more people out on short-term disability (STD), but that the disability period also tends to be longer. Therefore, the main reason you want to see a list of those currently/recently out on STD is because you are looking for people who show a pattern of being out more than most.

You are looking for a pattern, so start by reviewing when people take off for illness. Are they always taking Mondays, or near holidays, Fridays, or in the summer? I have run into two people like this over the years. The first employee claimed they had a problem with their back. Backs are a great thing to claim because it is almost impossible for a doctor to determine if there is really a problem. We have all had back pains and if you go to a doctor, they will tell you to rest.

They would go out for six to seven months and then come back to work for a couple of months before going out with another problem. It would be their back or shoulder or neck, but each time they would be out for months. They never claimed they hurt themselves at work, but rather that work aggravated the injury.

3. List every position each employee has held in the company since hired

Most people who join a company are hired to do a specific task, and even though they might move between departments, they never move up in position. These will be employees you will want to speak with.

If they were good at their job, they would be promoted and have more and more departments reporting into them. Instead, moving from department to department without being promoted to an even more senior position typically means someone who is not very good at anything, but the company is afraid to let them go — and for a variety of reasons but none of which benefit either the company or the individual.

I once ran a company who had a person moving from department to department at the director level. Long before I took over, HR should have stepped in when they saw this employee was being moved around to different departments. They should have realized that he was moved, not because he was any good, but because he was not. They should have looked at why he was being moved and why everyone was afraid to resolve the issue.

I once asked this person why they thought they were moving all around, never staying in a single position for more than two to three years. They told me they did not know, had never asked, and did not care as long as they kept their job until retirement. To do so, they would do whatever was asked without question or complaint. I asked this employee what they thought they were good at and was told they really did not know because they never held a job long enough to become really proficient at anything.

4. What everyone makes in the company

Part of why you want to see this is obvious: as President you need to know what people make, pure and simple. There is also another reason: believe it or not, you want to see if someone is milking the company.

One of the three VP's had started out as a shift supervisor, was promoted to plant manager, then promoted to head up the offshore office, and was currently in charge of sales in a very small territory. What happened? Come to find out when the small factory in which he was the shift supervisor needed a new plant manager, he promoted himself. He did the same thing when a VP position came up. He just gave himself a new title, told finance to increase his salary, and they all just did it. Now, here is the problem: After reading his file, he was not good at any position he ever held, but no one challenged what he was doing do so he just kept doing it.

5. Vacation policy

This one might seem a bit odd to have here, but it is another area where people milk the company and take advantage of policy. For example, people will not take vacation all year and expect to receive a payout of unused vacation at the end of the year. The company is strapped for cash and yet you have people expecting this payout simply because HR did not implement one or more viable vacation policies: "Use vacation during the calendar year or lose it," "One week only can be carried over, but will not be paid out if not used," "Company will close completely for a week in August/December and all employees will take vacation time then." This last is more typical in Europe, but is not without merit for the US. There are many different variations of vacation policies or PTO, all of which HR should be familiar with in order to recommend one that best benefits the company.

6. All pay increases for the past 5 years

Again, you are looking for people who are exploiting the company. It is not unusual for senior people to decide among themselves that no one in the company will get a pay increase except themselves. If asked, they will justify this by saying how much stress and responsibility they have compared to the rest of the company, that they deserve this because they are not taking their bonus, that this compensates them for all the travel or long hours. They will always have an excuse, but that is really all it is. In addition, it is important to know how all employees are compensated, if salaries are above/below/at market value, and if there is a policy for getting to market value. You can't keep good staff if they are consistently underpaid, as most employees these days have some idea of what market value is — plus or minus the experience and education they bring to the table.

After reviewing all these items, you can quickly see where the company places importance and how consistent it is when handling issues. I can assure you that when you get the detailed information provided by this list you will know if you should keep the HR person or let them go. This is after determining if they were incompetent or prevented from making HR improvements by the former president. Tell them you want this done by the end of your first week and that they need to be prepared to discuss any issues you might find from the list. HR will be the very first department you will interview, starting with the HR manager if there is one. And remember — the interview started the minute HR handed you the healthcare paperwork.

CHAPTER 6

Finance

Finance is the next department to be reviewed and the most critical area to be reviewed is financial integrity, starting with what policies the finance department adheres to. Policies should be in place for financial controls, covering everything from how bills are paid to what information is needed on a PO. What checks and balances are being followed? How much power does each position in the department have? Whether you are running a private or a public company, consistency is important. Generally Accepted Accounting Principles (GAAP) rules should be followed as well.

The same is true with in-house controls in the financial department. Most people would never steal from the company they work for, but sometimes life happens. Unexpected bills arise, mother gets very sick and Medicare will not cover the costs, or your child gets into trouble. You need just a little financial help, have no other options for obtaining it, and figure you will pay it back before the company ever finds out.

You must have internal controls, a system where everything in the company is handled in a certain way so that the unusual stands out and is easy to spot. Here are some basic internal controls you should have policies for:

- Sales
  - Processing orders through the system from receipt of credit application to shipment, cash application, returns/customer credits, accounts receivable analysis and maintenance of price lists.

- Purchasing
  - Processing of materials from supplier selection and price, requisitions and purchase orders, receipt of goods, payments, and maintenance of accounts payable
- Production
  - Processing of work in progress (WIP) through finished goods.
  - Maintenance of inventory records and physical inventory to include validation of all inventory.
- Fixed assets
  - Creation of appropriation requests with follow-through to close of project
  - Creating a fixed asset in your Enterprise Resource Planning (ERP) system, including the sale, disposal or relocation of assets in order to maintain proper fixed asset ledgers.
- Accounts receivable/accounts payable
  - If you are following GAAP, these two positions should be held by different people. You should not have one employee doing both jobs.
- Financial closing process
  - Month/year end closing process to include materials and inventory, journal entries, validating all balance sheets accounts, financial reports, and cash flow.

Investigate to see if people are getting around these policies. If so, it should stand out and be easy to spot. If people are working on getting around the system the question is why? This also can to point to larger issues throughout the entire company because, if the CFO is letting people get around the rules, why? Also, if you are told there are no internal controls, it just means your work review of this department just got harder.

Levels of signature authority are very important to review when it comes to purchases, checks, and funds transfers over $10,000. Many people ask why it is important to look at the finance department so thoroughly and the answer is easy. There is no employee in the company who knows the true status of the company better than finance, and specifically the CFO. If they don't, that's another issue to be discussed later on. However, the worse things are the more tempting it is for people to skim a little bit here and there because they know the company will most likely fold anyway.

I told a CFO once that I planned to move up the food chain in future companies and was curious how to discover corruption in the finance department. I was shown many things a corrupt finance department could do if they wanted. In addition, it was stressed to me that buyers were also people who needed to be reviewed from time to time. As luck would have it, I had worked there for about two years when I noticed a buyer no longer showed up to work and wondered why. I asked the CFO about it and was told that the buyer had been caught stealing from the company and offered to show me what they had done.

That afternoon we reviewed a couple of years' worth of POs and I was shown that the buyer had set up a shell company/supplier from whom our division bought 60%—70% of basic hardware. What no one at the time knew was that before the order was placed the buyer would have the personally owned shell company buy the product from this supplier. The buyer would then add a small fee to the price and resell it to the company. The buyer never made much from any purchase, but over the course of some years it became a large amount.

Corporate caught this scheme when they performed an audit and wanted to know why so much product was bought from a single source. I am not sure what was said or how they traced everything back to this one employee, but in the end, he was caught.

I have been very fortunate to work with very knowledgeable and competent CFOs in my life who were always happy to answer questions. For example, it was explained there are some basic giveaways if you are looking for kickbacks. The most obvious will be unusual loyalty to a supplier.

Many of the policies I use today not only protect the company, but protect the employees as well. We set up audits for buyers to help ensure they were not getting kickbacks from suppliers. This included no gifts, no lunches, and the mandate to have multiple bids. We force the buyer to change suppliers from time to time to see how much pushback we get. If the buyer has nothing to lose from changing suppliers, and the pricing is in line with pricing from previous suppliers, then they should not push back. Of course, nothing ever guarantees people will be honest, but you can make it difficult for them and try to remove the temptation.

The very first thing you need to get when you start is a five-year analysis of various areas of the company. Your finance employee will want to just give you the raw data, but politely state that you want this data in graphical form. The reason behind this format is simple. You are looking for inconsistencies, which will show up very quickly in graphical form versus raw data. Therefore, have your finance department graph the following:

- Sales dollars
- Gross margin
- Earnings before interest, depreciation and taxes (EBITDA)
- Maintenance costs against sales dollars
- Cost of goods sold (COGS) against sales dollars
- Top five raw material costs against sales dollars
- Inventory levels against sales dollars
- Inventory turns
- Scrap against sales dollars

With this data, there is a great deal you can discover. For example:

Sales

You really want the sales volume, gross margin, and the EBITDA on the same graph because this will tell you if sales is losing market share without you're even asking them. If sales volume is steady, but margins are decreasing, you might be holding market share by decreasing your sale price. This is the biggest contributor to your issue of cash flow.

If you are holding market share by decreasing your price, then you are sitting on a time bomb, possibly leading to the company's collapse. How much time you have depends, but the end is clear, and you will need to find a solution quickly.

Maintenance

The next graph you want to review is for maintenance costs. This will not be intuitive, so you need to see is if costs are steady or have even slightly increased over the years. One of the very first things most troubled companies do is to reduce preventive maintenance (PM) because it is viewed as a pure cash drain. Unfortunately, companies use flawed logic thinking this way about PM. Thus, when they do cut PM, they have just dug themselves a very expensive hole, should they try to get out of it. Let's look at why this is true.

Since you are a manufacturing company, you are clearly making something. It doesn't matter what it is, but why would anyone buy from you? Either you have unbelievably low prices, and I mean prices on par with those offered by China, or you have a good quality product that is price competitive with everyone else in your market. If option two, it means you have equipment either completely making the product or assisting in making the product. If this equipment is not working correctly, then how do you expect to make a good product? I have never understood why you would not take care of the very equipment you need to make the product you sell.

Cost of Goods Sold (COGS)

The next thing you want to look at is cost of goods sold (COGS), in hopes that it will explain the decreased margins. If the cost of goods sold is increasing, but your price remains the same, then you have explained the graph for falling margins. You have new problems, but at least you reset the timer on your bomb. When you get to the manufacturing group, you will need to cover this and understand what is happening to cause the increase.

One of the first things you need to make sure of is that COGS is really the COGS. This sounds funny, I know, but things are not always what they are labeled. I have worked at companies where the cost of manufacturing a product is in the month it was made even when the product might not be sold for months. When this happens, you have no way to determine if a product is profitable or not.

You might say "Who cares because, over the course of a year, it would work itself out?" The problem is that different products take different raw materials and different processes. This means the costs you were using that month to determine profitability of the product you just made are, in fact, wrong. These costs should be going into WIP, follow the product and move to the P&L when the product is sold, not manufactured. The idea is you want to know what the product costs to make. This means as the product moved through your manufacturing that costs associated with the manufacturing needed to be accounted for on the balance sheet and then moved to the P&L when the product was sold.

Top five raw material costs

Are you spending more on raw materials than you used to spend even when taking inflation into account? If so, why? Electronics go down over time while food, chemical, and animal costs fluctuate from year to year depending on any number of factors. The price of most chemicals used can be tied to market fluctuations and when you see a spike one way or the other you can tie it to the market. For example, natural gas, and natural gas prices can be reviewed over the years with nothing more than a google search. Natural gas prices have declined over the years, so you should see this in the financials. If you don't, then you need to find out why.

The other reason you want to see your top five raw material suppliers is because you will need to negotiate new prices and terms with them any some point, so you need to understand who they are, where they fit into the manufacturing of your products, and any options you may have.

It should be obvious that I have stated the top five raw material suppliers and not the top five costs. Chances are healthcare and benefits will be in the top five and these will need to be handled differently.

Inventory Levels/Inventory Turns

Finally, let's cover inventory and how often a product is sold from inventory which is called inventory turns. This is normally where senior management skims the company in many ways. You need to understand that usually senior people have a bonus based on the profitability of the company. If a company hits the budgeted profit, then senior people will get a bonus. The real question is, how do you take a failing company and show that it is making a profit so you can get your bonus?

The easiest way is to value your inventory higher than it should be. At several companies, the inventory was given an average value at the end of each quarter. Normally, to value an inventory you use the manufacturing costs. It is a straightforward process and typically hard to cheat, but can be done. Funny that I say this process is normally hard to cheat because, when you speak with auditors, they will tell you this is the number one area in which they find fraud.

Where people cheat is with Work in Progress (WIP), because values are a little harder to nail down. What people will try is declare WIP is higher than it should be, and this will drive the value of the entire inventory slightly higher than it expected. Since inventory is basically product you have sold to yourself the higher you make its value the more profit you have made, at least on paper.

Look for senior management bonuses every two to three years, the giveaway being that in those years, inventory, including WIP, was always high shortly before the New Year began. Why would inventory be high only on the years that management obtained a bonus?

At one company, every couple of years over the previous five years sales went up substantially the last 3 months of the fiscal year (January — March), but cash showed no corresponding increase in collections for these sales. Completing a deep dive for the months of April through June, sales dropped substantially and slow-moving inventory went up. Not by a small amount, but by millions and then it would slowly drop.

The CFO also was quick to inform me that they had always passed their yearly audit and so did not understand why I was asking all these questions. All this quickly taught me that he was not really running finance but, instead, was just a signature. Obviously, I needed to find out who truly ran the department. Turns out it was a controller calling all the shots and the CFO had no idea what was going on at all. Therefore, my discussions were with the wrong employee.

The reason I have included inventory turns is because many people fail to understand how much inventory a company should carry, and how much inventory costs. There is no magic number, which is why I use inventory turns. If you have a product that is not specialized and has 52 turns per year, then there is very little risk of building inventory. On the other hand, if the turns are three per year, I would question if you should carry it as inventory. At this point, it becomes more of a question of cash flow because to build inventory is expensive, and perhaps not the right step if cash is tight. Alternatively, if you have inventory that only turns one to two times per year, then this should be a made-to-order item with no inventory. Many people have fought me on this issue but, with a little thought it is easy to understand.

Inventory costs money to build, money you do not have, so why would you waste it making something that you only sell once in a while? There are also carrying costs to consider. Each foot of floor space has value; people must move inventory around, count it, maintain it, and keep it in good sellable condition. All of this costs money. It also means that for every month you have this product, its value goes up. By the end of a year the value of the product might go up 10%—15%, which means the profit of the product went down by the exact same amount. When this is all calculated, in you might find you did not make a profit at all but, in reality, lost money. Here are the two main arguments people have used with me to justify carrying inventory:

1) Manufacturing needs to run at 100% to keep costs down

2) The floor space and people are there no matter what, so they do not increase the value of inventory

We will cover item number one in the manufacturing chapter, so let's cover item two here. It's true that the floor space is a constant, but nothing says it needs to be used for inventory. Instead it could be used to expand QA or could even leased out until you need it. As for people? Perhaps if you did not have all this extra inventory, you would not need all the people employed in the warehouse. Finally, no warehouse is perfect and there is always a certain amount of spoilage that occurs. What if your product has a shelf life and you do not sell it in time? It gets sent from inventory to scrap. What if it needs to be moved and is damaged? Now it's scrap.

Scrap

There is no bigger consumer of cash than scrap. If you need to make 10 widgets and have a 20% scrap rate, then you really need to make 12 widgets. That means labor, material, maybe even overtime, were needed to make two widgets which were then put into the garbage. It also means that the cost of all the widgets went up, profit went down, and cash was wasted. We will cover scrap heavily in the manufacturing chapter but, for now, keep in mind that most companies do not put as much effort as they should into reducing scrap. Of all the sins in a company, this is number one.

What does your CFO really understand?

Determine whether or not your CFO really understands the numbers behind the data given to you, or did they have to ask their controllers for the answers. I doubt very seriously if the CFO, unless it is a small company, put any of the material together. Most likely they had one of their controllers do it. During the discussion with the CFO, you can see what they truly know and what they are taking as information without question from their staff.

There was no incentive for Operations to do better because they were not held accountable for any scrap produced. Just declare it the first of the year and don't worry about it. If the percentage of scrap was wrong, then finance would simply make a journal entry for the extra raw material and labor needed with no explanation in the journal as to why.

Next, look at sales volumes, gross margins, and EBITDA to see what the CFO knows. These are more questions for the sales department, but shouldn't finance should have some idea of what is happening?

Your finance department might be as honest as they come, on the other hand, there are companies where finance is not honest, which is the point I am making. Do not always think that the culprit must be at the top, either, because under the right circumstances it can be anyone. Also, don't just look at the last audit and assume that since the company passed, everything is just fine. Look at Enron if you think I am overstating things.

I once worked at a company that when they finished their audit, I came to realize it was one of the poorest audits of any company I had ever been involved with. I had only been hired about 30 days before the end of the year, so had not had time yet to really fully understand the P&L. They hired cheap auditors and it showed; given that they never discovered any of the fraud I discovered over the next few months.

Look for yourself and you will learn something about the company and the department you are relying on for the numbers. Even so, when I started, there was $3 million in the slow-moving inventory representing 10% of sales. It took about four months to unravel everything and truly get to the bottom of what was going on. In the end, I understood how the scheme worked and reported it to the board.

Profit

It has often surprised me how often people do not really understand profit or the fact that profit and cash have nothing to do with one another. I can understand if my directors and below do not fully understand how this works, but I would think that by the time someone becomes a VP or COO, they would have been taught, or learned on their own how profit works.

I cannot count the number of times senior people will look at me with a puzzled look when I mention profit. When I ask what is on their mind, they ask me why I am making this so difficult? You have certain expenses and certain cash coming in. Subtract the two and there is your profit. How is it that people get to the most senior positions in the company and think calculating profit is like going shopping or balancing your checkbook? If people do not understand how things work, you cannot expect them to help you fix the company's issues. Because of this, I have developed my right-hand/ left-hand explanation to try and explain profit in a very simply fashion. This is how it goes:

In your right hand you have paper profits. These are often in the profit investors see when they decide if they want to buy your stock. This profit comes from many sources, such as capital investments. Let's say you buy a piece of capital and, as we all know, it will be depreciated on the P&L over time. This time it could be five years, 10 years, or 20 years depending on what it is and what it will be used for. Computers, for example, are fully depreciated after five years while building improvements will fully be depreciated in 20 years. Consequently, if you buy a machine for $1 million and decide to depreciate it on a 10-year straight line, then it will reduce your profits in the P&L by $100,000 per year. At the end of 10 years this will stop, and your profits will go up by $100,000 per year. You did not make any improvement; the company is not more efficient. All that's happened is that a piece of equipment has been fully written off. Another way this might happen is that you are running your equipment at full usage to keep cost per element down, but much of this is being put into inventory. Putting things into inventory is like selling it to yourself, making your company appear more profitable.

I call this type of profit "paper profit" or profit for my right hand. It does not generate any added revenue to the company. You have not increased sales, reduced manufacturing costs, reduced the any costs of any kind, but the company appears to be more profitable. If you are a public company, this is important because people thinking about buying your stock will feel the company is doing better.

Don't get me wrong. The company is more profitable, and if you are a public company, this is important because investors are interested in buying stock from profitable companies. This profit, however, does not help pay the bills, give you cash for investments, or in any way help pay for maintenance, etc.

Left-hand profit, on the other hand, does in fact generate revenue for the company in the form of higher sales, reduced cost of manufacturing, reduced head count, and the selling of inventory. With this type of profit, you get a pick me up on the P&L which not only will provide real cash, but your investors and board will also like. This cash can be used for investments or new technology, or even just to pay off loans. Left-hand profit is the profit you need to be pushing for because it gives something back that can be used to better the company. Right-hand profit just looks good but does nothing else.

Capitalize or not to capitalize

I have heard more discussions on this topic from more presidents and boards than you can shake a stick at. Ultimately the rules for capitalization depend on where the company wants to go. If a company owns stock, plans to IPO, or wants to be sold, they capitalize everything they can. The reason for this is simple. When you capitalize things, your net profit only gets hit a very little amount. Going back to my previous example in profit let's again say you buy a piece of equipment for $1 million. Your profit does not go down by the $1 million you just spent but only goes down by $100,000 per year, every year, for the next 10 years. It almost feels like money is free as you can spend a great deal and only get penalized a very little amount.

Now, going back to my statement about companies who are public, plan to become public, or want to be sold, they will bottom out and lower the threshold on what can be capitalized in order to make the company appear as profitable as possible. When at the plastics company, they noticed the stock begin to fall due to low profits and decided they needed to turn their stock price around. So, they lowered the capitalization threshold from $10k to $1k. This meant that even laptop computers were being capitalized and, eventually, did boost their profit short term.

Like everything in life, there is a negative side to this policy. What if the market drops and you see a decline in sales? Maybe the country has slipped into a recession or someone new has entered into the same market space as you. There are many things you can do to lower costs in the company as you enter survival mode in order to give you time to figure out how to salvage this problem. What you cannot do is reduce the depreciation on the books. If you have a large value of yearly depreciation on the books, then no matter what you do it stays. When I worked for the plastics company, they lost an account and needed to really tighten their belt. The problem was they could have gotten rid of every employee in the company and still not made a profit. They simply had too much capital on the books, meaning that they had boxed themselves into a corner and there was no way out.

I have found that $10k seems to be a good decision point on what should or should not be capitalized. It will make you honestly ask if you really need to capitalize/not capitalize item X. However, $10k is big enough amount you will feel it at the end of the month, but it's also small enough that it will not hurt your year too much. More importantly, if the economy goes south or you need to tighten you belt for some other reason, your capital will not be out of control. You will be able to reduce manpower or find other ways to reduce costs, thus salvaging the company.

Setting the capital limit to low is like having a credit card with zero interest, no payments for a year, and a high limit. You don't notice you made a mistake by buying everything you wanted and maxing out the card until the first payment is due and you realize you screwed up.

CHAPTER 7

Quality Assurance

Quality is not a department. It is a lifestyle and your company either has it or it does not. There is no halfway, sort of, or working on it. It is an attitude and your company wants, above all else, to produce a quality product, or it does not.

You need to know up front that many of my ideas and practices come from the teaching of Edward Deming. After literally hundreds of hours of seminars and classes, it would be hard not to use most of what he taught. You do not hear much about Deming today, so for those of you who have no idea who he was, let me just give you a quick overview.

Deming championed the work of statistical process control, operational definitions. Deming is best known for his work in Japan after WWII, particularly his work with the leaders of Japanese industry. Many in Japan credit Deming as one of the inspirations for what has become known as the Japanese post-war economic miracle of 1950 to 1960, when Japan rose from the ashes of war on the road to becoming the second-largest economy in the world through processes partially influenced by the ideas Deming taught:

Better design of products to improve service

Higher level of uniform product quality

Improvement of product testing in the workplace and in research centers

Greater sales through side [global] markets[1]

[1] https://en.wikipedia.org/wiki/W._Edwards_Deming

Dr. Deming had 14 basic points that he taught and strongly believed in. Some I believe in and some I do not, but I want to cover them one at a time so that you understand why I treat quality the way I do. I also understand that if you ever take a Deming class, you will hear some of these points discussed differently from what is presented here. This is simply my interpretation of the 14 points he believed in. Nothing, including this book, is fixed in stone. You must modify the way you think to fit the needs you have, or the job you do. Since I work on stressed companies, the way I use these points fits that very well. The 14 points include the following:

1. Create constancy of purpose for improving products and services

2. Adopt the new philosophy

3. Cease dependence on inspection to achieve quality

4. End the practice of awarding business on price alone. Instead, minimize total cost by working with a single supplier.

5. Improve constantly and forever every process for planning, production and service

6. Institute training on the job

7. Adopt and institute leadership

8. Drive out fear

9. Break down barriers between staff areas

10. Eliminate slogans, exhortations, and targets for the workforce

11. Eliminate numerical quotas for the workforce and numerical goals for management

12. Remove barriers that rob people of pride of workmanship and eliminate the annual rating or merit system

13. Institute a vigorous program of education and self-improvement for everyone

14. Put everybody in the company to work accomplishing the transformation

1) Create constancy of purpose for improving products and services

This really belongs as number one because, if you don't have a culture for quality, then there is very little reason to do anything else. Everyone will tell you they care about quality, that they have a Quality department, and that everything they do is checked and approved by Quality. Most people are less than truthful about the first two and are really stretching the truth on the third.

There has to be records, so find them. If there are no records, how do you know any testing was done at all? How were they able to compare what they were testing to what they were using? How did they recall what tests were run, how well the tests were run, the conditions the tests were run in, and, without that information, how would there be any possible way to draw conclusions — right, wrong, or indifferent?

If there are no records, how do they know what is happening over time? Maybe they had equipment issues and the quality of the product has been drifting downwards for quite some time and the new plastic supplier pushed things past the limit. I work a great deal in China and the phrase there is "if it is not written down, then it is a rumor." As far as I am concerned, if you cannot show me the records, it never happened.

You would be surprised how many companies keep very limited data and even more have very little knowledge on how to statistically use the data. You can collect all the data in the world, but if you don't understand what it is telling you then it is worthless.

Often the mindset is to wait to see where the problems are and then put quality testing in place. This is completely backwards and solves nothing. In the first place, you will end up testing more than you need to test and spend more money than necessary. Remember you are working on a stressed company and cash is tight. You need to understand your process well enough to understand what needs to be tested and does not.

2) Adopt the new philosophy

So often issues drive Quality, not Quality driving Production. Remember, it always cost more to chase quality than to put some thought into it and do it right the first time. You can either pay for it once or pay for it three times later and perhaps, like the plastics company, lose customers in the process.

If your company had a philosophy of quality, then you would create a list detailing every quality issue that needed to be checked, changed, or engineered out. When I tell people this, their first reaction always is "then we need to check everything everywhere." That is just a dumb answer. If your company has a philosophy of quality, then as part of every discussion and decision ever made, quality would be a primary part of the discussion. No matter what you do in manufacturing, the quality of the part will change and this needs to be addressed. For example, if you change aluminum suppliers, the impact of this change needs to be evaluated to determine if any aspect of the aluminum is different from what was being used.

After World War II the US had the highest quality products in the world and the US prided itself on producing products of the highest quality. Other companies in other nations came to us to help them improve their manufacturing processes, which is a far cry from the way things are now. Today you see companies advertising for people who understand the "Toyota model," who know how to put Kaizen into practice, or they look to Germany for finely trained engineers. America has lost some of its competitive edge because we value quantity more than quality. Thus, it is no surprise to hear American manufacturers say that if they were to implement a fully-fledged quality program, they would lose money when, in fact, Quality does not cost you money. The lack of it will.

3) Cease dependence on inspection to achieve quality

This one needs a bit of explanation or no one will ever get their minds wrapped around it. Let's break it down and first see the flaw, as I interpret it, and then what a solution might be.

The classes I took on Deming said you need to force your suppliers to sell you quality products, so you do not need to do the inspection yourself. If you think about it, if everything you get is perfect, then why would you need to do any inspections? Makes some sort of sense so let's try it. I love thought exercises so we will do one.

Let's say you manufacture alarm clocks. Not the new fancy digital alarm clocks, but the old-fashioned, wind-up, hammer-hitting two-bell alarm clock, or better said, one that looks like an old-fashioned clock. You know, something interesting. We need a picture of this clock in our heads, so let's build it here. The housing will be plastic, the hammer aluminum, and the bells brass. There will be a windup knob in the back only for the hammer and the guts of the clock will be electronics made in China. This clock will have two hands, one for hours and one for minutes, an arm for the alarm and a face plate, also made of plastic. The face plate will be a simple piece of plastic with numbers written on it. The clock sits on four little legs and the plastic body is brown to simulate wood. Something you might see at a bed and breakfast to help make the room feel rustic.

This company does not manufacture any of the components themselves, but buys them all to make a dozen different-looking alarm clocks. They try to use many of the parts in different models in order to keep inventory of raw components to a minimum. This is why our clock uses an internal electronic circuit board, because that same board is used for the digital clocks they make.

They buy all the components just like everyone else does: the circuit board from either Taiwan or China, the plastic parts from both a US and overseas supplier, and the metal components locally. This is a normal small-to-medium sized company that makes mid-range clocks and sells them at a discount to retailers in the US.

According to Deming, you should make your suppliers ensure that they are sending quality products so that you do not need to do any inspection yourself. But let's see how practical this is. All the plastic parts are either made in the USA or overseas, and all they have been certified to meet your specification. The company relies on their supplier to send them the proper plastic blend, assuming that the plastic manufacturing was perfect. The dye used comes from another supplier who you must also assume has made no recipe changes, gets everything they buy from the same sources, and that all dye manufacturing was perfect.

Anyone who has ever used stains knows that just because two cans of oak stain say they are Golden Oak does not mean they will be identical. Stains vary from supplier to supplier and sometimes from batch to batch.

If you do not believe this, go to any place which sells Pergo-type flooring. Pull a box off the shelf and find the lot or batch number on the box. Now pull a box with a different lot or batch number and compare the color of the board in the box. Anyone who has installed this type of flooring knows you need to get all your boxes with the same batch number to ensure all the board color and hue are the same. Same is true of wallpaper, paint, stains, siding, etc.

When the body of the clock was made, how do you know there were no mistakes, no stress in the plastic which will crack? Doesn't matter if you assume that removal of extra plastic was perfect because the blade used for removal had been sharpened minutes before your products were made. But was it?

For the electronics, there is something called infant mortality, which is why most electronic equipment manufacturers have a burn-in period. Your electronics came from overseas where they may or may not burn in the board before it is sent. Even if they do, what about the shipyard? Was the container handled properly or was there an issue with the crane? If the company who makes your circuit board does not make the chips, can you rely on their supplier to make quality chips, and would your supplier even give you the name and address of their supplier so you could check for yourself? As can see, the list gets out of hand quickly, with too many variables to track.

I have changed this Deming point to read **"Take care of the front end and the back end will take care of itself."**

So now let's take the same clock and look at it another way. As each batch of parts come in, randomly take different items and check them. It is important to do random samples. If they are good, then that shipment can be cleared and used. If a single item fails, then the entire shipment is put on hold until some sort of resolution has been found. Typically, I will also make my supplier pay for all the labor used to check every part in the shipment and if they decide they don't want to do this, the shipment is sent back at their expense. Once they feel the financial pain, they will begin to police themselves and you will see mistakes drop.

Okay, so you say that's great, but my company makes things, we don't just assemble them, and so how would this work for us?

First, do audits at the supplier of all incoming raw materials to ensure the policies you have established are being used. All records are reviewed, talk to the workers, and watch a day or two of production. Nothing will tell you more than just sitting on the production floor and watching the people work. If they follow the policies you established for your product, the work being done will look natural. People will not be looking in a manual to see what the next step is. In addition, they will not be asking each other questions to understand a next step since, by now, they are experts. Honestly, I spend very little time looking at suppliers' books and most of my time watching suppliers prepare our product to see how the people work.

Next you have all products checked when they come in the building. If you ordered a specific brand of acid, verify at receipt that you got the exact item, or did they deliver the same acid, but a different brand? Their argument will be who cares where we bought it from; it is exactly the same acid you asked for. For your process it might make all the difference in the world.

Remember, you cannot inspect "in" quality. In other words, you can't make a finished product and only then sort the good product from the bad. If you have a need to check all your finished goods, then, by default, you are shipping a certain percentage of bad product into the field.

People always look at me funny when I say, "you cannot inspect in quality," stating that they do 100% final inspection to ensure quality. So what? First, you have just added all the costs to make something just to throw it away. Second, by default you are shipping a certain number of poor products unless you tell me that computers are doing the entire final check. To make this point clear, I'll use an exercise I developed at a company where I used to work.

I ran a test once at a company where we had inspections everywhere you can imagine. The company believed if it was touched in any way, it needed to be inspected to ensure it was not damaged. On the face of this, it does seem logical; the product was soft and easily scratched, so if it was touched or moved it could be damaged.

After a time, I came to believe two things were happening. The first was that we were trashing good product and second, bad products were still getting through the system. So, I set up a test between departments where we took 1000 products we made and numbered them. We then had our best inspector look at each product and write down the number in a "good" or "bad" list. Then we took two inspectors from each department and had them inspect all the products and remove all they deemed bad. When we were done, we looked at the products pulled out and had our control inspector go through them. She found that many of the items pulled were, in her opinion, good and should have never been pulled. We also found about 5% of the defective products were missed and marked as "good."

I have done this at other companies and have found inspection results consistent, no matter the product. I have labeled this my "5% rule." Anytime you have something inspected, about 5% will be pulled out as defective. If you do multiple inspections, one inspector might pull 3%, another 6%, others 5%, but if you average them all up over the course of a month, the total will be about 5%, and the same time about 5% will be missed.

Before you shake your head, think about it. You hired an inspector to find mistakes to ensure what is sent into the field is good. If they find nothing, they feel they have not done their job, and worse when you walk by and see they have found nothing, the first thing in your head is they are not doing their job. So quality inspectors feel the need to find something, not only to justify their job to themselves, but also to you.

Even with them pulling out good parts, they will not find everything, and I have found they miss about 5%. Might be the end of their shift, they have something on their mind, their back hurts that day, or maybe they had a fight with their daughter that morning. Who knows? But if you could check everything that goes out the door with a computer, you will see they do miss about 5% over the course of a year.

Since your goal is to not ship bad products and if you understand that 3%–5% of all bad products made will end up in the field, then the best way to reduce defects is to ensure that the process for making the product is controlled.

4) End the practice of awarding business on price alone. Instead, minimize total cost by working with a single supplier.

I disagree with this point on many levels and, frankly, do not use it. What happens if that supplier has financial issues, goes out of business, or has internal problems? You might remember what happened to Toyota in 1996, as reviewed below in a March 3, 1997 article by James B. Treece, staff reporter for *Auto News*.

JUST-TOO-MUCH SINGLE-SOURCING SPURS TOYOTA PURCHASING REVIEW: MAKER SEEKS AT LEAST TWO SUPPLIERS FOR EACH PART

You minimize total costs by working with suppliers in a way that will work for both of you. I cannot count the number of times a supplier has said that if I would change my process just a little bit, he could save money and, because he saved money, I could purchase for less. You do not want dozens of suppliers sending you the same product, but you do need to have more than one. I am sure we can all come up with examples of where a supplier let us down and we went scrambling to quickly find a replacement.

5) Improve constantly and forever every process for planning, production, and service

Most companies try to accomplish this in some way or another. The issue in most places I have either worked at or run is the statement that "things are running better than ever." I am sure they are, but normally these are the words used just before time freezes and no more effort is made to improve any aspect of the company.

I mean, why change something that is working well? Simple. Time does not stop for anyone and the minute you stop trying to improve, you are falling behind. The biggest issue of being good, top three in your market, having new products (basically anything you are good at) is that there are always people or companies working to knock you off your pedestal. No one tries to emulate companies at the bottom of the ladder, but everyone wants to emulate, and eventually beat, the company at the top.

Being at the top is a great place to be. Sales are easier, your company is driving the market, and, to a certain point, you will also drive profits because people always are willing to pay slightly more for the best. Not a lot, but some.

People at the bottom get leftovers, customers who cannot afford the better product or the newest and greatest innovation. They get what no one else wants, which makes them hungry — a hunger that will drive them to try to replace you.

6) Institute training on the job

I am of two minds on this one and will try to explain why. To begin with, I strongly believe in on-the-job training, which is something many companies do not do enough of. How do you expect an employee to do a good job for you if they do not understand how to do it?

I have always taken this concept a step further and tried to improve other skills in other areas knowing that it will help in the workplace. For example, the US has many Latinos who speak little to no English.

Therefore, in many of my companies I offered them free English classes. I believed that the better their English, the fewer misunderstandings there would be on the floor and the better their performance.

Many people have been critical of this practice thinking, incorrectly, that if the employees improve their English, they will leave for a better job. I have found the opposite to be true because they feel a certain loyalty to your company because you have shown you care about them. They know that better English skills will make it easier for them to function in everyday places so, because you care for their life, they will return the favor.

Now let's talk about my other concern about training: how much training is needed? Education quality is falling dramatically in the US, both in schools and businesses, and while I know people need to be trained to do a specific job, the "whys" do not need to be explained.

In the early '90s, I thought exactly the opposite, believing you could never train an employee enough on what they were doing. I held classes several times per year to explain the very complicated science of the product they were making in simple terms that most people could easily understand.

Albert Einstein is noted for saying "If you can't explain it simply, you don't understand it well enough." I believe this and understood many processes are very complicated, which means I need to understand what I am teaching extremely well. You would think that with this type of intensive training, yields would go up, production would be better, people would perform better. What I've found does not always support this.

People felt they could do better by not following the standard operating procedure and that these had been written for people who were not as thoroughly trained as they were. They will at times perform even worse than people who have been poorly trained. You could never convince them to follow the policy after the training because they were certain what they were doing was right. I stopped this training and, after a few years and as people left, things got better.

7) Adopt and institute leadership

The aim of supervision should be to help people, machines, and gadgets do a better job. For me, this really does not belong in quality as it should be a company philosophy, but it is one of the 14 points in the Deming Quality list, so I left it. I believe this should be a major goal for all supervisors and managers and yet is often severely missing in most companies.

I like to find the people who are really good at their jobs and promote them. The company can work with them and train them to be a good supervisor, but how can you expect someone to supervise an employee if they don't even understand what they do? Sure, they can tell them they are doing a bad job, but the real key is helping them do a better job. This requires some knowledge on the part of the supervisor, and another reason why I became trained on how make the product my company sells.

People who can, do.... People who can't, complain about those who can. I have found there are those supervisors/managers who walk around telling people what a poor job they do, how they are lucky to have a job, and basically berate people as the worst employees in the company. They do this to make themselves look good or, at least, to make other people look worse than they are. These individuals should have never been put into a supervisory or management role, and if they are, they need to be removed.

People who are competent will always reach out and try to help when needed. This is most important in quality. Quality is not about finding bad products or making sure bad products do not get shipped out to the customer. Quality is about not making bad products in the first place.

Most people want to do a good job and when they are not producing a good product, are open to having someone help them. At this point, they are in full learning mode because they want to understand what they are doing wrong and how to fix it themselves in the future. If your supervisors spend all day in the office, doing who knows what, then you do not need them. If there really is that much paperwork, then hire someone specifically for that purpose, or find what you can get rid of. Your supervisors should spend 80%—90% of their time on the floor, working with the people, making sure things have been adjusted properly, the equipment has been maintained properly, and answering questions from the people doing the work.

In an earlier chapter, I said that I am less concerned with what decision my direct supports make than I am with the reasoning they used to make it. This is done by training people to think about how their decisions affect the company as a whole, and not just what is best for the next 10 minutes. Supervisors on the floor need the same mindset. What is needed to make the employees do a better job? Do they need different tools or training? Is a specific employee a little slow, needing more one-on-one time? Every time a supervisor steps onto the floor they should look for an opportunity to help or train someone.

As you can see, I feel strongly about this and believe it is one of the biggest issues with companies today. People want to hoard power and control and if you train people, including training them to think, some individuals think they are giving away power. On the other hand, if people are poorly trained and not allowed to think, then they are forced to either produce low-quality product or come ask you for everything. This is will ultimately limit your company in terms of growth and flexibility.

8) Drive out fear

This one takes a little more explanation because it is a variable and something you will work overtime to achieve. Remember, you have just been hired to fix a company that is in dismal shape and losing money. This book is not about a company that is in great shape, well run, growing or healthy. Two completely different companies, so different cultures and approaches are needed.

When I first take over a company I rely heavily on fear, and explained such early in the book. Fear is a great motivator if used correctly and for short periods of time. That said, the term 'short periods of time' is relative because different companies will require different amounts of fear to get them moving.

I can recall the first week I was at a particular company, discussing a customer who was complaining about the quality of the product received. The VP of Quality was explaining that they had run all the normal tests and that the product had passed. In their view, the problem had to be the customer's fault, and not the company's, and therefore they were not going to put any more effort into this.

As we sat around the conference table, all the managers and VPs agreed with his statement. It was obvious to them that the problem was entirely the customer's and not with the product. In fact, the primary statement used was "we are not going to be blamed for their problem." They all patted themselves on the back, were very happy with this solution, planned to be nice to the customer, offer to help them fix their problem, but stopped short of doing any work internally.

When they were done, they all looked at me. Not sure why. Maybe they thought I would be pleased and waited for my response. To this day I recall this conversation clearly, and thinking back, it was this meeting that started the long road to recovery.

I looked at each employee one at a time, using the best poker face I could muster. I informed each Manager/VP sitting there that at the end of this meeting they should go to their office or cubicle, pack their things, and leave. Don't bother going to HR looking for some sort of severance because none of you will be getting any. Mic drop....

You are all sitting here talking about how good your product is, how this could not possibly be your fault, and that if the customer would only fix their problem, everything would be great. I reminded them that only 10 years before they had lost their biggest account because then, like now, you were convinced nothing was your fault.

I went on. In the first place, you run 20%—25% scrap so your product cannot be that good or you would not have such a high scrap rate. I understand, and have been told, this level of scrap proves that you are doing a great job of catching all the bad product before it reaches our customer. I am here to tell you these numbers prove beyond a shadow of a doubt that you are sending bad product to your customers. You have been lying to yourself for so long that you have now convinced yourself these lies are the truth.

And yes, I continued within a now dead silent conference room. For the sake of this discussion, let's pretend your fairytale and that all the product shipped is good. I can prove to you that it is not, and I don't even know anything, but for now let's pretend. Will it really matter if this customer walks and begins to use your competitor's product? Are you all going to still pat each other on the back, congratulating each other about how they switched suppliers but this issue sure as hell was not your fault? Is that going to help pay the bills? Is it going to pay your salaries? Even if you are right and they are wrong or they are right and you are wrong, if they start using a different supplier — YOU LOSE.

You all need to get your heads out of your collective asses and face some real facts. They are right and you are wrong, period. They are your customer and if they are not happy, then you have failed.

At this point, I stood up and started to walk around because I was now on a roll. All of you need to get this through your thick heads that your customers could not care less, doesn't give a shit, how good YOU think your product is, I said. I can promise you they are not sitting around their conference table right now saying that this issue must be internal because the supplier says their product is perfect. This customer is not saying it, thinking it, and does not give a damn what you think about your product.

What they know is this. They buy a product from you and it is not working for them. Because it is not working for them it is, by default, our fault. Period. The next employee who says this is not true can leave the company for good. What you think about your product does not mean a damn thing. If the customer is not happy, then WE have a problem, and you all better start thinking this way if we stand any chance of getting this company fixed.

Let go a lot of staff that day and in subsequent ones, and many discussions I had with groups at my company for the next couple of years were this bad or worse. Over that time, yes, I was invoking fear, and I do not apologize for this because it was what was needed at the time, but now we need to look at how things are today.

Today, things are very different because the company is very different. Today, I do work on driving out fear because I want a company where everyone is contributing, and for people to contribute, they cannot fear their jobs are on the line every time they open their month. I have not heard the words "it's not our fault" in years. Instead it has been replaced with "How do we fix the problem?" Today, no one cares who is at fault. Now, everyone understands a problem does not need blame, just resolution.

Here is the point. When you start with a company that needs to be turned around, fear is needed because it will motivate better than just talking. As time goes by, fear needs to be driven out of the company and replaced with respect for each other. Understanding problems should not be taken personally, and if a customer is not happy, then the company must take the lead.

9) Break down barriers between staff areas

Silos, as we all know, are one of the hardest things to remove from a company. People by their very nature protect what they view as theirs, and even though might say they care, they really don't want much to do with things outside of their area. I am sure we have all heard and maybe even said ourselves, "why should I worry about something I do not control?" I have said this in my early years and I am sure you all have as well at some point.

It is just human nature to protect our little world and the people inside of it. Areas outside of my world be damned, because nothing is going to hurt my world. This is not only true in companies, but generally true in life. Protect what is yours and what you can control and let the other employees take care of theirs.

This, like several other points Deming has, does not just relate to quality but to the entire company. They are listed in his 14 points of quality and so I have left them in the quality section. If you think about it though, quality is a company philosophy and not just a department. It is like safety. The company either believes in it completely or it does not.

One of the most used phrases I use is "I need players on the field, not spectators in the stands." Consequently, if you are not helping fix issues then you are not needed. This fits in perfectly here because a QA technician just sitting in their office issuing reports is of no real value to the company. The report has value, of course, but is it helping in any way to solve the problem? No. It also helps build silos rather than breaking them down.

In an earlier chapter, I spoke about how I got manufacturing involved in finance, specifically cash flow, so that they could better see how decisions they made were hurting or helping the company. Once Operations got involved, there was a different attitude when it came to buying things for production. To help finance better understand what was happening in Operations, I had them participate in the morning meetings. This got finance involved in making decisions in Operations and the two groups began working together.

The exact same thing was done with quality and manufacturing. I had an employee in QA begin working the lines with the manufacturing operators, looking at settings, flow rates, heater settings, and everything else on the lines. They would explain why certain things needed to be set a certain way and provided great training to the operators.

The QA department also found that some of their assumptions were not always accurate. For example, QA would say that an issue was caused by improper heater settings. However, when they started working to resolve issues on the lines, QA found out the heater had been set wrong because it was compensating for another issue. Once the main issue was resolved, the heater setting could be put back to normal, eliminating the problem of a poorly made product. At the same time, I took some of the best operators and had them spend some time in QA. They learned how the tests were run and what they meant. As a result, they better understood the QA reports that were issued, and when QA made bad assumptions or conclusions, the operators could have an intelligent conversation with them.

I did this throughout the plant, including sales. If a customer complained about a problem, then I would have someone from QA go along on the call so they could see specifically what the customer was unhappy about. I would also have QA and manufacturing along on yearly sales meetings with customers when they were updating the company on future plans they might have. By doing this, both QA and Operations heard things firsthand that were not interpreted by sales. The customer would be impressed because we cared enough to send the right people to the meeting. They saw people who were going to make their product, not just sell it.

This is what I consider "players on the field" and not "people sitting in the stands." They are actively solving issues, improving processes, and at the same time removing silos.

- Finance is working with manufacturing
- Manufacturing is working with finance, QA and sales
- QA is working with manufacturing and sales
- Sales, by default, is working with QA and manufacturing

This is not at a senior level. This is a supervisor on the floor, a QA technician, a regional salesperson, and a controller in finance. Everything has been pushed down so the people doing the work, closest to the product, are working together and making decisions together to make the product better. You should also easily see how this works with the previous topic of driving out fear, since it will not work if people are afraid of retribution or feel they do not have the support of the senior group.

10) Eliminate slogans, exhortations, and targets for the workforce

Right off the bat I have to admit that there is nothing about this point that I agree with. It is thus the one point from Deming I completely ignore.

I have never been into slogans, so there is no issue for me not to use them. I never liked it when other companies I have worked for had them. I know there are several variations of the definitions of exhortations, so, for the purpose of this discussion, we'll use the one from Merriam-Webster: *"speech or written passage intended to persuade, inspire, or encourage"*.

If you are working in a well-established manufacturing plant where quality is not only a department, but a fact of life, maybe and just maybe, this might be true. In our case, however, you have taken over a stressed company where 90% of the time, quality is not part of the way of life. Quite possibly the Quality Department was even reduced or eliminated to save money. Either way you will be persuading and encouraging quite a bit. You must encourage people to do a better job, make a better product, and reduce scrap.

There is no facility I have worked for, been president of, or visited that doesn't have targets set for the workforce. In fact, I will look to those targets as sources of things to celebrate, to ensure people are recognized for doing good work, and to encourage good behavior. Quite a contrast from Deming's following point:

11) Eliminate numerical quotas for the workforce and numerical goals for management

This is another Deming point which I have never seen implemented, either in the US or Japan. And Japan, as you read at the beginning of this chapter, is the world's biggest Deming believer. How are you going to know if your efforts are resulting in improvements if you don't have a baseline, target goals, etc.? Common sense thus dictates ignoring this precept.

12) Remove barriers that rob people of pride of workmanship and eliminate the annual rating or merit system

The "broken windows" theory is a criminological theory that says visible signs of crime, anti-social behavior, and civil disorder create an urban environment that encourages further crime and disorder, including serious crimes. The theory suggests that policing methods targeting minor crimes such as vandalism, public drinking, and fare evasion help to create an atmosphere of order and lawfulness, thereby preventing more serious crimes. The theory was introduced in a 1982 article by social scientists James Q. Wilson and George L. Kelling [1]. It was further popularized in the 1990s by New York City police commissioner William Bratton and Mayor Rudy Giuliani, whose policing policies were influenced by the theory.

I happen to believe very strongly in this theory and bring it to the workplace because it is my belief this directly relates to the quality of your product. If your workforce sees dirty floors, scrap lying around, tools left lying around, and general disorder in the factory, they will conclude management does not care. In return, your workers will not care. People are an extension of the management around them, meaning that the people who work for you take on some of your traits, both good and bad.

If you are organized, then you will tend to stress this in the organization you lead and, therefore, other people become organized and the people around you will also attach some importance to it as well.

Quality is an attitude and it will only be adopted if you feel it is important in the company. When I say it is important, I mean throughout the entire organization. (You've made this point above and below.)

If you want to start a quality program at work, then start by cleaning the place up. Show the people that you care about the place they work at and have no interest in anything but the best. They need to see this in you before you stand any chance of making Quality important throughout the organization. Many companies will use 5S, which basically states everything has a place and everything should be in its place. My mother told me this when I was five, and it is true.

This is how I define **"rob people of pride of workmanship."** If you are proud of your workplace, you will be proud of what you make. Once you get a sense of pride established people will actually become upset when they are not given the proper tools, training, or opportunities to make a good product.

Don't forget that, since you want quality throughout the company, HR should take pride in hiring the right people. Not just fill a hole but actually find and hire people needed in the company who make a difference. Finance, too, should take pride in closing the month quickly and accurately, so their results can be used to influence decisions made in the current month.

Merit systems are completely arbitrary and just reflect how one person feels about another. It does not truly reflect how an employee is doing or the job they are performing. Reviews should really be more of a discussion and the write up you do should simply be topics you want to discuss. I give reviews about every three to four years and mostly talk about trends I see happening, not necessarily about performance.

When someone is having issues, you do not wait for a review. Instead you walk into their office and discuss the issue with them in "real" time. If they correct it, then it is forgotten and never brought up again. You do not collect issues so you can use them later. You get them resolved in a timely manner by fully discussing what you do not like, why it is an issue, and what you expect in the future. You listen to what they have to say and at the end agree on a course of action.

The point to all of this is that people need constant feedback. I basically have a rule I tell people: the less you see me, the less I get involved, the less I offer input, the better you are doing. On the other hand, if I feel I need to go to all the meetings, be involved, offer constant suggestions, and make sure things are moving, then, by default, you are not going a good job. This in itself is constant feedback and people take great pride when I stop coming to meetings.

13) Institute a vigorous program of education and self-improvement for everyone

You will have very mixed results with this one. Over the past 30 years, America has put less and less importance on education and the need for education. This really hit me hard when I lived in Cincinnati where, in the mid '90s, they had two bonds on the ballot. Each was for $100 million. One was to help improve the schools and the other was for a new stadium. The stadium was approved by the voters and the bond for the schools was not. People want a place to go and have fun but don't care if their kids are educated. Might explain why the US is ranked 20th in the world for education.

I have started college reimbursement programs at several companies, but it is rare that more than a few people take advantage of it. Think about this, you work at a company that will pay your entire college education and you have no interest in going. Something that could change your life for the better and yet you turn your back on the program.

I will normally offer a variety of educational programs throughout the year, such as classes offered to improve skills on Microsoft products like Excel, community schools offering chemistry classes, or one of the local universities each year offers a food safety class. What I have found is that it gives me a pretty good indication of who will be a rising star (those who attend) and who will not (those that do not attend). The biggest challenge is that people who take advantage of better training or education will often leave the company for something better. This is fine and you should be happy that you helped someone find a better life. Believe me, word will get out to your employees and you will be viewed as an employer who cares. People work harder for managers that they believe care about them.

14) Put everybody in the company to work accomplishing the transformation

This should be a no-brainer because you cannot do this all yourself. If everyone is not working on making things better, then you have an issue. Don't get me wrong. When you start, you will have to push everyone, every day, about everything or they will stop. You are changing a culture, and this means it is completely up to you to get this started. There are days I go home completely frustrated and pissed that I must hound people about the same thing every day, but the next morning I get up and do it all again.

In time, the new ideas, concepts, culture will become engrained and will take on a life its own, but you need to be prepared to be the driving force on these issues for a period of time. When I came to my present company, it took almost three years before people fully and completely adopted this new culture and I did not need to push the issue any longer. It happened over time and every year things got better and now people in the company are coming with their own ideas on improvement.

While the preceding topics cover the 14 Deming points as I interpret and use them, there are other points I use as well. These are listed below.

Quality is a variable, not an absolute

People will tell you that quality means that the product was perfect and without defect. My response is you have no idea what you are talking about. If a product satisfies a need and then meets the requirement, it is of good quality.

Quality does not mean perfect. It simply means that whatever you are making meets the needs of the customer. A good-quality product for one customer may be a poor-quality product for another customer. It depends on what they are using the product for.

Keep People Focused

You will see this statement throughout this entire book because it is the hardest thing to do. People get easily distracted and to keep people focused on what you need is always a very difficult task. People will come to you and say they have a dozen ideas on how to improve quality in the company. Great. Listen to them all, then pick two or three suggested ideas and only work on those two or three. No one can succeed on six to eight items, let alone more, and will fail at all of them if you let them try. Keep lists small and achievable if you want to have success.

I cannot count the number of times as I was moving up the ranks when my boss would pull a group of people together, give us a list of fifteen things to accomplish in order to solve 80% of the quality issues we had. Some tasks took months to complete while some were so complicated that they took the entire year. Often, we would look at the list, pick off a couple, and accept that we would get an ass-chewing for the rest. The rest being items not done.

Give the enemy a name

Never talk about a quality issue in the abstract, but always name it. This makes it more real and brings it home. There is a big difference between saying we have a 20% scrap issue and saying 80% of our scrap is because of brittle or color variation. The first description is vague and meaningless, while the second description states what the issue is and what needs to be worked on. This allows you to more quickly focus people on a few very specific problems with full understanding about the problem.

A vague description with poor direction will just cause confusion. You want the entire company working on the same thing and you want them focused on solving it. The only way to do this is by naming the enemy you want them to defeat. Remember: 90% of solving a problem is properly defining the problem, and if you can define it, then you can name it, and if it has a name, then you can beat it.

CHAPTER 8

Manufacturing

Manufacturing is the heart of the company and, in order for new life to be breathed in to this company this is the department where it must come together. All the work we have done throughout the entire factory has been for our pride and joy, the manufacturing department.

I hear so many say that manufacturing is an art and, for it to work well, you must have a good feel for it. I think these people are a bit crazy. Manufacturing is not art. It is hard work and you absolutely must have a clear goal line that you are driving for. And believe it or not that goal is Boredom.

I know it sounds strange to talk about boredom. However, you know when you have achieved the goals you are seeking because your manufacturing department functions becomes routine. They know and understand exactly what they need to do to achieve the production requirements of the day.

This does not mean you are not always reaching for new goals, better output, higher yields, or lowering your costs. What it means is that the chaos is gone, the battles have been fought, training is in place, and, overall, the department is functional and predictable.

I was the sixth president in 18 years at one of my companies and with every new president before me came more problems. When I first started, I thought it was because they were hiring incompetent presidents, but later changed my mind. This was not the case. Each one hired understood what I did — this company was dying — but this is where we differed. They understood the place was dying and set out to take everything they could from it before it finally faded away, while I set out to breathe new life into the company.

There were no teams working on quality, no one was responsible for scheduling, and QA consisted of a single employee who primarily worked on International Organization of Standardization (ISO) documents. No one had any idea if the product going to the customers met specifications. If it was bad, then the customer would say something. If no one was upset, then it must be okay; a pretty dismal reality.

For me, I love manufacturing. It's a job where I not only get to make something, but it also gives me a place to go when I get tired of my computer in the office and need to create. When I say create something, I mean exactly that. Have you ever wondered why people like to garden or paint? In both cases they start with nothing and through their own sweat and love they create something that would not have existed had they not personally made it happen.

My background is engineering, and I spent many years in R&D as you have learned while reading this book. Over the years, my wife often asked me where I wanted to be in life — Engineering or Administration. As long as I stay in manufacturing, I get both!

Like the chapter on quality, many of what you will read here is not new. Virtually everything you will read you have either read or heard before. What will be different is how I applied it to achieve different results. Like everything you have read thus far, I have no interest in presenting studies of cutting-edge work previously documented and designed to change your manufacturing company into a high-performance superstar envied by all. For me, all of that is like weight-loss pills: look good, sell well, and make a great deal of money for the person selling the pills, but you the buyer never seem to get the results promised.

I am talking about manufacturing in the same way I would about gardening. You must prepare the ground, fertilize it, plant your tomato, keep the weeds down, and work at it until you pick the last tomato off the vine for the season. We have all lived near someone who seems to have the "green thumb" and produces unbelievable gardens and wonder how they achieve the results they do.

Manufacturing is the same. There is no magic pill, 20 steps, or 7 minutes to perfect management. This is something you work at, and if you are good, you will end up with a great company that will produce a high-quality product people want and your company will thrive.

If you love manufacturing as I do, you will become good at it, and like the person with the amazing garden, you will end up with something you can be proud of. If you are just doing this for a paycheck, you will be like the person who picks a single tomato off the vine, saying to yourself as you walk away that it was simply not worth it. From then on you'll buy all your tomatoes in the store. During an interview I was asked once why I only worked at stressed companies when I understood going in how much work would be involved to turn them around. I hope you are beginning to understand why: manufacturing can be the best of both worlds.

Everyone who has read this manuscript while it was being created indicated this chapter was simply too long and people would struggle to get through it. As a result, I decided to break this down into more palatable lengths where you will not be overwhelmed. This has been separated into seven sections which will make things easier to read and focus on. The first section will be understanding the capabilities equipment, then scrap, maintaining your equipment, people in general, teams / improvements, the goal post, and OSHA.

Section 1:
Present capabilities
Determine your equipment's' capability

Fixing a company is far more expensive and harder than taking care of it from the start. How will you know this is true? Is it cheaper and easier to change the oil in your car at the required time than replace the engine?

Tell your employees that going forward the focus will be on quality first and see if they push back. In all my years working with stressed companies I have never had a single person tell me I am wasting my time because the company already produced a great, high-quality product. They know they need help and are glad you are willing to commit, at least at first.

The next step is to see what the equipment capabilities are. My engineering background makes this easy for me, and by the time I have been trained on the equipment in my company, I will know better than anyone what the true capability of it is. I understand most people who read this will not have an engineering background so a good rule of thumb would be to take the information you are given and reduce it by 25%.

The reason to do so is because the people who you have tasked with collecting the data on the current equipment functionality will feel slightly embarrassed with the answer. They really do not want you to be mad at them, so they will inflate the number by 20%—30% to make things look a little better. They feel a low number will reflect poorly on them and they are probably trying to make a good impression.

No one wants to report bad news, especially an employee to the new sheriff in town, which is why they will inflate the numbers. In a couple of years when you have developed a good relationship with your employees, you can ask them WHY they inflated the number, which intimates that you know the number was inflated. Do not ask them IF they inflated the number, because then you are forcing them to lie. They will tell you then that things were worse than even they realized, and yes, you just forced them into telling you another lie. Give people a way out if you want them to trust and be honest with you.

The easiest way to determine the capability of your equipment is to take a product, look at the specifications, tighten them by 20%, and then keep slowing things down until you can meet these requirements for at least 48 hours of uninterrupted manufacturing. Once you have achieved this, you just found the capabilities for your first part. This now becomes your baseline and everything you do will be weighed against this baseline. The next thing you need to know is what the equipment was capable of when it was purchased. This becomes your goal. You now know where you are, and you know what you are working towards.

I once ran a company where our product had a specification of +/- .7mm which I then reduced to +/-.5mm, slightly more than 20%. We then began slowing systems down until we were able to meet this target. During this exercise I learned that there were several products that, no matter what was done, they would never meet this new specification as the equipment simply was not capable of producing it. This was not because of poor maintenance or even anything people had or had not done. The equipment simply was, and never was, capable of making this product to specifications.

In this case, I left the specification at its original numbers and about a year later, redesigned the equipment that enabled us to produce a product that met the required specification. During this time, however, I worked with the customer so that they gave us time to make improvements to other products they bought.

The fact they were seeing an improvement often times means that they may help you if they can. For example, one customer loosened product specifications that we had been struggling with for several years to give us the time to fix the issue. You will never know if you do not ask, and you cannot ask if you have no idea what your equipment is capable of. You also only get one chance at this. You cannot ask a customer to give you a waiver on a specification and then go back and ask for another one. You only get to go to the well once, so you better know what you are talking about.

Since they will see quality improvements in other products they were purchasing from you, it will give them confidence that you will keep your word and also fix the largest problem product. I have found that customers will give you time if they see you are doing what you said you would do. Don't lie to them or embellish the truth. Just explain what you plan to do, the timing you believe you will need, and that you will meet with them regularly to keep them appraised on how things are going.

The one thing you can never do, because it will backfire on you every time, is to tell a customer that other companies buy this product and do not have an issue. I cannot think of a dumber thing anyone can say to a customer. **They do not care what does and does not**

work for another company. They do not know what process they run, what equipment they have. What they do care about is their company and what works for them, and right now what is not working is your product. You will be surprised at how positively most customers will react to this honesty because they are used to being lied to, and not just by your company. They will find your honesty to be a breath of fresh air.

You must start building confidence in both the employees working for you and the customers you sell to. It does no good to tell people how you are going to reshape the company, improve quality, keep delivery promises, and be accountable and then allow production of the same garbage that went out before you arrived.

Never lose sight of the fact you are also building your own reputation. If you ever expect people to trust you, respect you, and work with you, then when you say something, they must be able to count on it happening. They are watching you and making up their own mind if you are worth following, because if no one is following you, then what are you leading?

You need to do this for everything you make, ensuring QA keeps records of every spec tested along with the results. This is only a starting point, but you need the baseline you are now creating.

The next thing you need to figure out is what it will take to get things back to full operation. Will good maintenance do the trick, or will there be capital spending? Since you have no money, chances are good you will need to get creative. I ran a company once where we slowed everything down and even shut a couple of devices off to pilfer parts for use on other equipment. I would rather have 80% of my equipment running well than 100% running poorly, causing me to worry about what to expect from it every day.

In every company I have ever taken over I found that the first thing prior management had done when things went wrong was to cut back on preventive maintenance. What this means is that the equipment the company is running will not be able to produce a good-quality product, the output you need, or both. You need to focus on going for quality rather than quantity because no one cares how much crap you produce. The only thing that is going to sell is quality. You need to come to terms with this right from the start. Quality outweighs quantity every time, and not only are you rebuilding a company, but you are also rebuilding that company's reputation. Keep in mind that people are quite good at deceiving themselves. As a result, prior management would have rationalized that even though the quality the company produced was not the best, it was also not *that bad*. In short, while they knew deep down it was bad, they were simply too proud to admit it.

Begin measuring your capabilities

If you cannot measure it, you cannot fix it. We have all heard this and no truer words have ever been spoken. Frankly, this goes even deeper because, if you cannot measure it, then you are not working on it, and if you are not working on it, you cannot fix it. Everything depends on your ability to understand a problem and the first step in understanding a problem is the ability to accurately measure it. In addition, how do you know if things are getting better if you have no reference point or baseline, and how do you know when you try something it works?

If you are going to improve your manufacturing, then you need a baseline. The words that make me cringe more than any others are "it is too complicated." I know that either the employee I am speaking with does not understand the process, or they are simply incompetent.

Measure what you are after. Over the years I have always found this to be an interesting subject. Most people measure scrap, which means they want the scrap line on their chart to go down. The line on your chart should continue to decline, meaning scrap is being reduced, until it reaches zero. For some reason this does not work as well as measuring yields, which is nothing but the opposite of scrap. The only difference is that, instead of wanting the chart to approach zero, you now want the chart to climb and reach 100%.

People seem to respond better to this, inevitably working to get the chart to go up. Having scrap go down is exactly the same as having yields go up. I call this measuring what you are really after, and it should be done for everything in the company. You are after 100% throughput in manufacturing, 100% control of the line, 100% productivity, and 100% equipment utilization. You do not say "downtime was better for the week." You would say instead that "we did much better with the overall uptime of our equipment."

Over the years, I have concluded that this has to do with peoples' "pride" and their need for respect for what they have done. Let's admit it. No one wants to be told they did a crappy job. People want to know they are appreciated and respected in the company. When you say "we had a bad week with 10% of unscheduled downtime" people will automatically begin to justify why that happened. Over coffee, they will talk about how you do not understand that there was a major bearing malfunction and that it took longer to replace because the supplier didn't have one in stock. If you really understood the hoops they had to jump through to get this done, you would praise them instead of making that comment. Every word they are saying is probably true.

On the other hand, if you measure yield, present this information while discussing how over the past year equipment uptime has been on an upward trend. Tell them that while there was a little blip, over the entire year the trend is getting better. I understand that you busted your butt to get this part in or things would have been even worse. Say that you have been reviewing the regularity of these blips and have seen that they are becoming less and less frequent, which is great to see. Emphasize that you recognize how maintenance programs, spare parts kept in house, and upkeep of the equipment is greatly improving.

Now, what the people will be talking about is the fact that you appreciate the work they have been doing. They will understand there was an issue, but your employees feel proud you know they worked hard to keep even that to a minimum. Your employees will now begin to discuss how to keep this trend moving in the right direction and how to keep the frequency of these blips further and further apart. You got the exact same message across, but you will get completely different reactions. Long-term, therefore, you will get more mileage out of the second approach than the first.

This does not mean you never say, "Things are not going well." I took over a company where scrap was out of control and I did not talk about how good things were, because they weren't. I told them that scrap was out of control, but that things were going to get better regardless of their excuses and feelings. I explained to them that I understood that they thought I was crazy, but that would not stop me, and I would demand their cooperation on this endeavor.

They did push back, and it was a real effort to move things forward but, as I have mentioned over time, we managed to get our yield up to 95%. We were proud. Think about going from 75% yield to 95% yield in about two years of hard work. In the beginning, everyone thought I was a nut case even thinking it could be done. Yet as a group we accomplished it. Your people deserve to be proud!

We never spoke of scrap again…only yields.

I would like to finish the 5% rule. In the chapter about quality, I introduced you to my 5% rule which very clearly states that each time an inspector is used they will find about 5% defects in the products they inspect. What is worse is that approximately 5% of those defective products will still make it to your customers.

If you follow the 80/20 rule (that 20% of your customers will generate 80% of your profits) then there is potential for the customers generating most of your profit receiving a large percentage of the low-quality products. This does not mean the other customers are not important, but if your sales information is truly analyzed, you will find that 20% of your customers generate most of the profit in the company, and even though the other 80% help keep the lights on, they are not the real profit generators. For example, I once read an article from United Airlines which said that 2% of the business flyers generated 60% of all the profit for the airline.

A customer might take months to decide they want to leave you for price, but nothing will convince a customer to leave faster than defective products. And here is where most companies go wrong because their solution is to increase the amount of inspections they are conducting in order to reduce the probability of customers receiving defective products. This, of course, is not the solution.

It is not how often you inspect. It is what you are inspecting that matters.

Examine workflow

You have looked at your equipment to determine capabilities. You have begun setting up programs to get this equipment back into proper working order. Now you need to look at workflow. This seems so obvious I am always surprised at how little attention is paid to this subject. People will tell you that they are always looking at ways to improve workflow, but the flaw with their argument is that they look at each area by itself rather than at the entire manufacturing process. The company is not a microcosm of little work areas. It is one organism with an inlet and outlet, and it's everything in the middle that needs to be optimized.

I worked at a company where they would run one type of product for months because doing so optimized production lines and would then switch over to the next product. From a production point of view, this process was optimized and created the fewest changeovers, fewest possibilities for mistakes, and overall resulted in the lowest cost product. All that sounds great really. What could be better?

Unfortunately, this process also created a maximum amount of inventory since they produced months' or even a year's worth of product, at one time to optimize production. Because they were making so much product of a single type, inventory was three times what it should have been. Inventory costs a company money because it costs to store the finished goods. In addition to labor and raw material expenses, there is a third cost — customer changes. Customers change their product lines as their business demands, and if you have made six months of a product, but suddenly they only want something new, what do you do? You have four months of product that you can no longer sell because it was made specifically for them. Now you must try to sell this excess inventory on a secondary market, which often means selling it at or below cost. Consequently, remember to find solutions but look at the entire process, not just a single department.

Section 2:
Scrap

We can afford the scrap, but cannot afford to fix it. It has always amazed me that people will tell you they cannot afford to either put in automation or modify equipment to eliminate quality issues. On the other hand, there always seems to be enough money to pay overtime, buy more raw material, or remake the product two or three times to get product out the door.

This is not only true in manufacturing, but also in life. Not so long ago I was having new tires put on my car and while waiting, was talking to a guy in the waiting room. He told me that his tire blew out, and because he did not have a spare, he had driven on the flat for about 10 miles and ruined his rim. I didn't think you could travel that far on a flat, but maybe I am wrong. Anyway, I asked if he had run over something that blew out the tire. No, he informed me. He should have purchased new tires months ago, but did not have the money.

I told him it was a good thing he had it now or he would be walking. He said he still did not have the money, but now he had no other choice. Bottom line is that now the cost was going to be much more than if he had just purchased the tires when needed.

Reducing scrap is virtually self-funding. By this I mean that, other than the first couple of projects to get started, reducing scrap will create enough cash to pay for itself. Not only will it pay for itself but, as your quality gets better, your existing customers will buy more, and you will have made it easier for your sales staff to find new customers.

I once ran a company that had a serious scrap issue. I asked them to list the three top issues they had in order of importance so that we could focus on one at a time. I then asked them to list on the white board everything that could cause each problem and ended up with over 100 potential causes! Next, they were asked to group the 100 by where they might happen in the system. They took some time and, with much discussion among themselves, put everything into five subgroups. Following that, they were asked to arrange the five subgroups in order of occurrence. While this took longer to do since they needed different dates, but that was fine because we were getting closer to a root cause. After reviewing the data, they decided that the five subgroups could really be three subgroups.

Now that we had a final list and supporting data, we could make sure the order was correct and put numbers next to each group. What we found was that over 50% of all the issues came from group one, making it the obvious place to start. Next step was to take the original list of suggested causes that made up this group and analyze the root cause for each issue using the "Five Why Concept" where you keep asking why until you get to a root cause. It might take three whys or it might take seven whys, but the average is five — hence the name of the concept.

The reason the "5 Whys" is a great tool is that it is extremely simple, which quickly helps identify the root cause of a problem. It will also help to determine the relationship between different root causes of a problem and is easy to complete without statistical analysis. For those of you not familiar with Six Sigma, which this is part of the 5 Whys, below is a simple explanation:

1. Write down the problem. Documenting the issue not only helps to formalize the problem, but also to describe it completely. It also helps a team focus on the same problem.

2. Ask why the problem happens. Write the answer below the problem description. If the answer just provided doesn't identify the root cause of the problem in Step 1, ask why again and write that answer down.

3. Loop back to Step 2 until the team agrees to the identified root cause. Again, this may take less than or more than 5 Whys.

For example:

1) Why is your car no longer running?

    a. Because it ran out of gas

2) Why did it run out of gas?

    a. Because I didn't buy gas this morning

3) Why didn't you buy gas this morning?

    a. Because I didn't have any money.

4) Why didn't you have any money?

    a. Because I spent my money going out with friends.

5) Why did you spend all your money with your friends?

    a. Because I was having a really good time.

When we were done analyzing the data and had gotten down to the root cause it was clear that with a few simple changes to the equipment and about $3,000 of sensors per system, this issue could be eliminated. Then we could stop inspecting and looking for any issues in group 1, saving 10x the investment. This savings could then be used to work on group 2 and so forth. It did cost to resolve group 1, but the return on investment was about two days running time. As a result, the cash savings could be used to fund fixing the next group.

About $20k per system was saved each year thanks to a one-time investment of $3k per system — well worth the money. Even better, this investment never showed on the profitability line because it was capitalized, so while it hurt cash, it improved profitability. Right now your board is looking at your bottom line and not as concerned with cash, so you have just showed them a major improvement.

We never sacrificed quality. Instead, we found the reason the test was done in the first place and fixed the problem, removing the need to do any other testing. How did I know this could be done? Easy. Whenever I hear people attempt to justify why they need to do a test, I know there is a good probability there is a solution.

Let's finish the discussion about the 5 Whys because the example I gave is extremely simple, making it looks like the 5 Whys will solve all your problems with very little effort. Unfortunately, it is not so simple. When analytically looking at something, regardless of the technique, the most important part is defining the problem and asking the right questions. People do not spend enough time defining the problem, nor do they really understand the answer given to them so they can ask the right question. Using the previous example let's change the answers to see why the right questions are important:

1) Why are you taking the bus?

   a. Because my car will not start

2) Why doesn't your car start?

   a. Not really sure

3) Why are you not sure?

   a. I am not a mechanic

As you can see the whys go off the rail very quickly. I mean are you going to ask why they are not a mechanic? The problem is that no effort was made to analyze the answer so that the next logical question could be asked.

4) I understand you are not a mechanic, but didn't you look at any of the gauges? Surely you looked to see if you were out of gas?

By spending some time and thinking about the answers given, it will help direct the next question. Even if the next question is not a "why" question, you are guiding the discussion back to a point where a why question can be asked.

Many people tell me they do not use the 5 Whys because their use doesn't seem to resolve anything. It does work, but you, the discussion leader, need to think about answers given and choose the right question to help narrow things down. Like many things, it takes time and practice because if you are not asking the right questions you will not get answers that lead anywhere. This is not just some mindless question game where no thought at all is needed.

Section 3:
Maintenance and automation

Invest in maintenance. Your equipment is the life of your company and to stop doing maintenance is the dumbest thing you can do. It seems when a company gets into trouble the first thing cut is R&D, followed by maintenance and the equipment runs until it fails. Then, and only then, do repairs happen.

There's a link between the costs associated with downtime and the time and budget invested into preventive measures. Your product is only as good as the equipment that produced it, so to cut off maintenance is to ensure the death of your company.

The idea is to reduce the incidences of unplanned work because they can cost up to ten times more than planned maintenance in rushed parts, service callouts, downtime, overtime and so on. The more unscheduled downtime you have the worse shape the equipment is in, the quality will suffer, and the higher your costs will be. Planned maintenance percentage (PMP) is a widely used measure for maintenance staff and shows the percentage of the total number of maintenance hours spent on planned maintenance activities in a given time period.

Not surprisingly you will receive a great deal of pushback to implementing a true PM schedule. When you propose it, everyone will be in full agreement and vote you man of the year but, as the implementation progresses, this will change with fewer people wanting it. The hoopla was initially because PM sounds good. People can plan when to do things, there is less recovery from unexpected equipment failures, and generally things run better. Alternatively, as you get the PM set, up people are now held accountable and have to explain why something failed before it was supposed to. Did the person who rebuilt it do a poor job? Was it not installed correctly? What is going to happen to prevent failure in the future? These are things your maintenance department will not want to answer, but should. Once you have PM fully up and running things will settle down and the maintenance department will stop pushing back.

Have operators involved with maintenance. I have heard many arguments on both sides of this issue. One side states that operators do not have the expertise to do the maintenance and the other side says doing the maintenance makes for better operators. It is true that most operators do not have the expertise to perform needed maintenance on equipment, but they do have the ability to help. They can also see how to make things easier for the employee doing the maintenance on their equipment. I have found that when the operator has to help maintain the equipment they operate they will take better care of it. It is not that they respect the equipment more, don't fool yourself. They simply do not want the headache of repairing it. In the end it will always come down to them and what makes their life easier.

Automation

Never partially automate. In my early days I used to think any automation was better than no automation. I was so wrong. The first time I realized my mistake was a company I worked at where they had two major initiatives in the company, both having to do with reducing the cost per part. These cost reductions included manpower and scrap. The thing both initiatives had in common was people, who are the biggest scrap producer in the entire company. Machines can be adjusted, fixed, or upgraded, but people are what they are. And that is a huge variable. Even your best employee will have a bad day or bad week for who knows why. Anyone who has been in the workforce more than six months can think of an example to prove this.

The best way to remove this human variable, and at the same time reduce labor, is to automate.

This is the most difficult part because it is very cash intensive and there is no halfway to automate something. If you try, and only partially automate, there is a good chance you will make the problem worse, not better.

Since automation is so expensive, we decided at this company to automate in phases. Thus, we started with something simple. We wanted to automate the flipping of components in a heated system. Seemed simple, which is why we started here and then moved forward process step by process step until we had the entire system automated. The key factor to keep in mind is that this was in the early '90s so all the automated gadgets we have today simply did not exist at that time. Sensors have come a long way and today can work in almost any environment, but in the '90s they were expensive and were very limited as to where they could be used.

Given these challenges, we put a sensor that would work through a quartz window on the outside of the chamber, using this sensor to count the racks as they flipped. When the system had counted the right number of flips the system would automatically start the operation on the other side. When it was first put into operation, we told the operators they no longer needed to watch the racks flip because this system would take care of it. It became obvious early on that the sensor would occasionally miscount, starting the second side before all the racks flipped. We worked for months to correct this but, try as we did, we could never make it work 100% of the time.

After some time, the decision was made that losses were too high, so now the operators were needed to count the racks. If the system started the second side early, they were to (1) push a button to pause the process and (2) press another button to force the system to continue to flip racks. We thought this temporary solution would work until we could determine why automation did not work 100% of the time. Unfortunately, by reintroducing the human element even more mistakes occurred.

When I asked what the issue was, I was told they did not know how to do what I had asked. I tried to explain that if the automation did not work, they should simply do what they had done before the automation was installed. They assured me that they had never done the flipping and had never had to restart the system after a flip. They explained there had always been some sort of auto flip and all they had really done is watch the system. It is easy to read this and think either I was crazy, or the operators were less than truthful, but the sad part is they believed what they were saying.

Try as I might I could never convince them that if the flipping failed under computer control that they simply had to do what they had been doing for a couple of years. I learned right then and there that you cannot partially automate something. Either do it completely or do not do it at all. I have partially automated several systems over the years and have always had the same result. Once you begin to automate, people seem to develop amnesia and can no longer do the job themselves. To partially automate something will create more issues than it will solve. I am a firm believer in automation, not because I do not like people, but because people are a variable. Good-quality and consistent product means removing all variables.

Section 4: People

In most companies, people are both a blessing and a curse. In manufacturing people are the biggest variable, they don't show up to work, their output varies from day to day, and the quality of their work varies tremendously just to name a few issues.

For example, certain crews are always better than other crews. It could be that some crews have more experienced people or a crew working days does better than a night crew. Perhaps certain crews always get stuck with startups or weekend shutdowns and, by default, have more scrap. In all the years I have been doing this, never do all crews have the same scrap rate as the others. Anyone who has worked in a factory running 24 hours per day, either five or seven days per week, knows all crews perform differently.

I was running a company once where we had finally gotten yields up to 95% after working on the issue for over a year. Then yields began to fall for an unknown reason, going from 95% to 92%. No one could explain why. When I asked the manager of operations he spent 30 minutes explaining that, on a bad day, yields dropped from 95% to 80% because of some issue or other. This dramatic drop would then cause the monthly average to drop below 90%. The team would then work hard for the rest of the month trying to get the average back to 92%. None of this was new, since it was why I asked what was going on.

Unfortunately the manager was justifying the poor performance, but not once did he mention what they were doing to get rid of the 80% days. At the next scrap meeting I put up the charts, explaining that I understood the math of a bad day, which is also why I never look at just a single day. Shit happens so, instead, look at trends. Continuing on, I said that by looking at chart, which goes back years, it is possible to see that for the past several months there has been a steady decline in yields and with no end in sight. This trend worries me, as does the fact that this group has devolved from a group looking for/resolving problems to a group more focused on justifying poor performance. That you feel the need to justify this performance says a great deal about why the performance is happening in the first place. You have gotten sloppy, lazy, and lost focus which is why I will be attending this meeting from now on.

When I started at this job, I did not sit around talking about how 20% scrap was good and that we should think of ways to improve this. This would be a waste of time and everyone would have just blown me off. I told them that this was unacceptable since, in actuality, they worked their butts off just so they could throw 20% of what they made into the trash. Basically, I rephrased my message by telling them that one week every month they worked just to toss what they made in the trash. That they were not home with family, drinking beer, or out with friends. Instead they were working here just to produce scrap.

Adding fuel to the fire, I stated that the raise you all think you deserve, the bonus I just stopped that you are mad about, and the other perks I have put a stop to are all in the trash you are producing. The reduction of that scrap will pay for the perks you think you deserve, but will no longer have, until they can be paid for. You are throwing all those perks in the trash but we, all of us, are going to change this.

It took time to get their heads wrapped around this change but the more improvement they made, the more I encouraged them. The stick I had to use eventually went away. I know people who do not believe in using any stick and that only positive encouragements should be used. Pay a bonus for improvements, have contests for ideas to improve yield, and other tricks like they are training their dog. This is a complete waste of time because people know when they are doing a poor job, and when this approach is tried, they know you are just blowing smoke up their ass and will completely ignore you.

You will get some small useless improvement and that's it. No matter how much you try to bribe people, they will never change. People do not change without a reason, period. Even worse is that when you decide it is not working and stop trying to bribe them to do better, they will complain even louder. Now they will say they have no reason to do better because you took something away from them.

There is a saying in sales that "you can always lower the price, but you can never raise it." The same is true about changing behavior. Once you have given something it is almost impossible to take it away. Before you say that I already stated I took perks away, let me remind you that I was not the one who gave them the perks in the first place.

The trick is to use these two methods of "encouragement" correctly and sometimes, like I am presently doing, you must switch back and forth to keep things moving. Remember, your company is stressed, and you are turning it around so it will take time to get things ingrained. People are going to slip and revert back to how they used to think, so they will need to be reminded that the old ways are no longer acceptable. This is also why I laugh when people ask me what kind of manager I am. I am what I need to be at the time — always!

Motivating operators

Of all the tasks you must do this is most likely the toughest. And if you have a union, it will be almost impossible. From the operator's point of view if they are a member of a union, they have no incentive to make improvements, work harder, change to a different culture, or help you in anyway. They will get paid the same regardless of how well the company does, and if the company goes under, then they will simply get another job. Since they are unskilled labor anyway, they see no difference between working for you or the person down the block, as long as the pay is about the same. In fact, it can be even worse than described here. In a union everyone is paid the same, so why work hard when you will be paid just the same as the laziest employee in the company?

Even at non-union companies I have seen things tried over the years, most of which have either failed or, at the least, not generated the benefits the company was hoping for.

Early in my career I worked for a company where low monthly output was causing per product costs to be higher than acceptable.

We put goals into place to correct the problem, adding incentive for hourly staff of a $100 cash bonus when these goals were achieved. The goal was based on increasing monthly output from the same time from the previous year. To keep people motivated we paid the bonus quarterly. Everything was set, the employees were excited, and so we were off and running. The first quarter the goal was achieved, an armor car pulled into the parking lot with two guys carrying a sack of cash. We wanted to make this a big deal which is why we paid to have an armored car. The company had about 1,000 hourly employees and each would get $100 = a $100,000 cash delivery.

Tables were set up where each employee signed their name and received a $100 bill. The company was loved by one and all and people were delighted. Note: only the hourly staff received this bonus — no engineers and no managers. The next quarter ended, and even though they did not do quite as well, they still achieved the desired goal and, again, were all paid out. People were happy, but not to the level they were the first time.

Third quarter came and they missed the goal so there was no payout. Then the employees started to complain about how we had reduced their salaries and we owed them the money. We explained, again, that the bonus was given out only when they achieved the goal, and since they had missed it, there was no payout.

Output became worse than ever and the employees were unhappier than they had ever been. They felt they were owed the money and that it was now part of their benefits. For the next six months life at work was miserable, and they never hit the goal again. In fact, for a while output in the company got even worse than it was before the program began. Consequently, the entire incentive program was eliminated. Throwing money at people to solve problems does not work. Lesson learned! A power of a monetary reward lasts until it is spent and then it is forgotten.

I have seen companies try "company picnic" day where everyone would meet at an amusement park. The company would rent a section with picnic tables, cook a meal and serve it to the employees and their families. Then the family could go out and enjoy the rides in the park courtesy of the company. I cannot count the number of times I heard people talk about how much this must have cost and they would have preferred to just have been given the money. Very few cared about the fact that the company was trying to do something nice for them and make work more like a family. Many people even resented going, feeling they had no choice because management would look down on them if they did not go.

You, on the other hand, have a company which is dying, and your people are not motivated in any way because they know their company is in trouble. Virtually no one in the company is motivated and it is much easier to improve something near the bottom than to squeeze more from a workforce that is already operating at 90%. You have nowhere to go but up with your people, making it easier to slowly get them to improve. More than likely they have been neglected for so long that anything you do will be viewed as positive.

They will give you some improvement with very little effort, but it will not take long for them to realize that, for the company to improve, it means they will also be expected to change and improve their performance. At this point the easy part is over, and you will have the same issue every company does regarding motivation.

At one company we started a summer work schedule that enabled employees to have a longer weekend. They still had to put in 40 hours per week so, instead of an 8-hour workday, we went to a 10-hour workday. Since overtime was based on 40 hours per week, there was no overtime involved. We also made sure everyone understood we would not pay overtime but were, instead, doing this so that they could have a more pleasant summer. People looked forward to this all year. It was a great motivator for the company. You could come in early or stay late to get the 10 hours per day, but the main criteria were that projects could not fall behind.

When we started the program, it was only half days on Friday but, over time, we moved to a 4-day work week over the summer. To this day, I think this was the best motivator I have ever used. Look for things that mean something to your people and which will have a lasting effect. They fully understood that to keep the 4-day work week in the summer, they had to get their work done, honestly done, in the four days.

One of the reasons I shy away from money is because once it is given and spent it is gone and forgotten. On the other hand, when people have Friday off, then the change is reinforced every Friday they do not have to come to work. They get reminded for three months that the company has done something nice for them, and if they work hard, the company is willing to do it again.

Demotivating people

When talking about motivating people, you also need to be careful not to do the opposite or demotivate people. One of the fastest ways to ruin motivation efforts is inconsistency. You cannot pick and choose who you will apply rules to, or who you will look the other way for. This goes for both good and bad; what is good for one is good for all, a concept that, believe it or not, is tough for most people.

I took over an extremely stressed company where all discipline was based on whether or not management felt an employee was a good worker. We were having an issue with people showing up late to work or not showing up at all, so I asked to see the attendance records to see who we had problems with. One employee was frequently quite late, but had never been written up. When I asked about this, I was told he was one of the best operators the company had. Regardless of his performance, I asked, how do you think the other employees feel about this? The answer was quick: "I do not care because they are not as good as he is."

The problem with this type of thinking is that other employees see what is happening, believe he gets special treatment (which he does), and this makes them angry. They now feel he is respected more than they are (and he is), so then they set out to work less. If management does not care, then why should they? When people feel they have been treated unjustly, whether or not that is the case, they will go out of their way to do less, create more scrap, and try very hard to make things worse for the company.

Get your minds around the fact that perception is reality and what they see as reality is fact, reality. If they feel cheated, they will react as such. Yelling, threatening, and finding a big stick only works for so long. In the end, you will need to deal with their reality, either by accepting poor performance, poor yields, poorly motivated employees, or by resolving what they perceive as unjust. Problems do not just go away. They fester and grow bigger.

I was told that if this wonderful employee was treated like everyone else, he might need to be terminated. My response was that he would be terminated. What is fair for 90 other people is fair for him and everyone needs to be treated the same. People tell you they like to be treated as special, but the truth is that people like to be treated exactly like everyone else — just as long as they feel like they are treated special.

Once this issue was finally resolved, people did improve their performance and we saw a reduction in discipline issues. You cannot expect people to care if they feel you have favorites in the company, and they are not one of those favorites. If you are treating someone well, then by default you are treating others poorly. People didn't see that they were being treated fairly while this one employee was being treated as extra special. What they saw was him being treated special while they were being treated unfairly. Not treating everyone in the company equally will kill motivation faster than you can believe.

Attitude adjustments. Motivating people, at least initially, in a company you are getting back on its feet is difficult but is easier than adjusting people's attitude. In a well-run company there is a certain culture that has existed for a long period of time and when people start, they either fit in or are replaced. Employees in that long-established company will not tolerate people who do not fit in.

You, on the other hand, are developing a new culture and a new way of thinking, both of which require change from people who have believed and worked one way for years. The attitude they had towards the company yesterday is no longer any good. Unlike a company that is well established, your company is failing and the culture when you arrived does not work, which is why you were hired in the first place. You are no longer interested in people who only care about how the company can better their lives. You want people who care about the company itself as well. I am not going to dwell on this because it really has been a theme throughout the entire book.

Believe it or not, tweaking the culture of a failing company is worse than gutting it and starting over. People will also fight you harder when you try to tweak things than they will if you scrap the culture and start over. I have never really understood why this is true, but when you tell people you plan to make changes to the culture to make improvements, they will argue with you for hours. They adamantly demand to know exactly what changes and your justification for making changes in that area.

On the other hand, if you tell people that the company is failing, in large part because of the company culture, and that you plan to start over and do it right, most people will agree. They know the company is failing and if you feel a change of culture will help, they seem fine with this.

Section 5:
Teams / Expectations
Startup teams

It sounds counterintuitive but teams can really help when turning a company around. The reason I say it seems counterintuitive is because your first thought will be to have no teams but to run everything yourself. You do not have the time to handle every little issue yourself, so you have teams which you do run, and let them handle the little things.

Teams can be used to work on many problems at once because the focus of each team is both different and specific. This is important: never start a team with an ambiguous goal. For example, you do not create a Yield Improvement team charged with "improving the yield of manufactured parts." That statement is not specific, providing the team with no defined target, no goal post to run towards, and no real win at the end. If yields improve by 5%, did they do a good job? How about if the yields improved by 2% or ½ %? They met the goal of improving yields in the company, so how could you consider their efforts a failure — if you did deem it so?

There are certain rules in running good teams:

1) Teams need to have very specific goals right from the start. If you start a yield team, then set a goal, for example, of a 10% improvement. State that you want yield to improve by 10% for six consecutive months and when once this is achieved, the team will disband. Everyone on the team understands what they are shooting for and that they have done their job well when the goal is achieved, and the team disbanded.

2) When a team is working, all the people on it are of equal rank. This means no disagreement is settled with a "because I am your boss" or a "because I told you." If there is a disagreement about something, then the employee running the team should switch from running the team to facilitator of the discussion. The minute people realize that disagreements are settled by rank, new ideas will stop flowing and the team will no longer be efficient.

3) All ideas are of equal importance regardless of where the idea originated from as long as it came from someone on the team. Just because a maintenance employee has an idea about quality does not mean it is a bad idea.

4) You need to be present when the team starts up to ensure the team is working on the right problem. Keep the team focused. Teams do have a tendency to start on a problem and then, over time, wander to something new that is out of their jurisdiction. This is proverbial "scope creep." Keep them focused on a single issue. If they discover something interesting, you can always start up a new team, but this team has to stay on point.

With number four you need to be there when the team begins to get things rolling and you will need to be present for a period of time once the team gets going. This gives you a captive audience to whom you can say why things need to change and why past performance is no longer good enough. It also gives you a chance to see the dynamics of the team and make adjustments, if necessary. For example, is one person dominating the entire time talking or does another have, at least in their mind, all the answers already?

When I started my first team at a company I was running, it was to solve an issue for a customer. The first thing the team wanted to discuss was that the problem was really the customer. This became lesson number one. Our customer is our customer. We are the supplier and they can buy our product from any number of other companies. Hence, if we wish to keep them as a customer then, by default, their problem is our problem.

They pushed back, explaining that the problem the customer was having could in no way be caused by the manufacturing process used at my present company. I replied that, "while that might be the case, it changed nothing because this was still our customer and our problem. Time to approach this from another point of view." Everyone looked at me like I had two heads, but I kept going. "Let's not prove this cannot happen; let's purposely cause the problem by making changes to our processes. I recall one of the team members telling me that (1) obviously I was not listening because it cannot be created by the process used and (2) I was telling them to waste time doing something that could not be done. "Humor me," I said. "Maybe we will learn something that can help our customer."

This is where I learned that we did not really understand how some of our products were actually made from a technical point of view. The team knew that if you did certain things a product would come out at the other end, but they did not actually understand the chemistry of what they were doing. All the experts I had sitting around the table knew no more about making this product I did, and I knew nothing. This, of course, meant that this team was of no use and it was disbanded on the spot. You cannot fix a problem you do not understand, and these people knew nothing. It also sent a clear message to the company that, if we want to keep a customer, then their problem becomes our issue.

Had I kept the original team going, they would have to work in every department, learning what had been forgotten over the years, and then figure out how that applied to our customer issue. All focus on the team would have been lost since they would not only have had to work on the customer's issue, but also work on learning why/how things worked in the first place.

We started teams in each department with the sole purpose of learning how to correctly do the jobs in that department. Each team developed processes for a specific area of the company and each team could stay focused on a very specific task. They could learn how things worked, why they worked that way, but after it was done, we had a faction of people who knew every aspect of the process.

Now a successful team could be created to eliminate the initial customer issue. The obvious question would be what we did about our customer during all this time. I will go into more detail on that in the next chapter, but basically I talked them into staying with us.

Never get caught in the dreaded 80% completion rule

Solve problems completely. This seems to be obvious, but it is also the least practiced thing I have encountered. I am all sure we have heard, or even said ourselves, "close enough." This is the worst phrase you can use; in fact, it is banned from use at any company I run. People always think they will get back to "it" later, that they will circle around and finish "this," or many other such statements — none of which ever really happens.

People will start fixing a problem, get about 80% done and then move to the next problem on their list. The belief is that they are getting a substantial return on the work done solving problem "X" and now they need to get onto the next issue. This is a big mistake, especially if you don't know whether the problem currently being worked on has a relationship to the any other issues you have. It could very well be that if the problem was resolved completely other issues might be reduced or eliminated.

When I took over a plant, we began to work on scrap as previously mentioned, and not being from this industry, I asked why they had a reverse osmosis (RO) system. One of the old-timers explained all the issues they had had with water and that this fixed everything because they could set the level of resistivity they wanted. Great! But why is only 50% of the plant using it? The old-timer told me that, while all the critical areas were using this water, because the RO system is only 70% efficient, they did not want to use it in noncritical areas.

What about all the other areas of the plant that used water to make our product? I could use any quality of water and everything would be just fine? His response was: "Well maybe not "any quality" but the other areas are not as sensitive to water quality. This we know." Really? Show me the data that supports this statement. Of course, there was no data because there had been no tests. They had started to use the RO system in certain areas of the plant, saw a major improvement, and then did not consider how the RO system might help in other areas.

We then expanded use of the RO system and saw major improvements throughout the entire process. It only goes to reason that if the process is sensitive to water in one area, there is a good probability it is sensitive in many areas. Of all the work the company did over the years to reduce waste, this was most likely the biggest factor to success, and had been overlooked for years. In fact, if they had lost close to $6 million in scrap since the RO was installed because it had not been expanded to be used throughout the entire plant. You might think this could never happen to your plant, but the truth is this is quite common.

Once at a company I had all projects which had been started but never completed pulled together for review. When we discovered projects had not ever been completed or studied, the next thing was to look at all the projects over the years and see which deserved to be finished. We based our decisions on the impact the project had for the product it was used on. If work had been done and the expected result was nowhere close to the real result, we moved on. If the results met or exceeded the expected result, we finished the project.

I call this the 80% application rule: where a great idea is used to resolve a problem but is only implemented to about 80% and then abandoned. Once people get to about 80%, they see big improvements, decide everything is done, and move on. The truth is, this same idea can be used in many areas of the plant if people would simply expand their thinking. Too often the most obvious is often the most overlooked.

Realistic expectations

If you have never taken on turning a company around before you may have no idea how much pressure you will be under from board members looking for profit, customers upset about quality, staff nervous about what you plan, and on top of it all, not being sure you can meet payroll. Everyone will be looking at you to solve all the problems and they will each believe their problem is the most important.

Pace yourself because the sure-fire way to fail is to give in to the pressure around you. In this book, things have been laid out in order of importance. For example, why start replacing poor performers if your HR department is not functional? Why start looking at cost per element or cost reductions if you cannot trust the numbers coming out of the finance department?

The board will want you to start getting sales improvements to generate revenue, and to make their investment in the company look better. I can tell you right now if you cannot help your board to see your issues in an honest manor, you will fail.

You can work on many things at once, naturally, but line things up so you are not working against yourself. You also don't want to redo work because you got ahead of yourself. For example, if you are working with customers to keep them from leaving, your introducing a new product might not seem like such a good idea. However, think about this. If you cannot produce the old product with good quality, then how can your customers trust you with a new product?

Actually, new product introduction could make things even worse. If you came to my company offering to introduce a new product while we were still trying to resolve issues with the old one, I would most likely cancel my order with you. If you are working on something new, then you are not working on fixing what you have. If you are not fixing what I am presently buying, then you have not been truthful with me because you promised me you would improve quality and asked for time, which I gave you. Now I find that you used this time to work on something new instead of resolving issues with my existing product. Don't misrepresent yourself to your customers or you will lose them.

Employ strong process discipline. Good manufacturing should almost be boring because everything should be done exactly as it was done the day before and the day before that. As the president of the company, this is really your goal post. It's what you strive to create. Everywhere in the company we have been talking about change — changing people, changing processes, changing culture, and pretty much anything else we can find.

We went after change because the company is failing and what they had been doing does not work. Previous management had either given up, were not up to the task of running a manufacturing company, and let it get away from them. No matter the reason the company is in the state it is, the company has degraded to a point where it is no longer viable. You were hired to change this and make the company both functional and profitable again. You have quite a bit of work yet to do but you also need to have goal posts in order to know when you have completed what you set out to do.

Manufacturing is not a "fly by the seat of your pants" operation. If done correctly it is more like a choreographed dance where every step is known before the dance even begins. To do this you need to have written processes and procedures in place everywhere in the company. There should be nothing open to interpretation or to guesses. And absolutely no winging it. Everything should have a written policy, and everyone should adhere to these policies, with no exceptions. If a better way is found, then the policy can be changed, but no one is allowed to deviate from it. Getting to this point is your goal and you need to make sure it is the goal of everyone you have working for you.

There is no way to achieve this other than having strong process discipline with no toleration for any deviation from the process. This will also mean that you have strong progressive employee discipline in place so that people completely understand what the cost is of not performing the tasks assigned to them and utilizing the process that has been established and documented.

Section 6:
Goal Post

Schedule/production attainment

You will not want to start this measurement until you have manufacturing running well. Remember, you measure what you are after, and if you begin to measure production attainment before your company is ready, you will force the company to make a choice.

A production or schedule attainment score is very simple to understand because it is nothing more than what the daily or monthly production capabilities are versus what was completed. This used to be called "plant efficiency," where you figure out what the plant can do without removing scheduled down time. Then you measure total plant capabilities, capabilities with scheduled down time, and what the plant ultimately did produce.

The problem is that if you start this measurement too soon people are forced to choose what they should be working on. Should they be working on improving quality or getting output up? The mistake many people make is to believe they can work on both at the same time, and this simply cannot be done. Once you have quality corrected then you can go after increasing your production numbers, but you cannot ever do this the other way around.

The most obvious reason for this is that people will equate the first thing you work on as the most important thing you are after. Thus, if you go after daily output first, they will feel this is most important and quality is second. I believe I have made it quite clear that this is not true, so go after getting your quality fixed first and then start on this. Remember, it doesn't matter how much you produce if no one wants it.

Perfect order percentage

If you read manufacturing books or go to seminars you know this is shown as the holy grail of manufacturing. Yes, it is important. Yes, it is something you want to obtain, and decisions about this will need to be made when you take over your stressed company. But are you going to hit this at 100%, even if it means purposely losing a few customers? Are you going to work with your customers and not make 100%? Hard call, as you might guess, because cash is tight, customers are already unhappy, and now you need to decide what to do next. No clear answers on this one, but there are some things you can do.

First you need to be brutally honest about what your company can actually do. For example, how many on-time deliveries can your company meet? Are you above or below 50% and how late are you? Do you miss ship dates by a day or a week? Let's take worst case scenario: that you hit on-time delivery 40% of the time and are late the other 60% of the time. Of the 60% the lateness varies from one to three weeks with some deliveries even later than that.

Next you need to do a full analysis of your customer base to identify which customers are profitable and which you break even on. The method I like to use is a comparison of gross margin vs. net profit analysis to make this determination. If you are making a positive gross margin, but negative net profit, then this customer is paying for some of your bills — not all of them, but some. These customers you will leave alone because they are helping pay bills. You do not want to lose them or even risk losing them at this stage.

However, if a customer has a break-even or less gross margin then net profit, naturally, is also negative, and that customer is clearly a non-contributor. With any luck, your biggest customer does not fit into this group, but more than likely they will.

I have found most salespeople are not very brave, and if there is the slightest chance of losing a customer, they will fight you at every turn to not address it with the customer. The bigger the customer, the higher the probability that you are losing money. The reason why is simple. No one wants to risk losing them because they are keeping people and equipment busy. Large customers know this and play that card all the time.

I got on a plane and met with the president of this company. You, as president of your company, have no interest meeting with a buyer or someone from finance. You will settle for nothing less than meeting with the president of your customer. Do not be afraid to use this very argument if there is some sort of pushback from your customer. For this discussion, anyone below president is of no value to you.

You also do not want your salesperson in the room either because there is a very high risk of them siding with the customer at the wrong minute. I was running a company where we had a customer who showed a negative net profit of 30% and I wanted to increase the price. I set up the meeting and my salesperson insisted on attending, which I really did not want, but ended up caving on. When we all sat down at the conference table, I was on one side and all seven employees for the customer were on the other. Where do you think my sales guy sat? You got it, he sat on their side of the table and during the discussion you would have thought he worked for them. Within the first 15 minutes, I sent him to the car to wait for me after the meeting was done.

Let's face it. The buyer is not going to be happy you want to speak with their boss instead of working with them. Actually, all your customer's senior staff will not be happy you are playing this card, but you need help and only the top person will be able to help you. They have no idea what you are going to tell their boss, but it cannot be good, or you would not demand the meeting, and with specific instructions that the buyer is not wanted.

When we met, I explained that we were going to have to increase the price of the product. Naturally, the discussion was more than this, as will be covered in the chapter on sales because you will need to be working with your sales team to achieve this. In short, we did get the price increase and we still have a good relationship to this day. I meet with the president once per year for no other reason than to catch up over dinner. Sometimes we discuss business and sometimes we just enjoy the meal. You never know what you can get unless you ask for it.

Section 7:
OSHA

Let me finish this long chapter and talk about OSHA

If at some point your company is visited by OSHA because of any number of reasons, for example, it simply has been neglected for years. Then you can assume anything and everything OSHA-related stopped long ago. Do not try to tackle this yourself. Instead, hire an outside entity to do an assessment of the company and issue a report which lists how many violations your company has. Keep in mind these people are being paid to find things. When selling your house, have you ever heard of a house inspection where the inspector comes back and said the house is perfect and nothing needs to be done? Of course not. When you sell your house and the buyer pays a house inspector to do their job, it is 100% certain they will come back with a list. The only questions are how big the list is and what on the list is most important. There is no difference when it comes to having a third party inspect your factory. They will come back to you with a list. Your job is to prioritize what's on the list and determine how quickly you can get the most important things done.

At the end of the inspection, they told us we were one of the three worst companies they had ever, in their history, inspected. The point is we started fixing things that required little or no cash so by the time OSHA did come, which they did because the union called them during negotiations, we were already working on areas which cost money.

The first thing OSHA does when they arrive at your factory is to meet with senior people, including your environmental and safety officer if you have one. They explain why they are there. For instance, are they there because you were unlucky and turned up randomly, or did someone call? If someone called, like our union, what was the complaint and what would they be looking at?

I explained that the call had come in during union negotiations, which they knew, and was done to hurt the company, which they also knew. I then told the officer that we would also fail, but that

I welcomed the inspection. I also wanted to cover what we had been doing before the inspection started. I did not hide the fact the company had almost gone bankrupt a few years before I arrived, and that anything having to do with OSHA had pretty much stopped. I explained that we were working hard at getting back into compliance with all OSHA regulations, but were not yet there.

They did a multi-day inspection and came back with a very long list. By this time, we had gotten our third-party inspection company and our attorney involved and both were present at the closing meeting. The lead inspector told us he really appreciated the honesty and that he would need to speak with his supervisor about how to proceed. In the end, we got a very small fine and OSHA worked with us to complete the list of items we needed to get done. We were forced to write monthly reports proving we were working on the list but, at the end, we got it all done and everyone was happy.

I will not say this would work every time. Our attorney stated I took a big risk by opening up to OSHA, but I find that honesty works more times than not. If you know you are going to get caught anyway, why try to hide behind a lie which will probably be discovered.

One thing I have never regretted was getting our attorney involved, as I do think it helped. At least with an OSHA-specialized attorney sitting at the table no one was going to intimidate or lie to us. I do not believe the officer we had from OSHA was interested in anything but helping us, but you never know. You can get stopped by one police officer who gives you a warning that your taillight is out or get stopped and get a ticket because your taillight is out. You just never know who will show up.

One last note here before we move on. The union did not call OSHA because they felt the plant was unsafe. They called OSHA because they were looking for some way to hurt the company during negotiations in hopes we would cave in rather than suffer one outlandish ploy after another.

CHAPTER 9

Unions

Let me start by saying that I have worked in companies with unions and companies with no unions. The first was when I left the Army and was hired by a company in Colorado as a technician. On the very first day I worked for this company the shop steward came by after lunch and told me I needed to slow down. Why? Because I was working too hard and too fast. Apparently, I was making other people look bad and they were upset. Cry me a river. Really?!

I told him that maybe they should work harder and then they would not look so bad. He got upset, told me these people were my brothers, and I should not try to make them look bad.

The funny part is that exact same thing happened many years later at a company I was running when we hired a housekeeper who quit on day one. She went to lunch and simply never came back. I had HR call her to find out why she left since she had been doing a good job. She informed HR that several union people had come to her telling her to slow down and not work so hard because she was making them look bad. She told HR that she had not really worked that hard, but they kept at her all morning, so she decided this company was not a place she wanted to work.

Think about this. Neither the housekeeper nor I were intentionally making the union employees look bad. They were making themselves look bad, but we were being blamed for their poor performance. At the end of the day, I too, left the company and never returned. Like the housekeeper I could not work for a company where a requirement was to lower my work ethics to meet the low standards of the union workforce.

Many people think I am against unions, which is not totally true. What I am against, are their tactics of "them vs. us" and that they often really do not care about either the company or their union members. Like all businesses they look for a profit, so they need to sign up as many people as possible while spending as little as possible.

I recall once watching the news as a union member was being interviewed. He was so proud his union had just caused a company to go bankrupt. He stated how the company president would not give them what they wanted so they went on strike, making it as difficult as they could for business to continue until he finally went bankrupt.

This union member was beaming with pride as he told the interviewer how they made it difficult for trucks to come and go and other ways in which they had made life difficult for the owner. No matter what they thought of the owner, his business provided their salaries, healthcare, and other benefits — a business they had just caused to close. I recall thinking this person is now unemployed, but was yet so proud of the fact that he and compatriots had hurt his boss. What none of them considered or cared about was everyone else who was impacted: non-union employees, suppliers, and customers. He was part of this aggressive union action because the union had convinced he and other union personnel that hurting people was the best way to get what you want.

If you really hate the company you work for or feel mistreated/underappreciated, then just leave. Find another company to work for that treats you better. Why do unions feel they have the right to hurt everyone else just because they cannot have their own way? If enough people quit, the owner should get the message and either change or go out of business, but either action will be because of the owner's choice of action, not because he was bullied into something. I never really thought all unions were this way, and maybe they're not. Perhaps this was an isolated case and most people have enough common sense to realize that when you force someone out of business ultimately you also hurt yourself. Maybe this was just unique to the car industry. I mean, surely people have enough common sense to realize they need the company as much as the company needs them — especially in an economically depressed area? Silly me....

What I have come to realize is that common sense, whether dealing with unions or not, is a rare commodity. Most people do not have enough common sense to fill a thimble, and if there was no one to tell them what to do, they would starve to death. I have no idea where common sense has gone but it just seems to be getting harder and harder to find.

This is where unions really get their power. People want to be told that nothing is their fault, that the issue is always with the other guy, and that they deserve better even if they don't. Unions are adept at convincing employees that, no matter what happens, they are always right, and the company is always wrong. This aids in convincing the employees that not only do they deserve more than what they get, but also that the company is out to get them. This tends to give unions almost unlimited power.

I once ran a company with a union which had been in place for over 40 years. After asking, I was granted a meeting with the local union representative who had a way of always making you feel like he did you a favor to meet with you. Within 10 minutes of talking to the regional union representative I understood three things very clearly. First, what I had seen on TV was not an isolated incident, and that the union really did believe hurting the company was the best way to get things done. Secondly, this union cared no more for employees than it did for the company. Thirdly, to turn this company around I would not only have to go to war with the union, but I would also have to win. I am often asked how I could come to these conclusions. Simple. The regional union representative told me he did not care what I wanted to do, what I wanted to change, or what reasons I had to do either. The union liked things just the way they were and would fight me on any change I tried to make, no matter what it was.

He had no idea what I had in mind, what changes needed to be made, or even the fact I told him from the outset I wanted to work

with him. When I took over the company, I fully understood what would need to be done to get the company turned around and the last thing I needed was another problem to tackle. I did not want to fight the union, which is why I told the union representative I wanted to work with him. The only thing he was interested in was to ensure I knew he was the "big man" and I would do what the union wanted, no exceptions, no discussion.

Over the years, I have come to realize that there are two distinct types of unions. The first is comparable to a mob, while the second is similar to a gang. Mob-style unions rule with an iron fist with such absolute authority that the members are more afraid of the union than they are of management. The union makes all the decisions, and if given any chance at all, will dictate even decisions normally due the company. Members stick with them because they view the union as stronger and more powerful than management. When you have a tribe/mob mentality the person with the biggest stick rules and all others do as they are told. Unions go out of their way to ensure members know who has the biggest stick.

A gang and a mob are similar with one exception: a gang convinces you that you are part of the family. From all the documentaries I have ever seen the number one thing that gets young kids to join gangs is the feeling of belonging to something. Gang members are often those who do not have a sense of family, real or imagined. They thus go looking for a person or organization that can provide this sense of belonging. Gangs too often are the only available substitute, making people feel they are part of something, that the other members care about them and that there is no greater purpose on this planet than taking care of the gang you belong to. I find that most people who join unions have this same desire: joining, belonging, and protecting the union they have joined. This seems to be the majority of union members, excluding the few who have no choice but to join since they are employed in a place where union membership is mandatory for the job they have. When I speak to people in unions, they talk about other union members like family, often referring to them this way. When a union is on strike other union members will not cross the strike line. I am told that they will never cross the line in support of their "brothers and sisters."

When I met with the local union rep, I tried to explain the current financial status of the company, stating that if the union worked together with me, I was sure we could get the company profitable again. Things would have to change, of course, and it would be easier if the union was in the loop. We never discussed what the "changes" might or would be, what the plan to move forward might be, or how we could move forward together. We never discussed the existing contract how to ensure the members would be protected, or how the union could help. We never got that far because, and I will never forget what he said to me:

"Rodney (he always called me Rodney), the union does not care what changes you want to make, why you want to make them, or what the company's financial status/viability is. The union will fight you on every issue as we are just fine with the way things are." Just as I stated earlier....

Seriously?? I had just explained that the company was in financial trouble, and if he wanted his members to continue being employed here — at all — then we needed to make changes. We pay above average for the area, which draws employees who have few other options as there is not much manufacturing left in the area. Finding new manufacturing jobs would not be that easy if my present company were to close or consolidate operations and yet the union rep cavalierly tossed that point of discussion out the window. Hard to believe that the union "cared" about members as anything other than a cash source with that attitude. If the union really cared, he and I would have had a conversation. He would have listened to what I had to say, discussed it, and made recommendations, and if he was still unhappy, he could have just left. Where would his people go? Not his problem. So, how was he looking out for them?

Not long after that meeting with the regional union rep, I had a companywide meeting since employees wanted to know what to expect from me and where I was going. This is normal since people are nervous when they get a new boss. When you have change at the top employees justifiably get nervous.

Since the company ran 24/7, I held some of these meetings in the middle of the night so I could catch all the shifts during their normal working hours. During one of these meetings one of the union members started asking some questions, always referring to the place he worked as "the company." I asked him why that particular use of words and was informed that he was union and I was not. I was part of the company and he was not. I said "So, you are telling me you do not get paid here? Get your health insurance from here? Receive any benefits from here?"

He confirmed that, even though the answer to all those questions was "yes," it was because "the company" owed them all to him. He vehemently stated that "the company" also owed all the union members a great deal more than this. When I asked why he felt his place of employment owed him and the union members more than what they were getting he told me "because we show up."

Look at the words used: "because we show up." Not because they worked hard or because they even worked, but simply because they showed up. Really? This would have been funny except I knew he meant it. This was not some 25-year-old who thought he was owed a free lunch. No, this was a 70-year-old person who was first-generation American and had worked for the same company his entire life.

I had had enough of the closed-mindedness, so I told him and the rest of the attendees two things. First, his union and the union members could either be partners to successfully make this company a viable company for everyone, or they could work against me, get fired, and I would still make this company a success — only without them. He stood up and informed me that I could not threaten him or the union members. I told him I was not threatening him or the union members. I was simply stating facts. I told him it didn't matter how things had run in the past because things were going to change. The company was in trouble, that I had been hired to turn it around, and that I wanted to do this together. That choice was completely in their hands because if I did not get their cooperation, then one of the changes would be them, and as anyone who knows me can tell you, I do not threaten. I may say things you don't like to hear, but when I say "x will be fixed," then "x will be fixed." "We are part of a union and we are not afraid of you," was what I was told and so I looked at him, snickered, and asked if there were any other questions. In three months, he was gone, retired.

Companies cannot be run by two different groups, and stressed companies even less so. I have often found Abraham Lincoln's quote holds so much truth when related to companies. "America will never be destroyed from the outside. If we falter and lose our freedoms, it will be because we destroyed ourselves." The biggest threat for most companies is not competition, but the very employees working in them regardless if there is a union or not.

As I stated earlier, I am not against unions and have, in fact, read where unions joined with management to help save the company their members worked at. This is the way things should work, hand-in-hand, so both sides get what they need and people stay employed. I am sorry to say I simply have never been privileged enough to have run a company with this type of union.

Shortly after the initial meetings with the union, I wanted to change our QA forms so that operators who completed a task would be required to initial the QA form to show they were the operator who had done the work. The union grieved the change because "I was trying to trap employees to later fire them." Remember from earlier chapters: if you are not measuring something, you cannot fix it and people need to be held accountable for their work to ensure you get their best work. Thus, if no one knows who did the work, how can you measure quality or employee performance in order to provide extra training, support, or tools to correct problems? If you are doing good work, then why would you worry about signing a form indicating you had done the work? I am not sure what they are so fearful of because, if people are doing what they are supposed to be doing, then there would be no way to trap them. The very fact that the union was set against this, however, told me there was a problem somewhere.

I have found that when people sign their work, they tend to do it better. This has nothing to with unions, it is just people in general. For example, take some clay and ask two people to each make a mug. The mugs will be judged by a person TBD.

One person is told to sign his/her mug while the second person is told not to sign his/her mug. Which person will try harder to make a nicer-looking mug rather than just slapping something together? I am not saying that one mug will actually look better than the other. Only that the person who signs the mug will most likely try harder and will probably have more pride in their work. When I use this analogy, I ask people which mug would be better if they were betting on the outcome? Without fail everyone always tells me they would bet on the signed mug. When you are accountable for your work, you typically try harder.

Think about why hotels, airlines, and restaurants send you emails asking how your experience was, how the service was, and would you come back? Yes, they are interested in your thoughts about the provider you used, but they also want their employees to know they are being watched and graded. If people they come into contact with did not like them or the service they did/did not provide, they will be disciplined.

There is, of course, the flip side of the coin. People take advantage of this all the time and this is, in fact, where having a union can help. I am a platinum member at a particular hotel chain so when I want something, I expect to get it. If an employee of the hotel says "no," what I want costs extra, then I could sit down and write a nasty letter to the manager of the hotel.

Hotels take every complaint seriously, but people with high status get their attention very quickly. Not hard to understand. You might use a hotel once or twice a year where I am there 50-60 times per year, so they really try to make people like me happy. When I send in a complaint, it is dealt with very quickly.

Now, I can say anything on the complaint, true or not true, but I am upset with the person I dealt with and want to strike back. The union will make sure they are not fired over this one complaint and they deserve this protection.

The other thing I learned over the years is that it is legal for unions to lie to their members. Amazingly enough, this is something that happens frequently. What surprised me more than anything is that during arbitration, the arbitrator supported the union lying if the lie was needed to achieve the results. Holy cow!! Of course, the company cannot lie, and if the union finds out or suspects the company has lied, they can take them to court. I have come to believe that if unions had to play by the same rules as the company, there would be no unions in the company at all.

During our contract negotiations one year the very first thing discussed was paying union members who were coming in on their off day for negotiations. Since my company was paying people who were supposed to be working during the contract negotiations, I felt the union should pay people who came in on their time off. After all, they did not come in on their time off to help in the factory. They were there exclusively for the union, so why shouldn't the union pay them? This seemed fair to me, and after a few days arguing the point, the union agreed. Much to my surprise, however, after the negotiation was over the union sent a bill for the expenses of paying the members during negotiations and told us we had to reimburse them. Needless to say, we contested this and refused to pay. The union took us to arbitration and won. Believe it or not, the arbitrator ruled that since their agreement to the payment issue helped move negotiations forward, it was in everyone's best interest that they lie. So, in this case, the arbitrator reasoned that the lie was permissible, and the company had to pay.

"At the first session of the negotiations the union agreed to pay for the members of the negotiation committee, but the union withdrew before the second session and filed this grievance and a charge with the NLRB.... The arbitrator finds the union had the right to withdraw...." American Arbitration Associations Case No. 01-15-0002-7420.

Unions are legally allowed to mislead both companies and workers, which benefits only the union. Who knew?!

https://www.redstate.com/laborunionreport/2013/09/30/unions-lie-shocking-isnt-it/

Another problem with having a union in place is that the union "mentality" seeps through the entire organization. For example, I needed some salaried engineers to work late on a project. They informed me that unless I was willing to pay overtime, they would not work. When I reminded them their-better-than-average salary included a certain amount of overtime, they laughed and informed me that if they were not paid overtime then they would not stay. They felt that since everyone in manufacturing was paid overtime for the smallest amount of overtime they should be as well, salaried or not — job description or not. They were correct that, no matter how little time someone in manufacturing worked in excess of their regular hours, they demanded overtime. We want our operators to be on the lines the full 12 hours so the union decided it would take six minutes for an employee to walk to the time clock. These six minutes must be paid as overtime.

You will be fighting a union mentality throughout the entire organization and this will make your work quite a bit harder. Salaried staff might not be paying union dues, but they can certainly act like they belong to a union. They see that union employees don't have to strive for results and, therefore, see no reason why they should either.

Past practice

Past practice is one of the union's favorite phrases. It means that if an employee has never done a job or task, then he or she cannot be forced to do it now unless this change has been previously negotiated with the union. It also means if an employee was allowed to do something in the past you cannot stop them from doing it in the future.

So, if a task or operation's procedure needs to be eliminated due to business changes, it too must be negotiated. In short, it means that anything you want to do that constitutes a change to current procedures the union can declare "past practice" to prevent the change.

At a company I once ran it was necessary to eliminate a position because it was no longer needed. While this meant change, it also highlighted that the union was focused on revenue, and not the employee. As a result, we had to keep a person on the payroll until the next contract negotiations which was almost two years away. Then we had to negotiate how to remove the position, what we would do with the person who was in that position, and how these changes would not reduce the headcount.

Remember, the bottom line is the union needs dues to be paid which means they need people on the payroll to make those payments. This is no different than a burger joint where a specific number of hamburgers need to be sold every day to keep the doors open. Therefore, the union wanted to make sure the employee was kept on, even if not really trained to do anything else.

In our contract, it clearly stated that employees had a specific amount of sick time per year. Not personal time or "go to the football game" time, but sick time. The minute I contested the fact that people were using sick time as they pleased, the union used past practice on me. What people used sick time for had never been contested before, therefore I could not contest it now, even though it was very clear in the contract how sick time was to be used. I understand many companies lump sick/vacation/personal time into one. How the employee uses the time is up to them and no one else's business. However, when the total days are done, they are done. The difference here is that in the contract, the union had sick time spelled out specifically and personal time as well.

If you have any doubts, let me assure you that anything you want to do that will increase money flowing into the union will be accepted by the union rep with very little argument. I wanted to implement a policy of light duty for people who had been injured, but could still accomplish something at work. According to the contract, there was no such thing as light duty based on past practice, so this normally would have had to be negotiated. My HR Director had barely gotten the words out of her mouth before the union rep stated it would be great and how soon could we start. You see, if a person is missing time because of an injury, they do not have to pay union dues, but once you have them on light duty, the payments to the union begin again.

So, the union was willing to make an exception to the contract within minutes of hearing what we wanted. In fact, they made a special trip to the company just to sign the paperwork. They had no idea what the light duty was or what the employee would be doing. Didn't matter as long it got money flowing back into the union coffers. By default it was a great idea....

Negotiations:

Chances are you will be negotiating a contract at some point in your life at some company. No matter how good you think you are with union negotiations you should always hire an attorney for this. There are firms that specialize in unions and they will understand the ins and outs of union negotiations better than you ever will. Be honest with yourself and recognize that you will need changes to the contract to help you turn the company around. You cannot afford to stumble your way through this, so you need someone who specializes in doing hard, and often acrimonious, contract negotiations.

You should also not even be in the room during negotiations so your people at the table have a reason to call a caucus in order to discuss something with you. It gives them time to think and to plan. If you are in the room, the union will expect an immediate decision since you are there.

At one company I ran, the union contract had not changed in over 30 years. You could review a contract from 25 years ago, open it to almost any page, and the wording was exactly the same as the contract currently in place. The only real changes over the years were in tangible items such as wage increases and time off, which the union always got more of. The health insurance the union had at was also a special plan maintained by the provider specifically for us because that is the plan put in place 30 years prior. The plan costs were also higher for the union members than for all employees at my previous company.

Because the company was locked into this plan for the union, it meant that the rest of the company was also locked into the plan.

These plans were extremely expensive and one of the goals I set was to change this. To accomplish this type of change you need a couple of things. A professional union negotiator, preparing in case there is a strike, and the balls to go all the way, no matter what. This is an example of why you need a good negotiator. At the end of negotiations, our attorney achieved a reduction in not only the wage increase, but also $500k of other benefit items, including health care.

The first step of pre-strike planning was to move our entire inventory off site since union truck drivers will not cross a strike line. They feel this action shows support for their union brothers and sisters. These are the exact words used by the union to me. Seriously this is support, for your brother and sisters? Sounds like gang mentality to me.

Step two was to hire an outside security group to come in. During past negotiation there were always mysterious issues that occurred such as equipment breakage or malfunctions, a reduction in quality, etc. Funny enough all these issues disappeared shortly after the union had its vote. Of course, for the company these mysterious problems were expensive. We found that, with security people in place, these problems did not happen.

Step three was to contact a temporary staffing company that specialized in staffing for companies on strike. Note: to get the temporary staff to the front door be prepared to have a pick-up point as many of the workers will not drive onto company grounds in fear of "accidents" to their cars in the parking lot. Even though these temporary workers are not trained in your detailed operations, there are many things they can do with minimal training: cleaning, emptying trash, getting supplies, moving product in and out of inventory, or doing paperwork. In any company there is always a certain amount of unskilled work that needs to be done. It is just as important as anything else and requires very little training.

Next, you train your salaried staff to take over all the production. You will have to cancel all vacation time since you will need these staff members to take the place of many production workers. You have spent months getting your inventory beefed up knowing that production in the plant will slow down with the work force you have. Slowed down, but not stopped, is the key point.

If the strike happens, union people will then see temporary drivers taking product to the off-site warehouse, so they know production is continuing even when they are on strike. You want the people on strike to know the company is doing just fine without them. Remember, they are on strike to hurt/cripple you, believing that the sooner they can do this the sooner you will cave and give them anything they want. On the other hand, if they see you can get along just fine without them, then they are more willing to come back to the table and negotiate.

Last, but not least, we also set up barriers with temporary security so the union employees could not cross onto company property if they went on strike. Key point: this cannot be done until the minute they actually go on strike or they can say you are trying to intimidate them, which is against the law. The law is very clear that you cannot intimidate union people in any way, so you must be very careful what you do in the open and what you do in the background. Some of this is done in the open, like the outside warehouse, but most is done quietly without the union knowing. It is not that you are trying to surprise the union. However, if you do steps two in the open, the union can claim you are trying to affect negotiations by intimidating the union members. If they can prove this, then they can file with the Labor Board, resulting in even bigger issues.

One of the favorites tricks unions like to do during negotiations is to call OSHA and file a violation. Normally OSHA will not come out until after negotiations are over because they want to stay out of that battle, but once called you know you will have an issue.

You should plan ahead and have your attorney employ an inspection company to determine ahead of time if there were any OSHA violations. Because they are employed by the attorney, the resulting report falls under client/attorney confidentiality so the union cannot demand you turn the report over to them. If the company had hired this outside firm, then the union has the right to demand a copy for review. A report is something they can use against you during negotiations. I have said this several times; negotiations have nothing to do with the employees. It is a war between the union and the company with the employees getting the spoils of the war, if any.

Once negotiations began, the security force started patrolling both the outside and inside of the building. After reading email and notes from past several negotiations I discovered that equipment downtime tripled, equipment failures went up, and accidents skyrocketed during negotiations. Having this proof, I was able to put security into place "for everyone's" protection, including the equipment." Even though the union took this to the labor board, it could not be stopped because I had proof from the past.

Those of you without unions you might think this is over the top, but one thing I have learned over the years is that unions do not care about the company, the equipment, the customers, or anything else related to the very business paying their members, who then pay the union. They are only interested in how much pain they can inflict so that you will come to the bargaining table and give them what they want. They know that the more money the company loses, the faster you will give into their demands.

You have an enemy, so name it. No one knows this better than the union, which is why they make the company, and specifically you, the president, the enemy.

I smile as I write this because once I came to grips with the fact that having a union has nothing to do with the employees, I focused solely on what was best for the company. The union took all the stress of making sure my employees were taken care of off my back and, in some odd way, freed me up. If the union did not get it, whatever "it" was, in the contract, then I simply did not worry about it.

I can say that non-union companies I have run had better benefit packages than a company with a union. At non-unions companies, I felt personally responsible for the future of the employees, needing to make sure they were taken care of. I understood those employees were depending on me for their future and I took this very seriously. If the union is unable to get things done, then too bad. I still look after my non-union employees, providing good benefits and a good future. However, I don't give the union workers a second thought because, hey, they have their union.

When working on a contract, the real key is to decide what you want to take away from the union and what it will require to accomplish this. Let's face it. Your company is in trouble and union people have more costs associated with them than non-union people. Generally, union people will most likely pay less for health insurance than non-union employees, yet union benefit packages will be more expensive.

Cash is tight so, by default, you will be taking things away so the company can survive. This all may not be true in healthy companies with a good bottom line and plenty of cash, but those are not the companies where I have worked.

Communications during negotiation

Communication is never more important than during negotiations though. During the first negotiations, we wanted to change healthcare because our insurance provider has this policy only for us. This made it expensive, not only for the company, but also for the employees. The union put out a flier stating that the company was trying to eliminate all health insurance and the members needed to stick together to ensure this did not happen. I will never forget what the union put out to the members:

"'They want flexibility in managing your health insurance coverage.' Translation: They want to adjust your benefit level at will and without bargaining with the union! They want to have the ability to reduce your coverage so they will not have to pay the so called "Cadillac" tax coming in 2018. You pay way more—you get way less. They want to do this to all the employees."

Of course, none of this was true, but it had the desired effect: the employees were scared. What we wanted to do was to find a plan that offered what they had at a cheaper price. Again, if union members realized the company was helping or looking out for their interests, then it is hard to make "the company" the enemy. While at no time did the union rep discuss the plan with HR, the union had no problem falsifying the intent of the change, thinking that union members would never know what was true or not. Consequently, on the first day of negotiations the following procedural changes were implemented:

1. My negotiating team were to publish the minutes no later than 30 minutes after the negotiations ended for the day.

2. The minutes were to be posted on the company board, with individual copies put in the cafeteria for people to take.

3. After every third meeting HR held a one-on-one meeting with every union member in order to explain what had been discussed and to answer any questions. There were no negotiations with employees which is against the law, only the answering of questions.

4. For topics such as health insurance that affected families, the spouses were invited to either come in or call HR so they could have the policy explained to them in detail.

5. If the union published something untrue when we had one-on-one discussions with the employees, then we would immediately correct the unions' mistake. Absolutely nothing the union put out that was baseless propaganda was discussed; only the proven facts were discussed.

As you can imagine, the union went ballistic over this. They said we could not do this because negotiations were to be private, which these changes made more difficult. Regardless, we continued the procedural changes through the remainder of the contract negotiations, and in the end, the final contract was radically changed and approved. It was approved because having this type of communication prevented the union from misleading the members.

There was also something else positive that came out of this. Our employees began to see us differently. We were no longer evil, but just trying to do our job. The younger employees began to feel they had some say because they were included in the same discussions as the more senior members.

Every meeting had a shop steward in attendance, as is required, but when you are explaining something, not negotiating with employees, which is against the law, what is the shop steward going to say? How can the union say you're not telling the truth when you have proof to the contrary? In the end, the shop steward had to agree with us because we brought proof to the table. This is exactly why the union was in a tizzy over our end-around. They could no longer post fliers of erroneous information because now people knew exactly what everyone was talking about.

Think ahead

Not everything can happen at the first contract negotiations, but the first one is where you set things up for the next one. You need to be thinking at least one, if not two, contracts ahead so that, during your first negotiation, you can put things in place that can be used for the next one.

As an example, all of union members received a week's pay as a Christmas bonus. I have no issue giving bonuses when the company is doing well, but I have a real issue giving a bonus when the company can barely pay the bills and all you did was show up, *sometimes*. Keep in mind that the union employees felt they deserved everything just for showing up.

As a work-around at the first contract negotiation, I introduced a work performance plan that would give the union members three times the amount of money as their normal Christmas bonus. And yes, I can hear you saying, "Say, what?!" I also knew three things about this plan: It was achievable, they could not resist it, and they were too lazy to achieve it. There was nothing dishonest about the plan as presented, and there was adequate notice about the what and why, so the union agreed to the plan. What I wanted was no different than what I had been asking for since I had gotten there. Show up to work and make a good product. Now I was willing to offer the union substantial money as a bonus to achieve just that!

For the first six months or so things went very well, and they achieved the results required on the plan to payout a wonderful bonus.

I had no doubt they would do great for the first three to nine months because they saw all that money they could get at the end of the year. Right on schedule, the union employees got lazy and started calling out. Quality and output also went down.

Of course, during this time data had been collected on all measurable criteria, which was used when the union tried to grieve failure to comply at the next contract negotiation. They had met every metric agreed upon for six solid months. Given that, no one could say the goal was too ambitious, that I had tricked the union, or that they had been cheated. They grieved this the very first Christmas when they were told they would get nothing because goals were not met.

Win! I now had something they wanted to get rid of at almost any cost. For the next 3 years there were virtually no bonuses paid to union members. You might say I lost because they went back to their old ways where yields/quality was down and every other issue I had was not resolved. However, since I felt strongly that the company should not pay for something it was not getting, the company was saving money because we did not have to pay a Christmas bonus. Even with a worst-case scenario, they produced the same quality as they had before, but remember it took setting this up at one contract negotiation in order to achieve your goal at the next one — playing the long game.

During this time, though, other changes in the contract were made to tighten up what they could and could not do. During negotiations we had reduced the number of sick days, callouts allowed, write-ups before termination, and a variety of other measures. All designed to make it harder for the employees to just not show up to work every weekend.

Key points to keep in mind. One: you must work on contract negotiations from the day you arrive at the company. Two: if you want to make a change to the contract, such as the number of personal days allowed because quality suffers, then you must have data showing the relationship between people coming to work and yields from production. You cannot just go to the contract negotiation saying you want something with no data to prove you are right. If you do, they will eat you for lunch.

At our next union negotiation, the union wanted to remove the performance payout and go back to a Christmas bonus. I agreed they could have it back at a flat rate rather than a week's pay. Everyone in the union would get the same amount. Sounds fair to me, you say. Not at all because unions are all about seniority. Not based on who is a good or better employee and should receive more income, but who has been there longer, and the payout would 50% less than the one they previously had.

A company paying employees a bonus based on seniority vs. a set rate may seem like a very minor variation but, the truth is, it sends a very clear message. Just because you have worked here 20 years does not mean you are any better than the person we hired one year ago. From the new employee's point of view, they now know that they are just as important to management as the 20-year employees. With new employees knowing they are just as important as more senior staff, you have now begun to swing their loyalty from union to management. They are beginning to understand the company cares for them more than the union does. If you ever want to decertify a union, this is critical.

I had been charting seniority vs. yield improvement for several years and was able to show that as the company seniority was reduced, yield went up. So how could the union penalize the best performers just because they were not the most senior? Seniority now went away. Older employees were mad while younger employees came to my office and thanked me.

An article I once read about union workers had an interview with a union member complaining that the company he worked for was always looking for ways to fire him. Well, he was wrong. The company was not looking for a way to fire him because there would be no benefit in that. The company just wanted their money's worth. Union people cost more, and by default, if a company is paying more, they feel they should get more.

If the company feels they are not getting better output, higher quality, better work ethics than from a non-union person, they feel cheated. Why would a company feel any less cheated than you would personally expect when you pay more for something? If you pay more for a luxury car, you would expect more from that car than if you bought a used car. It should have a smoother ride, better gas mileage, high-end bells and whistles to justify the extra cost. Paying more for labor is exactly the same. If I pay above market value for an engineer, then I expect an exceptional engineer, not an average one, and if I pay more for manufacturing labor, then I expect more.

Union people cost more, so they should provide more. Understand, the extra salary and benefits you pay for union people are just the beginning. You will also need extra HR people to handle all the complaining the union does. Your legal fees will increase because every time you say "no" to something, they will want to go to arbitration. You will spend a great deal of money for negotiations, if you want them done well, and you will need more people working in the factory because you cannot cross-train union people. You might also have to hire more people than you really need to compensate for high call-out rates from union employees.

Speaking with presidents of other companies, it seems quite common that when there are unions in a stressed company, more grievances occur than in a healthy company. I believe they do this deliberately because they know a stressed company cannot afford the legal fees associated with arbitration and will be willing to give in more often.

Communication is very important in every company and, typically, there is never enough of it. At non-union companies I have had no issue sharing finances, profitability, and virtually anything else about the company. Most people in the organization truly want to know if the company is doing well and what future plans might be. The more information you share, the more the employees will come to trust you.

With a union in the company, you must be more careful because every word you say can, and will, be used against you at some point. For example, to share profitability and the fact you have begun to turn things around means you have given them something to use against you at the next contract negotiations. No matter that there is still a long way to go since you have said the company is doing better, they will then demand higher pay, a reduced share of healthcare premiums, or more time off, or any number of other things. The company might still be struggling, or cash might still be tight but none of that matters. The company is better off than it was a year ago so they want more.

The work is worth it

The following negotiations took 16 hours which was four days and four hours per day. People often do not believe this, but I can assure you it is true. There are three reasons why this was accomplished:

1) I had something they wanted to get rid of desperately and that we pay for performance. If they had done the work, they would have been paid very well and I would have been happy to make the payment. My company had seen improved yields, improved plant performance, and improved profits.

   The employees would have been given three times their normal Christmas gift for honestly doing nothing more than their job. They had proven the goals were achievable because for six months they accomplished them.

2) I had built a reputation of being honest. Everyone in the company knew I would not lie to them, good or bad, and I always carried through with anything I said I would do.

3) The union employees came to realize the company was not out to get them, and in fact they came to realize we were often more honest with them then their own union rep.

Grievances

Here is why you will need extra people in HR because union people will grieve the strangest things. At one of my companies that ran 24/7 and we never shut down — not even for the holidays — I wanted to do something nice. Something I had done at other companies on the holidays.

The first year I started I wanted to do something nice for the people working on Thanksgiving, so I had Thanksgiving dinner brought in.

One meal for the day shift and one at midnight for the overnight shift so both crews working on Thanksgiving could enjoy a meal. This meal was fully catered with real plates and silverware, a turkey, potatoes, dressing and everything else you might have at your holiday table. There were people who served the employees and I let them bring their families in so they could have a real family meal. The meal break was extended to two hours so no one was rushed, and people could take their time

The union grieved this because I did not do the same for all the shifts, which they lost. Logically, I questioned why I should have a meal catered in for people who had the privilege of not working the holiday and had eaten their Thanksgiving meal with family and friends. What I was trying to do was give the people who had to work some time with family as well on this special day.

I assumed it was a one-time grievance, and now that they understood everything would be okay. Not so. We had a meal catered in for Christmas and it was grieved for the same reason. If I was going to do this for one group, I had to do it for every group. I also believe it was grieved to keep tension up between the company and the union. After all, doing something nice is not something "the company" would normally do. Needless to say, since that first year I have never offered another holiday meal to any shift. Simply not worth the aggravation.

Accountability

The one thing unions fight hardest against (what? Accountability?). For example, if you have a union shop, you cannot just start putting cameras on the shop floor so you can see what is happening. The union will fight this with every breath they have. Why is this so? If there are no cameras, then everything boils down to your word against the union member, which is a very difficult fight to win. The union at this point will say you do not like this employee, that you set this employee up or any number of other excuses. With cameras there is no discussion. Simply play back what happened and if the employee did something wrong, incorrectly, or even perfectly it is right there in full color. Period, end of sentence. There is virtually nothing the union can argue. Like I've said, unions cost you more money and this is just one more expense.

I wanted to do this at one of the companies I ran but, while the union was completely against it, the local union rep made two mistakes when arguing the point. We had had quite a few accidents at the plant, and it was impossible to see why. There is not a person alive going to say, "Oh, that was because I did something dumb." People are going to protect themselves by giving a less than accurate account of what happened. This is just human behavior and has nothing to do with the union, people are people.

We also had a rash of mysterious events going on that could not be explained such as valves turned just enough to ruin a run. A few weeks later the water temperature would be adjusted so it was too warm, reducing the quality of the product. These things never happened at the same time or on the same shift, but they all happened at night and they all had the effect of either reducing the daily output or quality.

The two mistakes I mentioned that the union rep made came into play here. First, he said that since we had no cameras, we could prove nothing. Then he mentioned that one of the other companies they represented put in cameras and there was a reduction in the quantity of accidents. He realized his mistake as soon as it came out of his mouth but, too late, the damage had been done! He then said that he was not saying we should install cameras or that we had the union's permission to install cameras.

We contested this and the arbitrator told the union that since the union rep had informed us how to solve the problem, he could not then tell us we could not use his solution. So, the cameras went in and the occurrences of accidents and mysterious operational problems went down. Today we have over 80% of the floor covered with cameras and accidents have declined by 70%, so the correlation is hard to deny.

Why unions will never attract really good people

Are you getting a feel as to why it takes so much longer and a great deal more effort to turn a company around with a union? What unions need to understand is that it is no longer 1920, when companies had no way to push back except fighting picketers with military/police forces or shutting down. Today, companies can decide it is just not worth the headache and move production offshore. It is not just higher wages or benefits that drive companies offshore, it is all the other issues unions create.

At one of the companies I ran we had a union employee who is disliked by even union employees. He is a below average employee, complains about everything, and probably would never hold a job without a union. When I discussed him with the local union rep, he asked:

- Does he show up to work every day?
  Yes.

- Does he do the job he is assigned?
  Much of it needs to be checked because often it is wrong.

- So, he does the work he is assigned.
  Already answered.

Then you cannot touch him because nowhere in the contract does it say he has to be nice, say hello to people, or even do a good job. He shows up, does what he is told, and does the best he can, regardless if you think it is good or not.

You have to ask yourself why anyone who is good, hardworking, has any drive to move up, or make more money would join a union, especially if it is not a condition of employment. The very best get the same pay as people who should not even be working for you at all. When people see others standing around and barely working, they feel they are being cheated because this poor performer is making just as much as someone who works hard. Before long, everyone is working at the same pace and quality as the worst employee.

You have heard me talk about the union mentality several times now, and for those of you that have unions, you know what I am

202 RoD MOORE · THE LONG GAME

talking about. For those of you who have never had the privilege of having a union, let me try and explain what this is. Because unions have contracts, everything you do or want to do is referenced back to the contract. If something is not explicitly spelled out, then people do not feel they can be forced to do it, whatever "it" is. Take, for example, cross-training. This is something many companies typically do to make their workforce more flexible, encourage employee growth, etc.

In a union shop, a person is given a specific job with a very specific job description. They not only do not have to do anything not specifically spelled out in the job description, but they don't have to do anything not spelled out even if it relates to the job they are hired to do. This is why you may see someone working hard digging a ditch while his or her buddy is sitting on the tractor doing nothing.

The person on the tractor has a job description that says he is only responsible for running the tractor. So, even though the guy in the ditch could use some help, he will never get it. This is also why union shops tend to require more manpower than non-union shops. In non-union shops, you can train people to do multiple things so if they have free time at one position, they can help in another. In union shops that person who has free time would just stand around.

Unions do a great job protecting the poor or mediocre performer that would struggle finding work at a non-union shop. A high achiever would never survive in a union shop because they would make everyone else look bad and would be pressured to leave, and they should leave.

Are unions evil? Absolutely not. Unions have a place, but they need to understand that today companies have options. If they cannot work with the union, they will simply move offshore or to another less expensive state, declaring the move was done to save money to allow them to compete. Unfortunately, the one who pays the price for this is the American workforce.

Unions need to work with companies so that both sides benefit, rather than taking advantage of the other. Unions need to stop making the company the enemy. Unions need to understand that a company must make a profit, or it will go elsewhere, while companies need to make sure salaries, benefits, and working conditions are adequate. Both sides need to work together and stop vilifying each other. Unions also need to start caring about their members more than the profits they take in from those members.

For example, where were the unions in mining disasters, either in the US or overseas? I have never yet read a report where a mine collapsed for no reason. In every news article I have ever read, workers had long been complaining about the mine before it collapsed. Everyone likes to blame the owner of the mine, and while they should be held accountable, so should the union that represented the workers. In fact, the union should be even more at fault because ensuring their members have a safe work environment is their job and what they are paid for.

Many of the benefits we all enjoy are directly because of unions. We all enjoy paid holidays, family leave, decent working hours, tuition reimbursement, etc., and most of these have come about because of unions. Unions do have their place in the workplace, but they need to work with people. I have never once received a letter from the union asking for anything; they always demand. Then they wonder why they are often hated.

How to get rid of a union may sound like a good idea. However, think about it before deciding if you really want to get rid of the union you have because, after a year without a union, a new even worse one could potentially come in. With a new union, all negotiations start at ground zero. Instead of getting rid of your union, you should concentrate on making them a union in name only but with little or no involvement in company operations.

If you do decide to work on removal of your union, then you need to figure out if your union is a mob or a gang. Depending on which you have will determine how you need to react. Remember, there is a real difference between gangs and mobs. They both work on fear, but how they get and keep members is completely different. If you decide that your union acts like a gang, then your goal is to replace that feeling of belonging that the union is providing. You need to prove to your employees they do not really need a union, that they can trust management, and that they will not be taken advantage of. They belong to a family and it is this family you are developing in the company itself. If an employee feels safe and taken care of, they will not feel the need to have a union.

This means you need to start to build a rapport with your employees so that they trust you, feel you are one of them, and that you have their best interest at heart. You need to get to know as many of your employees as you can, get to know their birthdays, and, most importantly, all their names. You, as the president of the company, should know every one of your employee's names. It's amazing what a difference it makes when you walk out to the shop floor, can say their name, wish them a nice day, or tell them they are doing a good job.

Think of yourself as their father or mother so that they see you as being the person in charge but, at the same time, you will protect them. You want them to continue to see their co-workers as their brother and sisters, but you are simply replacing the authority figure they feel they need.

You also need to have regular meetings with them, let them know they are going a great job, and provide updates on all the good things you have planned. In short, you need to develop a relationship with your employees and make decertification of the union your full-time job. It will take time, maybe two years, but it can be done. Remember, the union has labeled you as the enemy and what you need to show your employees is that the union lied to them. Let them see you are not the enemy, but someone who is trying to do what is best for them and the company, in that order.

On the other hand, if you decide your union is more like a mob, then this strategy will never work. In fact, you will be viewed as weak and things will get worse. The union in this case will rule the people with an iron fist and will want to be involved in every aspect of what is going on. If you post something, they will take a picture and send it to the local union rep so they can get their marching orders on how to deal with it. Union members will not think on their own, but will instead, take directions from the leader — directions they will act on. Anything you do showing the least bit of decency will be viewed as caving in and they will declare themselves the winners.

Mob mentality is exactly why the Thanksgiving meal was viewed the way it was. There was a show of kindness which the union needed to instantly turn into something bad. They viewed it as though I was not doing something nice for the people working, but rather as cheating the people who were off. The union must show that you always have an alternative motive for everything you are doing. They felt that I brought in Thanksgiving dinner simply to cause a conflict between crews. Nothing management does is ever viewed as good. It is always twisted into something sinister. These views signal a clear sign that your union has modeled itself as a mob.

You only have one choice in this case and that is to show you are meaner, tougher, and smarter than the union. You will have to declare a war. Stop thinking about what is best for the employees and start thinking about what you can do to create conflict that you can win. The union will take you to arbitration and you have to win. You need to read, understand, and know how to work around the contract so that the union never wins a fight.

When you have a union that has ruled the company with an iron fist for 30 years, you must work many angles to get the company back. You have no other choice. If you want to turn a company around and make it healthy for the long game, you must beat the union. Only one person can rule and that needs to be you. It's great if the union wants to work with you. If not, they need to go or at least be beaten.

CHAPTER 10

Sales: A Slightly Different Take

This chapter is not about how to increase your sales numbers or how to turn your average salesperson into the envy of salespeople worldwide. There are more than enough of these books and seminars telling you how to improve sales. Instead, I decided to write a chapter on how to sell yourself, which is the first step in becoming a great salesperson.

The first step is to be confident — not arrogant — confident. The difference is extremely important. Since many people do not fully understand the difference between the two, I copied some definitions from Merriam-Websters Dictionary just so you can see that there is a real difference between arrogance and confidence.

When customers know your company is having problems, they tend to spend a lot of time keeping in touch. It needs to be your number one priority to stay in touch with them. They must believe in you, not the company, but you. If they believe you can turn things around and get things moving in the right direction, they will stick with you. If they feel that you are arrogant, or a narcissistic loudmouth, they will leave. You need them and so I want to spend some time defining and explaining this single topic.

Arrogant is defined by Webster's dictionary as, "exaggerating or disposed to exaggerate one's own worth or importance often by an overbearing manner: arrogant official."

Self-confident is defined by Webster's Dictionary as, "confidence in oneself and in one's powers and abilities."

Narcissist is defined by Webster's Dictionary as, "an extremely self-centered person who has an exaggerated sense of self-importance."

You might ask why I am making such a big deal about this when it would seem obvious that everyone knows the difference between arrogant, self-confidence, and narcissist. The truth is most people don't know the differences between them. They just think they do.

People who are arrogant can also be narcissists, compounding the issue. Consequently, you need to ask yourself why you are doing the job. If it is just to feed your own ego, then, long-term, this is the reason you will never get people to follow you. You have a difficult job ahead of you to turn your company around and you need people to stand with you during it all. If you are pushing forward and the rest of the company is pushing back, then it is clear you will never get things done. This happens more often than people realize and is why most presidents who set out to turn a company around will fail.

At one company, I was the sixth president in 18 years and, with each one, the company slid further downhill. Some of the presidents recognized that the company was in serious trouble but were only interested in what they could get before the company finally failed. Others were so arrogant that the company fought back and pushed them out. Now the question becomes why I succeeded when so many before me failed. Do I bring so much self-confidence to the table that the world falls in line and will follow me anywhere? No, of course not!

Turns out there is something called a productive narcissist. Not being a psychologist, I can only provide the basic difference between someone who is a plain narcissist and someone who is a productive narcissist. According to Michael Maccoby, Ph.D. and author of "The Productive Narcissist," there are two types of narcissism: productive and unproductive. Productive narcissists make good leaders largely because they can see the big picture. It isn't hard for them to envision the road ahead for their company. But how can you tell the difference between these two types of narcissists?

Look who they surround themselves with. An unproductive narcissist needs to feel they are the smartest person in the room, even if they themselves are actually not that bright. They have a high need to have everything be about them and every win must benefit them in some way. If you have an unproductive narcissist on your staff as a supervisor, then I can tell you one thing for sure. In that supervisor's mind the only difference between he/she and god is that god is not your supervisor.

Nonproductive narcissists are interested in only one thing — themselves — which is why they tend to surround themselves with people less capable then they are. It is also why they have a high need to always be in the center of attention, feel they are smarter than anyone else, and take advice from no one. I mean why would they? If you consider everyone dumber than you, why would you seek advice from them?

On the other hand, a productive narcissist surrounds themselves with people who are smarter than they are. They will have a sidekick who will keep them anchored and not let them forget the people around them who are making their ideas reality. I am clearly a productive narcissist, but my ego is tied to the projects I am working on or the companies I am working for. Unlike the unproductive narcissist who sets people up to fail so that they, themselves, look good, I only see success through the projects I take on. Consequently, setting people up to fail or to blame others for my failures does not work for me because I have a high need for success, and realize my success is dependent on the people around me.

I recognized this in myself in the late '90s — that I was my own biggest problem. I needed to find a way to deal with this. There are very few things I have done in my life where I did not produce results, achieve or exceed expectations, and this success easily turns into ego. The trick is how to deal with it, which is where I came up with the anchor.

When turning a company around you need a big ego but, at the same time, you cannot forget that the very people you need are the ones you are driving away. So, I have always found a person who kept my feet anchored and never let me forget that the people who work for me are in fact people, with feelings, with families, and with needs of their own.

Here is the take-away from this. Do not worry if people think you have a big ego and classify you as a narcissist. It means you most likely have a great deal of charisma, can talk people into doing things, and, therefore, win more than you lose. Great, all good traits. However, you need to be honest with yourself, admit who you are, and find your anchor.

Let me take just a minute to explain what this anchor will do to help you be successful. In short, they need to ensure you never forget that the people around you are actually more important than you are. When they see your ego getting out of control, for example, by taking credit for everything, they need to sit you down and tell you that projects are successful because of other people's work. Yes, it might be your idea, but you did not do the work to turn an idea into reality. Others did.

They are going to remind you to say "thank you" when people do a good job and to find ways to reward people when it is appropriate. I realize this seems like quite a bit to ask from someone, and many people feel it shows a weakness in yourself. What I have found is that people are more than willing to take on this role and you will gain great respect from the person who agrees to do this.

Another point to keep in mind is that bullies are not narcissists in the pure definition of the word. They are childish bullies who get their way by threatening, intimidating, and pushing other people around. So, for you win, you will need buy-in from:

1) Employees of the company you are now running
2) The board who will be looking at your every move
3) Customers

You will see further on that I am all about the subtleties and the perception you are making. I have always believed that the battle is half won or lost before you have even opened your mouth when it comes to the following:

Selling to your Company
What are you selling?
Answer: credibility

Let's start with the company because if the people who work for you do not believe you can make a difference, then you will ultimately fail. Remember that fear will be a great asset and one you will lean on quite a bit. You need these people moving, you do not have time for a debate or a vote from a bunch of people who have no idea how to accomplish what you need done anyway.

As hard as it is to believe, you will have two groups in the company when you begin. The first group will hate you, push back, and basically be asking "who does he think he is?" They will be outspoken and try to rally people around them. Don't worry because you will have the second group who will be thinking, "it is about time," and they will support you.

Also remember that fear is short-lived and needs to be replaced with something else. This is where your selling begins because you have only one thing to sell — yourself. When I was in boot camp for eight weeks, fear was the only motivator used and, by the end of that eight weeks, even the drill sergeants were struggling to keep people motivated by fear. Their biggest problem was that, after this time, they had nowhere else to use fear as a motivator scenario. They could have you clean the grease trap at the mess hall, which is the most disgusting thing I have ever done or take on more guard duty in the middle of the night but, honestly, that was about it.

We have all read stories about how some of the most brilliant people in business yelled and screamed at everyone, and all staff was afraid of them. I am sure to some extent these tales are true. However, what you do not often read is that most of these people have a COO or VP directly under them who is the face of the company and the individual that most employees interface with. Even these difficult people realize that you cannot make everyone afraid of you forever. Consequently, they hire someone tough, but less high-strung to help run the company.

What you really need to ask yourself though, is if making people afraid of you is really all you have to offer? If you have no more depth, skill, or ability than fear, that appalls me, and it's surprising that you even made it to the top. Keep in mind this is not a door. You do not wake up one morning, say, "Ok, today we move from fear to belief," and head off to work. You are working on this the entire time. The fear will fade naturally as they begin to believe in you. Now the question is what do they believe and what are you selling?

When I talk to other people about this, they seem to think that all you need to do is explain what you have done with other companies and then your new employees will have confidence in you. The truth is no one really cares what you have done with other companies because they don't work there. Chances are they do not know anyone else who has ever worked at those companies, so how do they know what you are saying is true? Even if it is completely true, I still say most of the new employees will not care.

We had a very upset customer who complained that our product was not working. It was just before the Christmas season and one of their busiest times of the year. Our non-working product slowed their production lines down. Slowing the product lines down mean less daily production equating to a less profitable product.

Since this was a large customer, my sales manager suggested that the COO and I visit with them. He felt it would show the customer that not only was the company concerned, but the problem was being worked on by top management. Upon our arrival the owner cut loose, gave us what for, and then went into great lengths as to what this was costing him, how we had tarnished his reputation in the industry, and basically how much he really hated us at that moment. The language was strong and, to say there was some screaming would be an understatement.

My COO did something you never, ever do. He began to explain how our product was working flawlessly for all our other customers and that this customer seemed to be the only one with a problem. Obviously, that made things go from bad to worse very quickly.

This customer did not care how the product ran at someone else's facility. He cared only that it was not running at his facility. He did not know what type of product our other customers were using or what equipment they had. From his point of view, we might be lying to him just so we did not have to take responsibility for our problem.

You are what people perceive you to be

Your employees are no different. They do not care what you did, how well you did it, or how brilliant you are. What they know, the only thing they know, is that you are here now, they have no idea who you are, what your plans are, or how many will lose their jobs. Yes, they equate seeing you with lost jobs, so you have an uphill battle ahead of you.

One of the biggest mistakes I see presidents make when they have a company meeting for the first time is that they dress to impress. They will wear a suit and tie to the meeting, looking very impressive. This means you are going out to your employees for the first time while wearing a tie. Appropriate, of course for your position, but what do you think is going through their heads? "Here we go, another suit. That is the last thing we need here. He will just sit in his office all day and write emails. Like that is going to fix anything." I would never wear a tie to this meeting or, if I did wear one, it would be pulled down, so it looks like I did something that day besides write emails.

I am going to repeat what I said earlier in the book because I think it is worth mentioning again. It does not make a damn bit of difference who you think you are, what impression you think you made, or how well you think you did. Perception is reality and the only thing that matters is what your audience thinks. How you are perceived is how people will interact with you.

If people think you are brilliant, then every time they get stuck and need some help, they will come to you because you are the smartest person in the company. If people think you are a moron, even if you think you are brilliant, then they will avoid you and rarely take your advice. Who wants to take advice from a moron, even if you are the president?

I cannot count the number of times people have said it does not matter what the world thinks of you so long as you know yourself.

I hear this all the time on talk shows and at seminars and, let me tell you, they have all lied to you. It does not matter who you think you are because the world will interact with you in the manner which agrees with who *they* think you are.

Your job is to get things done and to accomplish this you can either come to work every day yelling at everyone, thinking people are following you even when they are not. They are doing what you tell them to do, no more, just enough, because they have no choice. Or you can come to work and find ways to inspire people, get them so they truly believe in you, and want to follow you. This group of people will, in fact, go out of their way to help you find solutions, make changes, and ultimately help you be successful. I have met people who are naturals at this, but for the rest of us, we need to work at it every day to ensure this is the image the people around us see.

For those of you that think this is crazy, just look at your congress-man. No one on the planet understands people better than politi-cians, or at least lifetime politicians. When they hold their town hall meetings, are they always wearing suits? No, they try to look like the average person they theoretically represent. A congressman from Texas having a rally or town hall meeting in rural Texas will wear blue jeans, maybe a western shirt, boots, and quite possibly a western-style belt buckle. He looks the part. On the other hand, you would rarely see a congressman from suburban Ohio dress like this. He will dress like someone who works in a clothing store or owns a small shop on the corner. He will not look like he works on Wall Street or as a banker, unless he/she represents an urban district. These people are always portrayed by Washington as the evil people and the people who have caused all the problems so they might wear Dockers with a button-down shirt. Look at any president who goes to a disaster site and notice what they wear. No tie, no suit, or in some cases no jacket, but they have their sleeves rolled up. What are they trying to say? For one thing, they are saying they are one of us.

They do this because they know that when they are on the news and people see they have their shirts rolled up, no jacket and no tie, we the people buy into it and think how glad we are that he/she is there helping those poor souls out. The truth is they are simply portraying what they know will inspire the feeling in you that will help them get reelected.

Different audience, different presentation. You need to be what the moment dictates you need to be. You do not want to wear a suit and tie at this first meeting, nor do you want to wear blue jeans. So, what is the look we are trying to achieve? I am in charge, but not afraid to get my hands dirty.

As I am sure you have noticed, I have only mentioned men so far in this chapter and for good reason. Women have known all of this since the beginning of time. Men are not so bright, but women are way ahead of us and have been for years. They look in the mirror every morning and decide what should be looking back at them. In fact, I have known women who will actually say that they are wearing their power suit today or their "get in the trenches" clothes. They understand the power of looking the part, because they have had to compete with men in a man's world.

They get up in the morning, decide who they are going to be at the meetings they need to be involved in and how they want to present themselves in these meetings. Then they will put on clothes that make a statement the minute they walk in the door. So, all you guys out there could learn a lot by watching how women dress and why they wear what they wear on any given day.

It should be noted that, over time, this becomes less and less important in the company because you have earned respect by the work you have done. At a company I used to run, the CFO wore blue jeans for years, but there is no doubt in anyone's mind that they were extremely smart, extremely competent, and respected by everyone. They had developed a reputation over the years and how they dressed was of no importance any longer.

Making the first impression

You have been at the company a couple of weeks and have decided it is time to introduce yourself and let everyone know what you plan. By this time, you have already met your direct reports and, most likely, gone to several meetings and met other staff, but what you have not done is make a company-wide address explaining who you are and what your plans are going to be.

You don't want to do this too quickly because you do not have enough information and knowledge about the company to be credible. Think about this. You are at the new company three days and decide you want a company-wide meeting to get the ball rolling. You get up and tell people you will be focused on solving the problems plaguing the company and plan to turn things around. To do this, you will be focused on plant yields, quality, labor, and sales. I can promise you most of the people sitting in front of you will not believe a single thing you just said.

You have been there three days. How do you know there is a quality issue or any other issue? They know you've essentially just arrived so there is no way you could have any idea what problems the company has, or not. Even if every single word you said was absolutely dead on no one will believe you and you just lost credibility.

Since you now have no credibility, it really does not matter what else you have to say during this company meeting because no one is going to believe you. You can get it back, but it takes time and effort, all because you were in a rush. On the other hand, if you spend a couple of weeks walking around, going to production meetings, speaking to the people in QA, and generally learning about the company, then people will believe you. They will believe you because they have seen you learning about the company you are taking over.

After a few weeks, people will be getting antsy to hear something from you. They have seen you at meetings, you have asked questions, you have listened, but you have not spoken to the entire company as the new president. Until you do, you are not really the president. You have the title, but you do not have the acknowledgment of the employees. You need the meeting because this moves you from having a title to having the position.

At the company where I was the sixth president in 18 years, the employees had a very low regard for the position as a whole. In addition, most of the presidents, from what I had been told, never left their office, never walked the floor, never learned anything about the product they made, or how to make it. I had been told there were a couple of presidents early on who had done their homework and gotten to know people, but that was years ago, and most of those who would remember that were gone.

By the time you have this company-wide meeting, you have been seen on the production floor by everyone. You have also been speaking with people so, even though you have not formally introduced yourself, people do know you. Part of the reason you have waited is not just to give you time to meet people and answer a few questions they might have, but you want them to be interested in what you have planned, where you see the company headed, and if you believe the company can be saved.

Remember, people always go to the worst place when they lack information. They always think and assume the worst. By the time you have your meeting, people will be hungry to hear how bad it is, or if they will lose their job.

Before I ever became a President, I would be one of the people who rolled their eyes at most of what was said during the president's meeting. Either they talked about the glory days ahead or the company was on the brink of collapse, with hard decisions needing to be made.

If you get the "glory days ahead of us" they will talk about all the companies they have turned around, how well they are doing today, and it was all because they could see opportunities that others had missed. They will go on and on about their past, how they had killed the dragon over and over and how everything they touched turned to gold. They will include how they now have full support of the Board and freedom to move this company in the right direction and open new markets for them to grow in.

Many will buy their speech hook, line, and sinker — and the new president is counting on that. This buys them time to make some quick fixes, collect their money, and get out before everything collapses. They are not in this for the Long Game, but for a quick win to make themselves money.

On the other end of the spectrum is the new president who talks about the tough decisions to get things working again. They might use those exact words so that the employees they are speaking with will get the picture. Remember, perception is reality, so put yourself in the place of the people you are speaking to. They are not board members or shareholders, but people in the trenches. They may not really know how bad things are, but they know the company is in trouble. They also know you were hired to clean up the company and make it profitable again. Some think you will fire everyone, some think you will fix the company enough to sell it, and others have no idea, but are hoping for the best. So that you do not lose the very people you need most, the trick becomes to tell them enough to give them hope but not enough to scare them. At this meeting, you will want to discuss what the company will be working on as a whole.

Never present more than three needs

In 1956, Bell Labs reached out to Harvard professor George Miller, who published a classic paper titled "The Magical Number Seven, Plus or Minus Two." Miller argued that we have a hard time retaining more than seven to nine digits in short-term memory. Now you know why a phone number is seven digits.

I believe the number of items we can easily recall is three "pieces" of information for a single topic. When someone leaves a phone number on a voice message, most of the time you can recall the first three digits before playing the voice message over to write down the rest of the number. Even the Declaration of Independence has three items of importance: life, liberty, and the pursuit of happiness. A list of three items: short, powerful, and easy to recall. No one today knew this better than Steve Jobs, who did pretty much everything in groups of three. The original iPhone offered three different memory sizes, 4, 8, and 16 GB flash memory. He understood that the number three seems to be a magical number when dealing with people.

The best way to take advantage of this concept is to pick three items you plan to focus on and give your entire talk about these three things. When I say three, I mean three, not four and not two, but specifically three.

At most companies, the three items tend to be scrap, equipment up-time, and people's commitment to the company. Are these the only things needed to be worked on? Of course not, but when these three things get fixed, they would see progress, which is what you are after. These three issues are clearly complicated and have huge project lists behind them but, today, in that meeting, you are talking about only these three things and why they are important.

The meeting began as any meeting should — I explained my background. Then I moved on to my three items. I begin explaining the attendance problem and show graphs depicting how many people from each crew were not showing up to work. When there are crews where 70% of the people never worked a full week, it means everyone else needs to work harder to make up for it. Then I show how these call outs affected yields in the plant by simply overlaying one chart over the next. It was very easy to see that when people were not at work yields fell. You would think this was obvious.

People often respond that it was discouraging to come to work when the equipment did not work correctly. That they were always fighting old equipment that had not been kept up. I agree and state it was why it was on my list. By the time you have this meeting you should be able to anticipate the concerns people have, or better said, the arguments people will make and ensure at least one of their concerns is on your list.

As you might recall, preventive maintenance (PM) is something that companies in trouble always seem to eliminate in order to save money. I have never taken over a stressed company where this was not true. To save money in a declining financial environment, previous administrations had all but eliminated PM within the company. While a review began on the PM work that had been in place when the company was healthy, I started the old schedule up. It would take months to do a complete review and determine what changes, if any, needed to be made to the PM schedule, but the existing schedule could be put back into place until then. Your people need to see activity, not committees, if you want them to believe what you say about getting the company back in order. If you want their commitment and emotional support, they need to see it from you first. Get things moving and you can modify details over time — but show activity.

I informed them that, since poor yield had been an issue at the company for years, it was harder to easily assess and that a team would be put into place to focus on fixing this single issue. The team would be a mixed group of both engineers and operational workers so that all aspects of manufacturing could be addressed.

Lastly, I showed them that work schedules would be modified if the chronic weekend illness problem continued. Every Friday, Saturday, and Sunday people were calling out sick three times more than for the rest of the week. This was completely unacceptable and a big factor resulting in low yields.

Because the persistent lack of coming to work directly related to product yield and quality I informed manufacturing that I was considering a schedule change, cutting four crews down to three crews which would work 12-hour schedules. Doing so required fewer people to cover the shifts for our 24-hour/ 7-day schedule. In this way, I could better cover for the chronic weekend illness issue. There is always more than one way to skin the proverbial cat....

You have now had your first meeting and addressed scrap by starting a remediation team. This team will be very visible and will be making changes quickly. You know this because, at first, you will be running the team to ensure it is functioning in parallel with the way you are slowly moving the company.

You have addressed equipment uptime by getting the maintenance schedule back up and running. You will be working with your Maintenance and Operations people to update this schedule but, for now, you have something in place and visible to the people on the floor.

You have addressed the issue of people coming to work, or not, explained why this is an issue and what needs to be done to resolve it. You have taken your time with this one, showing one or more schedule options to accommodate the weekend issue with the same number of people. More importantly, you have told the union and its members that the ball is now in their court. You will be happy with any schedule they pick as long as people show up to work.

They now clearly see that, not only do you have a plan, but you also clearly know how to get the company out of the mess it is in. While they might not believe you in a single meeting, you have laid out what needs to be done, why it needs to be done, and made it clear that you are in full control.

Now you wait for the pushback and who will decide to challenge what you have put into place. Here is the most important thing to understand. You will get pushback and you will be challenged. Remember, weak management in the company for years put it into the shape it is in. It does not matter whether or not there is a union. Pushback and challenge are coming, and you need to make sure that your reaction is precisely what you said it would be. When it comes, do not take weeks or months, act immediately. As hard as this is to believe, doing so will increase your credibility, not reduce it. They are learning that you say what you mean and mean what you say. People do not change easily. They will struggle with you, but hold strong. You have begun the long road of teaching people a different way of thinking, which takes time. You need credibility and they need hope, so this is a perfect match between the two.

Selling to your Board

What are you selling?
Answer: no buyers remorse, and a bright future

Buyer's remorse includes the first few meetings where the board is going to decide if they made a mistake in hiring you. Most will make up their mind in the very first meeting, but there may be a few hold-outs that extend to the second meeting.

Remember that I suggested you should speak to at least one board member during your interview process? That comes into play now. In the first few days on the job you should give this person a call and talk to them about what the board thinks is wrong with the plant. You need to do so in a subtle, rather than direct manner, but this is what you are after.

You might say something like "I am sure many on the board have strong feelings about the company and it would help if I better understood their concerns." This needs to be part of a discussion, not an interview. Remember, board members talk to each other, so your call lets the entire board know that you value them and their input. Make sure it does not sound like you want them solving your problems. They may be clueless, but they do want to be heard and respected.

It is no secret that I place very little value in boards, as I find most are liabilities rather than assets. If your board has eight people on it, there might be one or two who bring real value. Your mission is to find these individuals and make friends with them. Funny as it might sound, they often are the quiet board members who say very little.

I need to clarify something at this point. I am quite certain healthy companies have remarkable boards who really contribute to both the health and growth to the company. I am sure these healthy companies relay on the expertise of board members to help guide the company forward, and if not guide the company, at least find possible pitfalls the company needs to watch out for. I honestly do not believe you can be a top 500 company without a strong and competent board.

This competency is not on the board of companies I hire onto. The companies who want me to work for them are companies which are failing and are looking for someone to turn them around. Just as great companies need strong boards, companies who are failing are doing so partially because of a weak board. So do not think I hate or have negative feelings about all boards because I do not, but failing companies are failing because of poor management decisions in the past, including decisions made/not made by their boards.

I once worked at a company where the chairman of the board and his right-hand man monopolized 80% of the entire board meeting. They would spend hours talking about why the cost of insurance had gone up 1% from last year and what the CFO needed to do about it. They might spend four hours talking about whether or not the company should change banks because they did not feel the current bank respected the company enough.

They brought nothing to the table, but had an extreme need to be heard. This ensured that people were spending time on pretty much useless activities. I fully understood they did this because, somewhere in their subconscious, they knew they were incapable of helping resolve issues in the plant. Therefore, they fixated on things they felt they did know something about. I would let them talk and discuss meaningless subjects for hours, knowing full well that to try and move things forward too quickly would be disastrous. However, if they were allowed to talk themselves out, I would receive either a small list or no list at all.

Part of your job is to manage your board. To do this, you must understand them. In the end they are just people, and people want to feel respected, needed, and that they are contributing. Your job is to make them feel all these things without letting them get in your way.

Going back to the board member you are cultivating, you might ask why this board member would tell you anything? You are working there because they voted for you. The odds of you getting this job if this individual had said "no" would have been slim, even if this is a private company using a board. I say this because, if this is a private company with a board, it is because the owner wants something to hide behind.

Listen to what the board member who voted for you has to say. Right now, they will be in your corner because they do not want to be perceived as having made a mistake with their vote to hire you. Use this to your advantage to get a feel for who the other members are, what they think, and their positions on certain topics.

It does not matter if you agree or disagree with a single board member, only that these concerns are addressed in the first board meeting. Also call all the board members three to four days before each board meeting so you can hear what they had to say and do as much as you can to calm them on the phone. Also make sure to include what they said on the phone in your presentation. It may have been only a single slide, but they knew they had been heard and that you are taking them seriously. You will literally see the pleasure on their face as you begin to talk about a subject they had discussed with you.

No matter if what board members have said is useful or completely off base, try to find some way to use it so you can report on both their concern and the solution to that concern. Be smart about how you discuss these concerns at the board meeting. You do NOT start putting names on issues. You do not say "Mary" suggested this and, after I investigated, Mary's concern is a big deal. This is just dumb.

Mary knows this is a concern of hers, so she does not need to hear it out loud. She may also not want others to know it was a concern to her, for whatever reason. Therefore, you should simply say: "In a former company, we experienced an issue with employees cheating when clocking in/out of work. To ensure that is not a problem here, over the past few weeks all the timecards have been audited. The audit validated that this is an issue with very few employees. However, in order to eliminate the problem, I am thinking of putting a camera over the time clock just to make sure there is better control."

You have now addressed Mary's concern, investigated it, determined there was not much of an issue, and you are moving onto the next item. Mary is happy because you did investigate an issue that was on her mind, and you must have found something, or you would not be thinking about installing a camera. I can promise you that offline Mary is going to say this was an issue she was concerned about and that she is quite pleased you are addressing it.

You have also left yourself a way out if you decide not to put in a camera, because you never said you would do it. You said you were thinking about doing it. Therefore, if you decide in the future this is something you do not want to follow through on you have a way out. "Upon doing further audits, we have found that the abuse is extremely small. I also thought about what message we would be sending to the employees if they saw the camera installed. They would want an explanation, and if we did not have an actual list of people who cheated on the time clock, they would feel that we did not trust them. As you know, we are trying to motivate the employees to improve production and this might work against that goal. Therefore, we have decided to leave things the way they are, at least for now."

Let's review why this response is the one to use. Mary feels vindicated because you acknowledged her concern that there might be a problem. However, you said the problem is not overwhelming. The board is happy because you have shown that you study issues and do not waste money on problems with little return. The board also feels you take them seriously because you investigated one of their concerns and came back with a decision. You have shown that you are not afraid to act if the problem warrants it, but, on the other hand, you are willing to take a different approach if the data indicates that would be a better choice.

You have impressed the board and did not have to do anything to achieve it. The most that will be asked from you now is to continue to monitor timeclock use to ensure it does not become an issue. This must be said for no other reason than for Mary to continue to look credible, so accept it and assure the board it will be monitored.

Over time, things like this will become less and less important as people stop challenging you during board meetings and begin to build on ideas and thoughts you present for the future. The goal is for board meetings to be about *your* vision of the future and less about theirs, but if you don't have the confidence of the board, this will never happen. Keep in mind that this type of activity, even though you might think it is a waste of time, gives you time to get something completed so that you can show the board some success, no matter how small.

Within the first three meetings, you need to move away from ensuring there is no buyer's remorse to selling success. Assuming you have a board meeting every three months you basically have six months, or two board meetings, to show the board that something you have done is showing success. It does not have to be huge but it does need to be something you have been reporting on so they have grown accustomed to the numbers and can clearly see that progress has been made.

At this point, you start moving away from buyer's remorse and begin to move towards your agenda because they can now clearly see that you do know what you are talking about. Just as important? They will also feel that you are having this early success because you listened to what they had to say, which is guiding you to succeed. In short, they are going to take credit for your early successes. Suck it up and know that you are succeeding because you have been successful at managing your board. This success now gives you the opportunity to make bigger and bolder moves in the company.

In time, you will only talk about your approach. As you move on, you will get more and more credit. Since this might take a year, you need thick skin if you really want to play THE LONG GAME. By the third board meeting, you should be talking about small ideas or changes you would like to incorporate into the company. If you have a big idea, keep it to yourself because at this stage, the board is not ready for it. By this meeting you should spend less time talking about what they want or think and spend more time on what *you* are thinking.

You need this foundation because, in the next chapter where we talk about strategic thinking, you might need them to take a leap of faith on very little but your word. Take the time to build a relationship you can use at a future date. You will never regret it.

I was working at a company where one divisional president was always pushing back on the board. Interestingly enough, though, he was right more than he was wrong. This made him untouchable for the most part, because no matter how much you might dislike someone, you simply do not cut the head off the goose laying the golden egg. The board tolerated him for quite some time but there finally came a day where he was wrong. Wrong by a small amount, but he cost the company several million dollars. If he had built any type of foundation with the board, he most likely could have survived this. In fact, you might even have argued that the board should have looked at how much he had made the company over his career versus this one mistake.

This, of course, is not what happened. Instead, he was portrayed as having lost his magic touch and that this was the beginning of a long, expensive decline for his group. He was out in a single meeting, with no second chance, after not even much discussion.

He personally needed every applause, every pat on the back, and all the credit for everything that was done. While he did deserve most of the credit, people are people, and everyone wants to share in the glory. However, because he had always left so many in the dark during the good days, they dumped him the first time they had a chance.

If you are really playing the Long Game, then you need to be honest with yourself and understand that, at some point, you will make a mistake and will need the people sitting at the table. You may need them to look the other way and forgive you. And perhaps they will if you have not isolated them, beaten them down, or ignored them in the past. Building rapport and working relationships is never a bad thing....

A bright future

By this time, you should have figured out the direction you believe the company should move in. You should have also figured out which members of the board can help you move the company forward. As I said, these people are often quieter board members rather than those with the biggest mouths. Not always, but often.

If your plans only include taking care of the people side of the plant, then this part is easy. All you need to do is report on the changes you have made, what you plan to change and why. Show the board how things are improving and how customer complaints are being reduced.

As you will see in the next chapter, there are many things you can do and many things you should look at, but the board will want to know and understand what you are doing in the company and why. Remember, pick out three items to show the board and, over the next six to nine months, discuss how your moves are strengthening the company. By doing this, you are building a foundation that will allow you to make bigger and bolder moves. At some point, you will need the board to trust you and this will only happen if they believe that you have good judgment and make solid decisions. The board now sees a future.

Selling to your Customers
What are you selling? Answer: You
What are you buying? Answer: Time

You can be assured that most of your customers heard promises from your predecessors that were not kept. If they had been kept, you would not be here; your predecessor would be. They have heard how the company would be turned around and how things would get better. They now view you with a great deal of well-founded skepticism. Before you get defensive, just think how you would feel if you had been lied to many times over the years. Before you say that is not fair since you never lied to them and you should be given a chance, understand that your company has lied to them so, by default, as the face of the company, you have lied to them. You need to show you are different right from the very start of a conversation with each customer, maintaining this advantage throughout the entire meeting. The real question is, how do you do this?

Start the meeting with a list of the three most pressing items this customer is concerned about. I realize they may have more than three issues, but you want to go in with three — and those three in detail. In other words, if Quality is one of the three issues, you might have a dozen documents showing where they have had quality complaints. Even though you will not be giving any of this to them at the meeting, you will take it a stack of papers out of your briefcase and put them on the table. They will see you gave this meeting some thought and have come prepared. How? Because you just put some hand-written notes on the table.

After a discussion with your salespeople, you know that the three biggest issues this customer has are quality, on-time delivery, and consistency. Broken down, these issues include some or all of the following, which originate in your manufacturing environment:

1) Quality
   a. Size control
      i. Reduce the standard deviation

    ii. Not following specifications in QA department

    iii. Confirm all test equipment has been calibrated

  b. Product meeting customer expectations

    i. Develop testing more closely aligned to the customer's equipment

    ii. Improve raw material control

    iii. Ensure customer requirements are understood.

2) On-Time delivery

  a. Equipment issues are causing low output. Identify which ones and why.

  b. Scrap is high which limits the amount of good, shippable, material

  c. Extreme absenteeism creates manufacturing bottlenecks

3) Consistency

  a. No standard operating procedures means each shift is running equipment differently

    i. Equipment is run differently, not only from shift to shift but also between operators on the same shift

    ii. No SOP's = no ability to train

    iii. No SOP's = no ability to properly test materials

While you do not necessarily need three sub-items under a main topic, you should never have more than three. If you have a single subtopic, then find a total of three to keep things consistent. The list for On-Time Delivery has three subtopics, but no topics below them. In Consistency, there is only one subtopic, but it has three items further breaking it down. In other words, always work in groups of three.

Keep in mind this is not a list you are ever going to give to anyone, much less a customer. This is a list you, personally, will use to develop the narrative during the meeting. This is just like where you instruct your salesperson, who has 100 ideas, to keep it to a maximum of three. You need to have enough detail that you can formulate a succinct story with the customer. Most of your customers will have lists of their own which may be very close to yours, so maintain consistency.

Always be honest and truthful to your customers. This will always come back to bite you, so you want to be truthful at all costs. Saying something like "the company is a wreck, but don't worry, I will fix it," makes you look stupid. Unlike at your first employee meeting you will be talking to your customers about your past as this is all you have at this point. You have nothing else to sell them but your past and your accomplishments.

I like to use what I call the "Tennis Shoe" approach to selling. If you watch any tennis shoe commercial, they never talk about how well they fit, how fast they will make you run, or how much better you will perform wearing them. What they do is show you someone wearing them and doing something amazing. If they are showing a design that looks great, then they might show someone dressed up wearing these shoes. It gives you the dressy look while maintaining a casual and comfortable feel. You can then wear different color shoes that draws people's eyes to your shoes. You look fashion-forward, but still comfortable. Maybe they are selling a sport shoe, so they show a basketball player making an incredible shot while wearing this company's shoe. The point is they never mention the shoes, they just show you a look or an act that you wish were you. Your brain will put the rest together. If I have these shoes, I can do or look just like the person I saw on TV. They know people are not totally dumb, so when you see this commercial you know you are not going to be as good looking or as good a shot as what you just saw, but you're certain you will be better than you are right now. That is worth money to them.

This is what you will be doing with your list and the customer problems. Your goal is to take this list and get the customer to think it is very short. You will do this without talking about either your current company or his company but, instead, will help him associate your past with how you will fix his issues. This is the big difference between your employee talk and the customer you are sitting in front of.

Your employees do not care about anything but themselves and the job they are doing. They do not care about your past or the amazing things you feel you have done because none of it affects them. The customer does not care about your company or your employees. They only care about their issues and the problems you are creating for them. They only want to know when you are going to resolve their problems, not how you are going to do so. Because you are new, you only have your past to make your points with.

Now it is time to take the list of three main complaints, the breakdown you did and build a true story around everything. Basic introductions have been done and business cards passed. Try to identify the Alpha person in the room, which might not be the company president. He may be sitting there observing, but having his VP or COO take the dominate role. If so, great, because you will know the effectiveness of your discussion if the president does not ever take the primary role. He might ask a few questions, but never takes the lead until the very end. If the president takes over the alpha role early on, however, then you are not doing so well. Conversely, if the president takes the lead right from the beginning you will just have to judge how you are doing by the questions posed and whether or not the president's attitude softens during the discussion.

Without talking about your current company's specific issues, talk about a problem from your past, how you solved it, and also confirmed that quality issues often cause late delivery times. It is your goal to talk about your past, show how things were remedied, and, at the same time, get your list down from 15 to three or four items.

If you are successful, your customer will understand you do not have a huge list of issues but, instead, a small list which is driving every other problem they are seeing. At the same time, they can see how you have solved issues like this in the past will feel confident you can solve these. You have also shown them that you are logical, understand technology beyond the obvious, and can get things done.

There are two points here. First, is you do this at the largest or most frustrated customer first and, second, you do not practice, or even discuss, what you will say to the customer with the salesperson you are taking along. The reason is simple, and it is because your customer is going to be watching your salesperson. If he has a "here it comes again" look on his face, then your customer may not believe most of what you just said. On the other hand, if your salesperson has the "new car smell" look on his or her face your customer will see this and believe.

I call it the new car smell because I have never met a person who, after buying a new car, signing the paper work, and driving off the lot for the first time, doesn't take a minute to breathe in the distinct smell of the new car they just bought. There is no missing the look on their face.

You want this from your salesperson and, just like a new car, you only get this once. After you tell the story, you hope the salesperson says something spontaneous like "That is pretty impressive," or "You did that?" or anything similar. Once your salesperson has heard this story, or any variation of it, you will never get this reaction again. This is a one-time thing.

You recall I said that, with any luck, the president of the company was in the meeting because if he or she was, this is where they will speak up. The president will ask a couple of questions or make a couple of comments, but will end asking you how much time you need. You need to ask for something realistic, and in months, not years, because if you ask for a year then things have been made worse. However, if you also just ask for a month, they will not believe you because it will seem unrealistic that long-term problems could be fixed that quickly. If you have done your job well and your customer believes not only that you can turn the company around but also give him the quality wanted, then they will give you the time.

In every case, you are selling yourself and the plan you have for correcting the issues which have plagued your new company. For the people in the company, you are giving them hope for a future, that the company can be saved, and that their jobs are not at risk. For the board, you are validating that they made a good decision in hiring you and that you can achieve what they want. For your customers, you are selling the belief that they have been heard and you will resolve the quality issues they have been complaining about.

CHAPTER 11

Strategic Thinking

At my past jobs, there was one overwhelming factor that caused all of them to be in the dismal shape they were: ineptitude. Companies do not just fall apart for no reason. They fall apart because operational management fails to understand the changing needs of its customers while top management fails to acknowledge issues within the organization. This is the reason why, when you step through the door, you have an extremely difficult task ahead of you. It's also why you must be thinking years ahead of where you and the company now are.

Many years ago, I was working at a company that decided the market was changing faster than the company was. Senior management decided the company had lost its ability to think strategically, just gotten lazy, and was existing based on past abilities. One of the VPs was told to start and run a strategic planning team. He handed out a document written by Michael Stanleigh, which I have kept all these years because Stanleigh understands strategic thinking extremely well. It's a document I have referred to many times over the years. For those of you who do not know who Michael Stanleigh a quick introduction is in order. He has written many documents and books on how companies can fine their strategic direction, manage change, and become more innovative.

If you are working at a well-functioning company, I would just suggest you buy his books and begin implementing what he suggests. The difference between those books and this one is that they focus on evolving a well-functioning company, while this one deals with the opposite: fixing a company that is in trouble.

In a well-run company, you are looking for a strategy that helps transcend borders, extends sales from national to international, and gets you ahead of the competition. In the company you have signed onto, however, your initial strategy must get you out of financial problems, run day-to-day operations with little to no money, and motivate a work force that has no idea how they will get through the next six months. In short, you are not in what you once considered your dream job. You are now tasked with turning a company around.

What is strategic thinking?

Even though everyone pretty much has their own definition of what strategic thinking is, most people will agree that strategic thinking is the "What" and the "Why." This is extremely important to you because you have taken on a new company that is on a downward spiral. If you are going to move it in a different direction, you need a clear vision that allows you to be able to answer "Why" and then "What."

I believe real strategic thinking is when a person has a clear understanding, from beginning to end, of the interdependence of all the different aspects of an idea. A strategic thinker may not have the minute details of these aspects, but they do have a clear understanding of where they are going, why they need to go there, and what is required to achieve the desired end results.

Strategic thinkers are always looking for new opportunities, ways in which those opportunities could help the organization they are running, and how they could be implemented. They are capable of planning years in advance, adjusting plans as time goes by / events dictate to ensure they arrive at the desired results.

Can you teach someone to think strategically? There are many people who make a great deal of money selling seminars that say you can. Like so many things in life, you can probably teach someone to be a modestly successful strategic thinker, but they will never be as good at it as are people who do it naturally.

In any given situation, I am always thinking what could happen long-term. I anticipate the future in any given situation, enabling me to develop not only a clearly defined and focused business objective, but also to identify what is needed to achieve this objective. Not only am I naturally able to think things through strategically with regard to objectives, but I can also understand the vision process needed to achieve the objective. A vision process is a clear and succinct description of what the organization should look like and what it will take to get there. Because these are complementary, I do not believe vision process can be learned. That makes natural strategic thinkers far better at the process than people who have learned the skill.

I have found there are some people who are very good formulation thinkers, but only in a limited way. If an idea is presented to them, they are very good at determining if it is a viable idea or not. On the other hand, they do not have the ability to come up with the idea themselves. In fact, when they are presented with an idea, they may take weeks to ruminate on it, showing you every plus and minus associated with your idea. Some view this as being very negative and wish these people would just go along with the idea. You should actually praise these people because they have done you a great service by beating your idea against the rocks to see what fell out. Do they typically come back with more negatives than positives? Yes, and so what? You now have a more solid platform from which to plan for all the possible outcomes you might face.

You need to decide which of these people best describes you, if either. Can you think of new opportunities and strategically move the company in such a way as to take advantage of this? Or are you an individual who can take someone else's idea, work through all the angles to determine if it is a good idea, and then identify how to use it? The third possibility is that you are a person who can do neither. You are not good at finding new opportunities or at determining how to position the company to take advantage of a new opportunity. You need to understand which type of person you are because it will tell you who you need to hire to strengthen your weak points.

If you excel at taking someone else's idea and figuring out how to move the company in that direction then why would you hire someone else who is also good at this? If you do, it is just for your ego so you always have someone around who will agree with you. You shouldn't need, or hire, sycophants.

There is nothing wrong with having shortcomings, as we all do. What is wrong is not admitting to them. If you will not admit to yourself what weakness you have, then you stand no chance of finding the support you need to move forward.

Strategy planning — answers the "how" and "when"

After coming on board, it is not unusual for me to replace over 50% of the people in a company over a period of time with fresh employees who really want the company to succeed. Existing employees may say they want the company to succeed but, if that were the case, why is the company in such bad shape? You need to decide who stays and who goes, but only when you are certain what type of people will be needed to move forward

You will be replacing people with individuals who will help you move into the future which is why it is important to quickly asses what you plan to do with the company. The people you hire are a very large part of the how you will move the company into the future. They have the knowledge needed for the move.

Even though you want people who have knowledge that will help you get where you want the company to go, that is not the main factor I look for when interviewing direct reports. The first thing I want is someone who has a deep need to succeed. Secondly, do they fill a void I have and, lastly, are they very passionate about what they do?

Believe it not, there is a huge difference between people who do not want to fail and people with a deep desire to succeed. People who do not want to fail will not think beyond the scope of the project they are working on. They will not consider other possibilities and, if things change, they will just continue along and finish. These people do not take chances, think outside the box, or consider any actions they take unless it brings them closer to their personal success. In fact, they are so focused on not failing that they will often throw anyone or anything under the bus just to make sure they are successful.

Their success, not the company's, is paramount and nothing will get in their way.

People who have a deep desire for success, on the other hand, tend to look at the big picture and understand the end results you are looking for. Since these people tend to be big-picture types then as the picture shifts because of market, sales opportunities, new business, or any number of other factors, what they are working on will also shift. If the reason for a project changes or evaporates, they will come to you and explain why they are going to stop working on this project, whereas people who are afraid to fail will just plod on. I hope you can see these are two completely different types of people with two completely different ways of working.

As I indicated earlier, 80% of solving a problem is to properly define it. With this new definition of the company, I had my strategic objective and could then begin the process of transforming the company. At this point, I had not even been at the company for 60 days, so I was working on HR and finance issues, but it was critical to get this new definition of the company clarified, documented, and published to all employees.

If my objective was to compete strictly on price, then I needed to hire people who understood just-in-time inventory and Six Sigma and had experience reducing costs to absolute rock bottom. If all I had was a "me too" product to sell, then I would need to get rid of every extra person in the company, make it as lean as possible, and take whatever profit possible. On the other hand, if the objective is to transform the company to a value-added company then the need is for creative people. You want people who can redesign on the fly, create a masterpiece from a pile of Legos, and find solutions where others see only problems. You would be looking for people who were not afraid of "what if," but who fed off it.

I want to throw something new in the mix here, intuition, which I count on very heavily. Intuition does not just happen because you are a lucky person and plugged into the cosmos in a special way. I believe that people with great intuition tend to be people who read a great deal on a variety of topics. People who read books on economics, science, about people and how they succeeded, and even books on how things work tend to have better intuition than people who do little or no reading at all. Intuitive people have discussions with people who have differing points of view and not afraid to admit someone is smarter than they are.

Your brain takes all of this disparate data, finds pieces that fit together, and helps resolve issues you are now have. If I am not the smartest person in the room, then I need people who will be. The more information you have and the more open you are to new information, the better intuition you tend to have.

Now the "When" needs to be answered, which is simple. While you are slowly bringing the company back from the downward spiral, you begin to implement the long-term changes you are really after. They both need to be done at the same time and, even though this does not seem the correct move, it really is. If you are not doing both at the same time it means you will need to move the company twice, first to right the ship and then to change course. It does not take much more effort to do both. It just takes good management.

Operational planning

Strategic Planning is a process of breaking down the future into steps, detailing each step, and knowing how each step could be implemented. Operational planning is a short-term, highly detailed plan formulated by management to achieve tactical objectives. This task is often done by directors and/or supervisors who can take the planning and break it down into very specific tasks. These are very detailed people but, most importantly, it takes people willing to totally commit themselves to the project.

Over the years I learned one very important lesson. People who say they will try ultimately tend to fail. They will fail because they have already given themselves permission to fail when they indicated they have no other commitment to the idea than "to try." On the other hand, people who say they will "do it" or "you bet, I am on it" or any other words of commitment are winners and will almost always succeed. You can walk into a room, stop, look around, and then walk out again and declare you tried. That is what someone who "will try" does. On the other hand, people who hate giving their word on something and then not coming through are the "doers." And you need doers, not those who will try.

Everyone fails from time to time, but if they do fail you know they gave it their best. You also know they might just need a little more help, perhaps a fresh set of eyes, a little more knowledge on the subject, or some outside assistance. When they come to you and inform you they could not make it happen, review it with them and see what you can do to help them turn it around and be successful. You win twice doing this. You get the result you need, and you have a very loyal employee because they feel you cared enough to help them be successful. Now they want to be on your team and will tell people how you helped. Losers say they will try, but winners commit, declare they will succeed, and do.

Conflict is not bad

You might think talking about conflict in a chapter about strategic thinking a bit odd, but you will not get to where you need to be without it. And, frankly, everything you are doing is going to create conflict. Conflict is not a bad thing and change will not happen without it. The trick is to never make it personal, never let it get out of hand, and always have a reason for letting it happen.

Many people hate conflict. They feel a simple brainstorming session is good enough and, after you have a few ideas, rate them and move on. I will then tell you that the best idea was never uncovered and that you simply settled. We are not talking about arguing, yelling, name-calling, or any form of personal assault. We are talking about people with different ideas openly facing each other concerning those ideas.

When you start turning around the company you will be telling people what you want and how you want it done. This way everyone will work exactly as you have instructed. As time moves on you will begin to tell people what result you are looking for and that you expect them to achieve it. People will have different ideas and ways to get the results and often, because of the conflict this creates, they will need to find some way to all agree.

This agreement can be a hybrid of ideas or something completely new, but ideally this new idea is what you are really pushing for. This new idea is innovative, which is how companies grow. For this to happen people must listen to each other, find ways to achieve results, and think outside the box. This will build trust among your team, especially when each team member realizes that the person sitting across the table is not trying to make them look bad, steal the glory, or has a hidden agenda. Instead, the team is simply trying to resolve an issue. As this trust grows, so will innovation. People will feel free to throw ideas on the table, knowing bad ideas will not going to be used against them.

I find it useful to use a consultant at this stage because it enables people to feel free to speak their mind. They know that what is said in the room will stay in the room and that, while they are talking, everyone is of equal rank and everyone's voice carries equal weight.

You have actually been planning for this day (or should have been). The reason I say this is because you want to find a consultant you trust so that he or she can learn the company culture before being called on to assist with team building and change. Consultants are like everyone else; for the most part they are looking for the easiest way to achieve a result you are looking for. For them, your assignment means using programs and work sheets they have used 100 times at other companies. The problem is this is utterly useless because your company is not the other 100 companies. If the person you hired insists on this approach, then get rid of them and hire someone new. Your company is developing a culture of its own, unique unto itself, and your consultant needs to fit into this culture or be replaced.

Remember the customer who was told how our product worked everywhere but at his facility so the problem must be his process? He was quite upset, justifiably, because he did not care where our product worked at. What he cared about is that it did not work for him, and it was our problem.

Very few consultants have worked at a company in the midst of being turned around and, more than likely, do not know that the people in these companies are not being managed the same as in a well-established company. What has been used successfully in many companies will not work in your company, his programs will not work, and the approach needs to be different. In short, you do not really care what they have done at other companies. You need a program that will work in your situation.

I hired a consultant two years before I knew I would need him. They worked on small, but extremely important tasks, learning who the company was, who the people were, and the culture of the company. This was not a wasted two years but fruitful, as this consultant could help HR get better at their job, the VP of Finance to be more productive with operations, and operations to trust other leaders in the company. In this way, he is getting people to better trust each other and to trust him as well.

Many people ask why I need this person and why can't I do this myself. The answer is very simple.

1) People don't like to argue with or have confrontations in front of the boss

2) If they do, they want to win so they can look good

3) They are looking for you to take sides or resolve issue for them

4) There may be personnel issues which causing the problem.

Your goal is for your people to resolve the issue of teamwork by themselves, work their way through conflict by themselves, and learn how to manage conflicts. All of this should happen without you. The consultant can work behind the scenes with people and help them move forward better than you can.

If you get involved, then people feel you have taken sides. You meet with one VP and have a discussion and, as soon as you enter the next one's office, they feel they are in second place. If they were not in second place then why would you not have spoken with them first? With a consultant in place I can avoid this because they know him, they have seen and talked to him for two years, and he knows them. They trust each other and both sides know that what is said is said in confidence. You don't have to worry about the consultant destroying the culture of the company because they have been working with you for several years, know how you think, what you are after.

Here is the trick to get this part started. Pick a project you want resolved, one that you know your people have strong opinions about. Do not pick a subject you do not have interest in because your people will feel like you set them up, which you did, and you will lose their trust. This must be a subject you care about and want resolved. Now, you have given them a real-life project to work on that you know is going to create conflict and, that to resolve this issue, they will have to work through this conflict. You will now see all the time and effort you have been putting into your consultant pay off and you will have a stronger team at the other end. You are doing all of this because the other option is company stagnation, one of the issues that originally got the company into trouble.

Decide

Making a decision seems to be the biggest issue people have with strategic thinking. Most people fall into one of two camps:

1) They never feel they have enough information to make a decision
2) They make "gut" decisions with little or no information

I have worked for people who seem to have a constant need for information. It does not matter how much information I give them on a subject it never seems to be enough. There is never enough detail or there are never enough examples of other companies doing it. They never seem to feel they have enough information to make a good decision, yet always seems to feel they are taking huge risks on every decision they make.

Unfortunately, by the time they are capable of deciding the timing is gone and the deal they could have made slipped through their fingers. Then they wonder why the outcome they had expected doesn't happen. I feel they set themselves up for failure, the very thing they are desperately trying to avoid, because they are so afraid of making a bad decision that they are incapable of making any decision.

Over the years I have met people at other companies who have the same issue, becoming paralyzed by the facts. This is the big reason why they need so much information. It has nothing to do with having all the facts available and everything to do with delaying making the decision. They allow themselves to be paralyzed with facts and, in many cases, set out to accomplish this very thing — even if subconsciously.

Then there are those at the other end of spectrum who, with few to no facts still make decisions. This is just as bad as never having enough because these people rely on "gut feel." When asked why they made the decision, they will say it just felt right. There is a company I was involved with in which the owner used to say that, if it passed the smell test then it was a good decision. What's crazy is he made more bad decisions than good by a pretty wide margin but, like most people who go strictly by "gut feel," he also always found some reason why it was not his fault.

I find these people make just as many bad decisions as people who never have enough information. So, it all boils down to how much is enough information to move forward. This is why I so often say, "let's break it down." If you break a problem down to its basic parts it will help you make a sound decision. The other tool I use is to take decisions to an end point and see what it looks like. Many people will tell me that my end point is ridiculous and could never happen, but what if it did? And even if it doesn't happen no matter where things land you know you made the right decision.

Give your team freedom to become more engaged, but continue to coach them

As I indicated at the beginning of this chapter, people who are good at strategic thinking are unique because they think about problems and opportunities differently than most people. To some extent this can also be taught. Consequently, unless you want to be the only person in your company who thinks strategically you need to spend time working with your staff to help them develop this trait. They might never have the strategic thinking capabilities you do but it is always usable on a day-to-day basis. You want them to think through issues, understand how decisions lead to certain conclusions, and what people's reactions will be to those decisions.

Let's review how failure to strategically plan for the future made the action of one individual a poor one. Sadly, if it had been thought out it could have been a very good action. You recall from an earlier chapter how buying a reverse osmosis system really helped the quality of the product at one of the companies I ran. The idea of using the RO water was a good idea, but the person in charge of the project did not look at the consequences of what that meant. Would this move pay for itself? Was the increased use of water justified by a substantial improvement of product? Did the customer complaints go down, returns go down, or was there any measurable improvement from our customers? The answer was no to each question.

This is a lack of system thinking, which is a composite of strategic thinking is. Did this make his decision a bad one? At first glance, no. However, not anticipating increased costs when looking at the consequences of moving more of the plant to the RO system was compounded by not investigating potential new opportunities.

After I saw the water bill, I began walking the plant trying to figure out how to ameliorate this unexpected new expense. It so happens that I walked into the area where we clean some of the raw materials used. Some of the material used is natural and dirty when it arrives. Normally about 30% of all the water used in the company is to clean this raw material. It dawned on me that the discharge from the RO system could work perfectly for this purpose. The discharge was plumbed to the area where we clean the material and has been used there ever since. The result of this not only reduced the water and sewage bill but we also had better water being used all over the plant, along with reduced manufacturing costs. This is an example of why strategic thinking is needed at every stage of the business. Not just in moving the company from poor markets to better markets, but in everyday operations as well.

An Idea is not a plan. It is an idea.

Many times people feel they have a plan that would succeed if people would simply follow it. Most of the time, however, the plans were never more than an idea with no strategic planning behind it at all.

I once did some consulting for a company in Massachusetts. They hired me to help them eliminate a backlog of products, help with cash, and keep the company together until the big idea they had come to fruition. They had decided to make a very difficult coating for the fiber industry, which could make them quite profitable, even though they had no idea how to make it. This coating had been around for several years and companies would pay almost anything to get it. To say these coatings were more valuable than gold would be the understatement of the century. This company had been working towards this objective for a couple of years before I started. Even though I was not working on the project, it was in my field, so I knew quite a bit about it. I asked them why they were pursuing this filter and was told that this "will put the company on the map." I then asked the president of the company what his plan to achieve success was.

He told me that they had a coating engineer working full time on this and were sure they could achieve success. When I asked why they felt this way I was told it was because the engineer had assured them that he was very close, and he did seem to be getting closer.

I again asked why they were continuing an attempt to make this coating, and at that point, the president became quite upset. I said let's talk through this idea. For two years you have been working on an idea with no plan, just trying different methods in a hope of success. This coating has been on the market for several years and you are right: one good run can make you hundreds of thousands of dollars. However, your equipment is old and not optimized to make the coating you are trying to make. You know this since 25% of all the runs you make have to be aborted because of mechanical issues with the system. You are pushing your equipment way beyond anything it was ever designed to do. The next issue is that you have a mediocre engineer on staff who has never in his career made anything this complicated. You have asked him to invent a workable coating but making that type of coating is beyond his ability. I told the president that between these two issues alone the possibility of success was almost impossible.

The third reason I said I would walk away from this project is because it would collapse before long. At the type of price he could get for this coating, it guaranteed other, non-coating companies were working on a cheaper, better product. If you know nothing else, the price alone ensured other companies would work on this for no other reason than that fiber would be around for years. They all wanted a piece of it and what's better than taking the most lucrative piece. In fact, within one year another company did come out with a product that could replace these filters for a fraction of the price. The coating they had unsuccessfully worked on for years was now worthless.

A company I worked for brought on a new president and the very first thing he did was to announce his new plan for the company. Instead of all the subsidiaries working on what they wanted, he decided that the company would focus on a few markets. He wanted the company to focus on food, medical, beauty, and other "feel good" products. This was a great idea, but it was only an idea. All these areas are multibillion-dollar industries, so which aspect should we focus on? What is the best fit for the company in each category? What will the company specialize in and where will we put our resources?

Beyond presenting his idea, he did not work on how to make this idea into a plan, and, with no plan, there was no chance for success. An idea is only an idea until it has been completely thought out and a plan put into place to achieve it. How do you move forward when no one knows what direction forward is?

The idea he had was a good idea, but not achievable because it had not been thought out. The company was not a large company so resources were not unlimited. He should have hired a few experts to help him flush out a plan, understand what each piece was, and how each company would focus their energies in making the plan successful. For example, one of the ideas was to develop something in the pharmaceutical area because he had read that collagen was good for the body.

There was not a single person in the company who understood this industry. He wanted this to sell into the US so he would need an expert for the FDA. There was no single person who understood the rules, regulations, reporting, or another aspect of the FDA. Would the factory have to be changed to meet requirements? What testing would be needed? What does it take to get FDA approval? These were just some of the questions that needed answers and he was relying on people searching the internet for those answers.

Might he succeed? Perhaps, but the odds were against him. In addition, overall costs would be higher because mistakes would be made. Just because you have an idea it does not mean you have a plan. You have a plan when you can lay out the entire scope of what needs to be done to achieve a result.

Desperation breeds inspiration

Let's end this chapter with one of my favorite sayings: desperation breeds inspiration. There are companies that seem to long for change and whose very livelihood depends on it. Look at companies like Apple, Google, and Microsoft. They not only embrace change, but also live and breathe it.

This is not true for most of us who loathe change, or for whom the very thought of strategic thinking scares us to death. I have found that when the company is desperate, or a project is failing, people get very creative. Not everyone, of course. Many people will throw up their hands and give up without even trying, but there are a few who will become inspired and suddenly have ideas that you never thought possible.

This is exactly why you spent the time developing your team, gave them space to have ideas — many bad, but all embraced. You might be surprised to find that a bad idea three years ago is now perfect. Always encourage your people to find a solution and teach them how to develop those solutions.

One of the best practices is to develop scenarios where the very future of a project is dependent on finding a solution to a problem. Like all projects this cannot be a made-up activity just to help train people but, instead, should be something real where failure means jobs, bonuses, or something else they want. No one ever really steps up to the plate until they must because no one wants to put their reputation on the line until there is no other way.

I typically start small. People need to become used to having to think, which may be a new concept for them. For example, the company needs to achieve a certain profit for anyone to obtain a bonus. Never tell people you will increase the bonus if they succeed because they will most likely fail. That is the same thing as "I will try." They already have a bonus so if they fail, they will simply shrug their shoulders and be glad they are getting their regular bonus. In their mind, they did not lose anything.

The goal of Strategic Thinking is to outthink, out plan and outmaneuver other forces or competitors. Without comprehensive Strategic Thinking, the organization risks making quick decisions that lack the creativity and insights derived through a Strategic Thinking process.

CHAPTER 12

Leadership Style Must Adjust To The People You Are Managing For Optimal Organization Growth

I think one of the dumbest questions I get asked when I interview is what my management style is. The reason this question shows a real lack of intelligence is that it presumes the company is stagnant and whatever the company is today is exactly the same as it will be in five years. It also presumes that everyone in the company is the same and needs to be managed the same. This is a ridiculous statement and I find myself cringing every time this is asked.

Every company goes through changes brought about by a variety of things: the economy, being sold, or simply a changing market. Look at Detroit where most American cars used to be made as an example. Years ago, it had a thriving economy because of the auto industry, but now it is almost a ghost town. I was there a few months ago and was told population had dropped by 55%. So much of a decline that the city would give you a home for $500. The deal was that you had to live in it and fix it up. I am sure, depending you and your bias, you can give some reason for the downfall of "Car City."

There were companies like Montgomery Ward, which started out as a catalog store and then went brick and mortar, and today is just a memory. There are many reasons why this happened but, in every case, change happened. For whatever reason the company or industry struggled to change with it.

To some degree, small or large, changes are happening to every company no matter where you work. If they are not changing, then your company is doomed because the world itself is changing. Who would have guessed in the early 2000s that Amazon would dominate the marketplace as it does today?

Now you are reading this and thinking, "who cares"? He is talking about huge companies and macroeconomics and I am just trying to turn this midsized company around. What does all of this have to do with me? Well, frankly, everything.

Companies have life cycles and once you achieve a point where happy, inspired employees make the difference between a good year and bad year, you have reached a very import and crucial phase in the life of a company. Not to put your employees first means high turnover. While this is expensive, it also means you are losing creative talent in the company, and it may be to your competitor. Wherever your employees are going the ultimate loser is you and your company.

Other management styles such as pacesetting, coaching, inspirational, results-based, and example-setting are all tools you need to be using from the beginning. The need to use a variety of management styles (or tools) never goes away, and you will use them your entire life.

No matter what size a company is only one thing is certain: either the company will change and grow or stagnate and die. I am one of those people who really does not believe a company can stagnate and hold its own because the world does not sit still and so, to even to just hold your own, you must change. Not only do companies change but so do people. Each generation is different than the one before it. Just look at the young people today, for example. Things we did back in the '80s would be considered completely unacceptable by today's standards and in 20 years what goes on today most likely will not be acceptable to that generation.

If this is true for a normal, healthy company, it must be true for the company you are turning around. In fact, it must be even greater, with both much more change and much faster change than in a healthy company. When you have been hired to fix a stressed company, people are not going to give you 20 years to make things happen. Your board is going to expect to see changes quickly. Just think about nothing other than demographics in a company and how diverse it probably is. Not everyone in your company is 30 years old +/- 5 years. While this might be great because they grew up in the same generation, it is an impossible thought. Some will have college degrees and others might not even have a high school diploma. However, all these people need to contribute to the future of your company. You are hiring an almost completely new senior staff. Some will be firefighters while others will have an eye on one or two years down the road and what your company will be when the firefighters are gone.

I have worked in both healthy, thriving companies and in companies which should have gone under long before I was ever hired. I can say with 100% certainty that no place you have ever work will there be more diversity than in a company being turned around. Even in this book you read that there are people who see their company as nothing more than a place to hang out until they retire to people so high-strung that you practically have to tie them up just to get them to sit still.

Over the years people have been brainwashed into believing one type of leadership style is better than any other. People call authoritarian leadership "a thing of the '50s" and that companies need to be more progressive today. They point to many companies in the tech industry and tell you should manage more like they do, treating your employees like partners and less like employees. Give them more freedom and work on becoming more self-directed.

This mantra, of course, is preached by people trying to sell books or seminars and who need something interesting to say that you would be willing to pay for. They show graphs and charts, quoting studies that have been conducted to prove what they are selling. If you ran your company like the ones in the picture, you too could have a billion-dollar company.

As I had indicated from the start, this book is not based on "studies." It is based on what works in real life: good or bad, hard or easy, new, old, or a combination. I have turned around several companies and, more importantly, have been able to observe the failures of the people before me. I have never been so lucky as to be the first person found when the company got into trouble, which is why I have seen, and inherited, the mistakes made by my predecessors.

Any person you ever meet who has successfully turned a company around will agree that nothing in this book has been embellished. In fact, it was probably toned down because the average person simply would not believe the truth. Throughout the book I have discussed various styles of management. Which style best depicts me? Some folks who know me think my style varies based on the need at the time. However, this is not true as I do have a very specific style. That said, we have all heard of many common styles, some of which I have included below.

- Directive
  - Autocratic style. This type of management is characterized by a top-down approach. The manager makes the decision and all others below must fall into line.
  - The manager that utilizes this style will expect full compliance from subordinates. There's little room for error here, and discipline for mistakes is often swift and severe.
  - The directive manager focuses carefully on the performance of employees and isn't afraid to deliver threats in the face of failed standards.
- Authoritative
  - The authoritative, or visionary style employs the use of providing tangible, long-term direction for the team.
  - The manager in this role will make clear the vision they have for the future and will also set about a concrete plan for how to get there.
  - Employees are given more freedom under this management style, although an authoritative manager isn't afraid to step in to give fair and constructive feedback.

- Affirmative
  - This style puts the greatest emphasis on the well-being of the employees. A "put people first" manager seeks to make subordinates feel valued and satisfied.
  - With this management style, employees are put first and output is placed second so there is some risk of mediocre employee performance. However, some arguments suggest that an affirmative management style may actually increase employee output due to a healthier, happier mental state.
- Participative
  - This style, also called the democratic style of management, encourages the active participation of all employees.
  - A participative manager will seek to receive the contributions of all their subordinates before making decisions. This may sometimes slow company progress, but it does help boost team morale, as all employees feel valued and trusted.
- Pacesetting
  - In the pacesetting management style, the manager sets the pace of production. Often, the pace will be swift, and some employees will find this challenging.
  - A pacesetting manager will complete tasks to a high degree of excellence to serve as an example for employees. This management style has high expectations of its employees, but production is often high quality and efficient.
- Coaching
  - The coaching manager, or developmental manager, is highly focused on the professional development of their employees.
  - In this managing role, the manager will have a hands-on approach to coaching and encouraging new skill sets in subordinates. This often fosters a strong bond with employees, and they come to view their manager as a coach or teacher, as opposed to a boss.

- Inspirational
  - To be an inspirational leader is no easy task, but it is extremely effective when accomplished. The inspirational type of management style requires superb people skills, a big heart, and an honest desire to help your employees develop both in and outside of the workplace.
  - In this case you might need to adopt a more authoritative type of management style, but having an authoritative style of leadership doesn't mean you need to be rude. Remember that you can give orders with a smile and a "please."
- Results-Based
  - The magic word for results-based managers is efficiency. You're not concerned with how things get done as long as they get done well and in the quickest way possible.
  - You don't feel the need to create every rule and method yourself. If an employee comes up with a superior way of doing things, you're happy to make changes to company policy. The only thing that matters with this type of management style is results.
- Example-Setting
  - This management style is exactly what it sounds like: you lead by consistently setting an impeccable example of the kind of work standards you expect at your business. The bar is set by your actions and your actions alone
  - In some cases, this may even transform the ethics of and working environment of your business. Example-setting leaders are definitely not afraid to roll up their sleeves and get their hands dirty to show the crew how things should be done.
- Strategic
  - Strategic managers aren't interested in the minute details of basic tasks. Instead, they're focused on the bigger picture and long-term success of the business they manage.
  - If you have a strategic management style, you're comfortable allowing assistant managers and shift leaders to oversee the bulk

of everyday responsibilities. While the crew gets the mundane work done, you're planning marketing campaigns and preparing for expansion.

- Charismatic
  - The charismatic management style, sometimes called the persuasive management style, is built around the personality and charm of the manager.
  - If this is your type of management style, you're focused on developing personal relationships with your staff and building a team in your workplace. Employees are cooperative because they respect the fact that you're interested in getting to know them as individuals.
  - Ultimately, any manager worth their salt will use a combination of these types of management styles. Leaders who know how to lead are flexible and quick to adapt to their environment.
- Transformational
  - Transformational leaders tend to be emotionally intelligent, energetic, and passionate. They are not only committed to helping the organization achieve its goals, but also to helping group members fulfill their potential.

These various management styles all emphasize different approaches to handling and guiding employees. Which of these management styles speaks to you the most?

Over the years I am sure everyone has heard of these styles. Everyone has a personal favorite and can tell you why one is better than another. I am not going to go over each one as you can look them up or buy a book if you are interested in anything more specific. What I want to look at is what should you be and why every manager, regardless if you are turning a company around or not, should strive to become. I hope before I am done, you will see that one style outshines all the others and for good reason. People are dynamic and not robots, and companies are just as dynamic.

Most people do not promote the harshest of styles like authoritarian or directive any longer, as they say this is out of touch with what people need in the workplace. Yet this is one of the first places I went at the beginning of the book. In fact, I stressed that you probably would not succeed, or least in any reasonable amount of time, if you did not use these. I believe this is still true, and if these two management styles are not used initially, I am not sure you will ever really get a company on the brink of collapse turned around.

When you take over a downtrodden company you could decide to use the Participative style but remember people do not like change and that is exactly what you will be doing. So, ask yourself how the very people who created the problem will participate. In time they might, but I am talking about in the first six to twelve months. What are you expecting them to do?

If you use the Example-Setting and Coaching styles they could work if you are willing to take much longer to begin to see results. On the other hand, you were not hired to take years to see the smallest results just because you are afraid to take control. You were hired to get results in a very short time span, so you need to take absolute control.

Many times, when a new rule is put into place one of the first things people will say is that it will never work until someone is made an example. Sometimes this is said on the back end where people will say they are not surprised someone was fired because it seems an example is always needed so people know you are serious. People seem to have a need to test the system, to see if you are willing to back up what you are saying, and they will challenge you. Regardless if you are in management or not, we have all seen this. Even when I was working on the floor and had not started to move up, we would talk about who would be fired when the company announced a new policy. I can recall people making bets on which they thought would be the first one fired because of the policy and the fact it would be challenged.

So rather than write a book telling you how to negotiate this or describe how people are so sensitive that you cannot be this way, I am just saying people have not changed that much and the odds of being hired into an enlightened company is so remote that there is no point in pretending. Admit the truth about what you have hired on to and get in front of it.

This leads to the basic question: what is the right management style needed to turn a company around? The answer is all of them. I believe the Situational management style should be the only style ever taught and used. As you have read several times now **you need to be exactly what is needed at the time it is needed, and nothing else.**

I would love to say I coined the term Situational management, but I am sure it has been around for years. What I can tell you is when I use the term people look at me like I have two heads and have no idea what I am talking about. Or they think I just made it up. The only style you ever need to master is the Situational and to do this you must be good at every style I named above.

- Situational

  Stress the significant influence of the environment and the situation on leadership.

  Primary styles of leadership, including:

  - The telling style is characterized by telling people what to do.
  - The selling style involves leaders convincing followers to buy into their ideas and messages.
  - The participating style is marked by allowing group members to take a more active role in the decision-making process.
  - The delegating style involves taking a hands-off approach to leadership and allowing group members to make the majority of decisions.
  - The directing style involves giving orders and expecting obedience but offers little in the way of guidance and assistance.
  - The coaching style means giving lots of orders, but leaders also give lots of support.
  - The supporting style is an approach that offers plenty of help, but very little direction.

So, what exactly is a situational manager? The very best definition is you are what you need to be exactly at the time you need to be it.

When you take over a company that is drowning, I stressed that you need to be a bull in a china closet because people need a wakeup call. You do not have time to take a vote on every decision and, frankly, why would you even be interested. The very people you are coming down on are the people who ran the company into the ground. You need them to do what you tell them to when you tell them to do it.

You will be assuming complete control over the entire company. You need to have this control before you stand any chance of turning things around. In fact, one of the very first things I always do is enforce people to "CC" me on every email they write, whether it is for internal or external use.

There is absolutely no question this is the Authoritarian and Dictatorship type of management style. There is also no question that when you took over this is exactly what was needed at that precise moment. You need to be 100% sure everyone knows there is a new sheriff in town and the rules have changed. You don't care what the rules were before you arrived. You are here now, and things will be done differently. As hard as it might be to believe not only will the people let you take control, but the really good employees will also feel it is about time someone did. They want to see the company turned around and will welcome your hard approach as they will view it as something long overdue. One thing you need to understand though is if this goes on too long these same people will be the first to complain.

We saw in several chapters that fear is not something you can rely on long term since it will burn itself out quickly. If you cannot use fear for the next two years, what will be your fallback position? This was covered in many chapters but ultimately you will need to sell your vision to the people who work for you. You need them working towards the future because they believe in your vision and they believe in you. This is when you will get the absolute best you will ever get from your people because they have a goal and a mission they are working towards.

People always work hardest for something they believe in, and it does not have to be work. Look around and see where people really make time to make things happen. People who really believe they owe society will find time to work at churches or soup kitchens to feed the homeless. You see these people giving up their own holidays to volunteer where they can give back to people who have less than they do. People who feel they can help shape the youth in our country will lead organizations like the Boy/Girl Scouts, giving up some of their own vacation time to take these kids camping or helping them earn a badge for swimming. If you can get people to believe in something, there is nothing they will not do, no matter any suffering they will endure, to achieve result. This is not just for a company you are turning around, but for any company you are running. You need a vision and then you need to sell this vision to the people so they will follow you into the future.

Unless you personally want to run everything forever, you will be coaching people to help them improve their skills. You do this so you can first have them participate in the decision-making process and then later delegate responsibility to them. The problem you will find is that most people have never been coached on how to do the job you want. The phrase I hear often is "throw them into the deep end and see what they have got."

I know people who complain that their company has stagnated and is not moving forward. It takes just about 20 minutes of walking around to see why. The company has never moved forward because the president has never stopped being the dictator of the company. They never took the time to coach people and teach them how to make good decisions and, because they could not be trusted to make good decisions, nothing was ever delegated to them

If you are taking care of every single issue in the company every day, then how will you ever have time to work on the future? The short answer is, you will not, and the company will deteriorate. For this you have no one to blame than yourself. Either you are too insecure to give people the power to make decisions or too lazy to teach them how.

Either way your company will never move forward beyond a certain point, not because there are only 24 hours in a day, but because you only have a finite amount of ability. I don't care what ability we are talking about: creativity, technology knowledge, sales skills, udor just finding solutions to problems. For a company to move forward you need the people around you, and you need them to take over running the company day-to-day, so you have time to focus on the future. You cannot do both.

People will tell you that you need to strive to get your entire company to where everyone is working at the highest level possible. I consider this the big con. There are many problems with thinking that everyone can be taught to make good decisions and be self-directed. The first problem is unions, who realize everyone is different. Some union members will excel, and some will not, so they find the worst employee and make this person the upper and lower bar. No one should ever be expected to be better than this person, and as long as no one is ever worse, they cannot be fired.

Even if you have a mature non-union company that runs quite well everyone in the company is different and will grow to a certain level. There will be people that will always need more direction than you care to give and others who need only the basic instructions. There will be people who will suck up your coaching like a sponge because they want to move up in the company and be given the opportunity to incorporate their own vision into core of the company, and others who don't.

I was on a plane recently flying home on a 14-hour flight from India. As much as I do not really care to talk to my seat mate, there are times when the person sitting next to me feels differently. Just a quick side note. When sitting next to a person on a plane who does not seem interested in you or what you have to say, then back off. Otherwise you should expect the less than pleasant response you might get, but back to my point. At some point we got around to what we each did and when I told him I specialized in turning companies around, and was writing a book about this very subject, he informed me that "people like me" made too big a deal of this. Get rid of everyone and hire some good people and the job was done. Okay, he is an idiot, but I had not lost my composure yet.

I informed him that people "like him," who had never done this always felt just turning the company upside down and giving it a good shake was all that needed to be done. Since it was obvious he had no idea what he was talking about, I asked what he did and was informed he ran division X for a large firm. Okay, this sounded promising.

I figured since we were talking, this would fit into the chapter I was writing, asking his style of management and how he dealt with people. I was informed he delegated everything and got rid of anyone one who was not absolutely the best. First off, he would need to define the best and by what standards was this definition used, which he did not in this case. I felt this made no sense and showed he had no idea what he was talking about. End of conversation, but it did prove interesting. ...

Let's assume you have a company where everyone is an A type personality. Type A personality traits, including competitiveness, time urgency, and a tendency towards workaholism, can be seen (particularly by Type A people) as beneficial for career success.

- **Time urgency and impatience**, as demonstrated by people who, among other things, get frustrated while waiting in line, interrupt others often, walk or talk at a rapid pace, and are always painfully aware of the time and how little they have to spare.
- **Free-floating hostility or aggressiveness**, which shows up as impatience, rudeness, being easily upset over small things, or "having a short fuse," for example.

Additionally, Type A behavior often includes:

- **Competitiveness:** these people need to "win" at everything from work to relationships, even if these activities aren't inherently competitive.
- **Strong achievement orientation:** Type A people tend to get their feelings of self-worth from what they achieve.
- **A need for dominance:** Many Type A people try to show dominance in business and personal interactions, disregarding the wishes and needs of others in favor of their own.

https://www.verywellmind.com/type-a-personality-traits-3145240

Can you imagine if everyone in the company was competing about everything and needed to be the most dominant person in the room?

Nothing would get done and no one would be doing it. The only thing people would be interested in would be how to outshine their neighbor. This is not what you need.

No question, when you start turning things around, you will be hiring many senior people who have these traits because this is what the company needs at that time. As time goes by the need for these traits will decrease. As you might recall, in an earlier chapter, I talked about who you need to hire and that at times you need a firefighter who most likely will not be a long-term employee. Once the fire is out then they will need to go. Even when the company has been turned around, people are all different and there will be some who will always need to have a great deal of supervision and those that do not. To ask how any individual management style is going to work in a vibrant company full of people is an ever-present question. You need to be as dynamic as the company you want to lead.

Also, as with every other aspect of the company you need to decide what you want the company to look like when you are done. How do you want your team to function? Even with people you start at the finish line — the end result you want — and work your way forward. How much of the company do you want to delegate, how much authority should department managers have, and so forth throughout the company.

Remember that at my start with present company one of the largest accounts had been having quality issues and the company had been ignoring them? My present company, as had been mentioned, was of the mindset that the problem was because the customer had made changes in their plant. What would have happened if they had been told to take a step back and ask themselves to consider if it might actually be an in-house quality issue?

The customer had been complaining for six months that there was an intermittent issue and the entire company had ignored them. Why would they be willing to change their minds at this point? In fact, at the very first meeting I had with the quality group they presented a list of reasons why it could not be a casing issue and had to be an issue at the customer. The customer was convinced it was a casing issue and, key point my present company was not considering, since they are the one buying, they had the right to go somewhere else.

What the people at present company needed was to wake up and realize that regardless of whose problem it is, when the customer took their business someplace else, we would lose their biggest account. I guess they could be proud of the fact they were right, or at least convinced themselves they were right, but is that pat on the back going to keep the lights on? It does not matter who is right and who is wrong. The only point is to make sure the customer does not decide to spend their money somewhere else.

I called a meeting with all the senior people, QA people and every director. They were informed that I was not interested in hearing that this was not their problem and that the problem had been created by the customer. I did not want to hear a single word about what a pain in the ass this customer was, how they were always complaining, and if I just ignored it they would eventually stop.

They were in fact told that this was OUR problem because when this customer left we would not have the money to make payroll and hard decisions would have to be made. In addition, since the people in the room were the highest paid, they would be the first to go. They had all better get off their high horses and find a solution to this issue. I could buy us some time, but this problem had to be solved.

They were also informed that the best way to solve this problem was to assume the issue was our product and begin to work it from there. One of the directors spoke up and told me this was silly, that they had been doing this for quite some time, I was new, and they knew this was not their problem and had no intention of assuming a customer problem as their own. He informed me that I was wasting their time and they had better things to do than chase an issue which clearly was not our problem. He understood I was new and that I wanted to look good and solve this but "trust him" I did not know what I was doing. He was fired then and there. I walked him to HR and informed HR he was to be out of the plant in the next 20 minutes. Needless to say, the attitude was quite different when I went back into the room.

Yes, I was authoritarian and a dictator but that is what was needed right then and there. What he had done was make a power play and there clearly had to be one winner and one loser. This was not a coaching or persuasive situation. This was the first of many tests to see who was really running things. In fact, this did not even have anything to do with the customer. He assumed the group in the room would stand behind him and that I would be pushed aside. As for the people in the room, they were waiting to see who looked more dominant and that was the person who they were going to stand behind.

I started up teams at each of the major manufacturing step looking for what could possibly create this problem. Within a couple of weeks, it became apparent to even my employees they were lacking in knowledge. Once they accepted this then they also accepted that they might, in fact, be the cause of the problem. Real progress began to take place.

Each person from the main team was assigned to lead one of the secondary teams, which ensured both harmony and pressure. Harmony, because each leader of the five teams was part of the main group and therefore had reason to compete. If any of the five sub-teams failed, then the main group would also fail, ensuring the people leading the teams failed. The main group reported back to me and they clearly understood I was not interested in failure or people who failed.

You know the saying "the enemy of my enemy is my friend"? Universally across the company I was the enemy. This was okay because it created a certain unity in the company. Like fear, this does not last forever but, if used wisely, will kick start the company movement. I was the enemy and there was absolutely no doubt in anyone's mind of this. Remember, always give the enemy a name.

In addition, while I sat in on the secondary group meetings being authoritarian on these groups served no purpose. They had been started because it was acknowledged by all that they needed to relearn some of the engineering required to make a casing. I did not tell them they had lost all this knowledge and were no longer experts. They had come to this conclusion themselves, therefore yelling or being a dictator would only do harm and hurt progress rather than helping it.

Now they needed to be encouraged to stay focused, to be taught how to properly run experiments, and to interpret the data from those experiments. They needed someone who would coach them and teach them how to run a team, how to motivate people on their team, and basically how to be a leader.

On only one point was I authoritarian with the main group, demanding results and pushing people for those results. At the same time, I was assisting the other groups with being retrained and learning what had been forgotten. On experiments I was coaching and teaching. Note: no management style covers this range of activities other than Situational.

After about two years some people began to step up and take responsibility for their work, even looking for more responsibility. They now had ideas of their own on how to make the company stronger, cut costs, and produce a better product. Now was the time to delegate responsibility to give these people room to grow. A divide then began to show up in the company between those wanting more responsibility or looking for ways to improve the company and those who were still trying to catch up. This was true in the teams at the company as well as departments within the company. How can this diverse group of people be managed with a single style?

If you, as the president, are unable to shift your style, not just from group to group, but from person to person, then the company will stop growing. Ultimately, you will not be as successful as you could have been. Your company is only as strong and capable as the leader who runs it. As the company changes your style must change as well.

When I arrived at my present company nothing happened in the company that I did not know about or approve. This, of course, meant that I worked very long hours to keep up with everything. Eventually and slowly I replaced my senior staff with competent people, and they were able to share the load. Even so, nothing moved in the company unless either I or one of my senior staff reviewed/approved it. The company was still struggling, and this level of control was still needed. People needed to be assigned tasks which were watched very closely and managed with an iron fist. Over time this process was relaxed a bit, but senior management still sat in on all team meetings and still made most of the decisions.

This being said employees began to get excited about the future. Teams which were started to develop a new casing, improve product accountability, review our accounting method had people volunteering for them. They were excited about being part of something new and seeing how their actions were making a difference to the company as a whole. There is nothing like the joy of seeing a company shift from forcing people to get involved to turning people away because so many want to join a team and help make change. You know then that you have made a difference and the company is viable.

When your company has reached this level of development you know that it is time for the company to take the next step. Now you pull back and give people more authority to make decisions on their own. This is harder than you might believe because you and your senior staff have become accustomed to making all the decisions. However, if you do not pull back, and your senior team continues to make all the decisions, all the enthusiasm you created will die off. People will begin to feel there is no longer the need to get involved because someone else will make the final decisions anyway, so "why bother." These are the two words you want to listen for above all else because when you hear them you know you are behind in the development of your people.

It is extremely important for you to understand how this sequence will go.

Phase 1 is when you are forcing people to get things done.

- Over time some will begin to take responsibility on their own and you will begin to manage them a tad differently. However, as a whole the company still needs tight management control.

- You are authoritarian and control every aspect of the company.

- You are making changes in the company and most likely the company is pushing back. This is why some of the changes will come by force of will.

Phase 2 is when people are very enthused and want to be involved in everything and want to be a part of the future of the company.

- You will know when this happens because when you want to start a new group to work on an issue there are no complaints about being asked to join the group. In fact, most often people will volunteer to join because they are excited.
- At this point you are doing more coaching people to make decisions and what it takes to make a company run.
- You have pulled back slightly and have begun to rely on your senior staff and some directories more and more.
- Very few decisions are made without your review, but you welcome the engagement of others.

In phase 3 people are not as excited about being a part of the future and once again you will have to ask people to get involved.

- People begin to wonder why you spent so much time working with them if you are not going to trust them.
- Your senior staff still makes a great many of the decisions.
- People will no longer be excited about joining teams created solve problems.
- People will be asking why no one ever listens to them and why the ideas they have are not taken seriously.

When you have reached this phase, you know the company needs to evolve and this means you and your senior staff must give up control. Your style needs to change and how you approach your people needs to change. If you have not been working towards this spot from the beginning, then you will ultimately fail because no one will have been taught how to take on increased responsibility. This goes back to the chapter on Strategic Thinking where you have to decide what you want the future to look like so, as you hire people and work with them, everything is moving towards the end goal.

In the late 90's self-directed teams were all the rage and I had a new boss who decided this is what all the departments reporting to him should do. No department should need supervisors because the people working should be able to make decisions on their own. His feeling was that they knew what the problems were and, therefore, should be able to understand how to fix any issue.

I vividly recall the meeting where he announced this to his department managers, and someone asked how he expected people to make all the decisions. He thought this was a ridiculous question and asked why the person asking did not believe their people could not function on their own.

His felt that if all the SOP's were up to date and people were properly trained, all they would need was the authority to accomplish the tasks handed to them. He felt the only reason we, as department managers, would not want this was because we were afraid of giving up control. We had the power and we wanted to keep the power. We were told that all the books he had read indicated studies had been conducted to validate this method, which meant our management structure was very inefficient since self-directed teams were the future.

Then someone asked how we were to go about achieving this goal. It was a logical question since none of us had any idea how to do this. His response was simple. As your supervisors left, do not replace them and, instead, work with the people on that shift to make their own decisions. Of course, this was no answer at all because it was obvious to all of us he had no clue. For instance, no one knew who had the authority to decide who made calls for something as simple as overtime. Do the people working take a vote or does someone get fed up because they are working hard and just call someone? How do you manage how much overtime is being used for the month? What about vacations and ensuring half the crew working a specific shift does not go on vacation at the same time? How are the people working going to make the decision on who gets what weeks for vacation? These are just a sample of questions that need to be resolved, but the real issue is that even though no one knew how to make this work, we were ordered to do it anyway. Of course, the entire project failed.

I recall being called to his office, which he never left, because he wanted to discuss my failure. My costs were up, my daily output was down, and scrap was going through the roof. When I tried to explain that I was running the department as a self-directed team, as he had demanded, he blew up. I was informed that he would not tolerate either himself or my people being blamed for my failure to correctly implement a self-directed work team.

His style of management was not to manage at all. He was not a situational manager but only believed in delegation management. The sad part is that he believed in delegation, not because he believed better decisions could be made by other people, but to ensure he was never blamed for any bad decisions. He had read some books, gone to a couple of seminars, and had been told this is how you have a highly efficient team. He did not train anyone how to achieve this nor had he done any planning beforehand. As he used to say, you just needed to jump into the deep water and learn to swim.

He was right about one thing. Decisions do need to be pushed down, but people need to be trained how to do this. The first step for you will be teaching your direct staff to give up control. Getting your staff to give up this control will be harder than you think. Your senior staff will push back and say things like "how do you expect me to be responsible when I am not making the decisions?" It is very hard for people to give up control once they have it. What they do not understand is that by doing so it allows them to take on a bigger role themselves. You cannot worry about everything going on today and at the same time be thinking about the future.

Now your management style will switch to the coaching and supporting style for your staff. You will need to help them make the transition from Authoritarian to Coaching and Trainer. You need to work with them both as a team and individually to help them train their staff to assume more responsibility.

Here is where people go wrong. You work with your direct staff and they work with their subordinates. You do not work with their subordinates because then it looks like you are going around their boss. You must look at this from their perspective. If their boss is doing such a great job, then why are you getting involved? Why are you pushing the decision making to the next level down? Obviously, you are doing this because their boss is not doing such a great job and you might even be looking to replace them. The only perception that matters is the one that the receiving person has. They are going to react to what you are presenting as the truth, so if they misunderstand what is going on it is because you presented it wrong.

Now I realize it sounds like you are moving an entire company in one direction, but this may only be partially true because people are not like robots and they cannot all be programmed. People move at different speeds and some people simply cannot make the transition at all. This is the real power of the Situational management style which, at the same time, is a real burden. I feel it may also be a burden because you have taken all the responsibility of managing people on yourself and will manage each one in a style which will get the highest output.

People are different and you will never get everyone at the same level. You need to ask yourself if you really want everyone at the same level. In companies I run I personally want people all over the spectrum. Some people are laid back and go with the flow, hardworking, but just want to do their work and go home. Some people are extremely assertive in the way they attack life and finally, some people are in-between. These people all need a different type of supervision if you want the best out of them.

One of the big mistake managers make is that they expect the people who work for them to adapt to their style of management. I cannot count the number of times I have heard managers say that they expect their employees to step up and work in the manner with which the manager is comfortable, or they can leave. For me this is completely backwards as a good manager should manage people in a way to get the best out of their employees. This is why the only management style you really need is the Situational style. You are what you need to be the moment you need to be it. If you believe this and live by this, you will always appear sincere, because you are.

(Okay, I'll give you this last part of the chapter, BUT please cut it back and/or relate the points made back to the management style BRIEFLY. Simply too many examples and you started to lose me which means your readers will be antsy....)

CHAPTER 13

Shaping The Company

We have covered a great deal in this book and have discussed virtually every department your company may have. As you complete the process of taking over a troubled company and turning it around, you will see the logical approach to the process in this book. There are very specific steps you went through to get to the positive results you will finally enjoy. YOU

1) took decision-making away from everyone in the company

2) showed the company that you are a person of your word

3) looked at the company, the market, and then decided what the future of the company should be

4) systematically went through the company and replaced everyone who was not contributing to the future

5) found the right people to help move the company in the right direction

6) began to work with people, teaching them how to make good decisions

7) slowly released control of the company and began relying on your people to run the company.

8) steered the company to use strategic thinking throughout the entire organization

9) adjusted your management style as the company moved forward.

10) decided if you will stay to further grow the company or will move on

When you first arrive, you will be taking away the right for anyone to think for themselves. The thought process that has been used in the company is the reason the company is in such bad shape now. This is the why you are taking control of decision-making. If you think they will begin making good decisions just because you have arrived and are fluffing your feathers, this takeover will fail. You need people to understand that you represent change, some easy and accepted, and some hard and disliked by all.

At first, you will have support from very few because no one is sure which way the wind will blow or if you follow through on your promises. Most likely, you will not be the first person that was hired to turn things around, and if you are not, then you need to understand that these people have heard all these promises before. You will have warned them that they might not like your answer. They may actually hate both you and the answer, but they can be 100% assured that what you tell them will happen. When I started at my present company you could see everyone roll their eyes when I said this, but over the years they have learned it is true.

Not so long ago there was a rumor there was going to be a major layoff in the company. Even though HR and every VP told them this rumor was not true, the people in the company still wanted a meeting to ask me directly. They knew if I said there is no layoff then there would not be one. Now you might say they simply wanted to hear it from the top, but I could have lied to them as easily as anyone else.

Once you have this trust there are many things you can get done which many might have thought impossible only months before. At one of the companies I ran there was a union workforce. I was scheduled to meet with people at corporate the next month and so told the union that we had until I left to get the contract done and ratified. Our normal contract was not due to expire until the fall, so this meant we needed to get this done five months early.

Because people now had trust in me, we accomplished the final contract in four days, with a total of 16 hours of work. The union members knew that I was telling the truth and that I was trying to help them by getting this done quickly. Everyone came to the table with an amazingly small list of demands and both sides were willing to negotiate in good faith. The contract was ratified before I left and as a second positive note, the overall summer was more enjoyable for everyone because the stress of contract negotiations had been taken off the table. Trust, as you can see, is well worth having.

From the start, you demanded to be copied on all emails and you will be attending virtually every meeting, regardless of the topic. Even though this may build resentment in the company you must shoulder this and keep moving. You are not only judging the quality of the people but determining if they are accomplishing anything during these meetings. There is not a single aspect of the company you are not involved in and virtually every decision made is by you.

One of the worst reports I ever got was a few weeks after I took over an extremely stressed firm. The report was seven pages long, two pages explaining the problem and why the group was started, two pages covering who was on the committee and what they were working on, and two pages at the end talking about what the group planned to do at some time in the future. There was only one page that explained what they were actively working on and the results being achieved. This by far was the most worthless report I had ever seen. What it did show was that there was lots of activity but little results at the company. This explains why you must be at all the meetings.

I fully understand that initially people will feel there is no point in making a decision since you will judge it and quite possibly change it to what you want anyway. This is ok. In fact, it is better than ok. It is exactly what you want because to mold something you need it in a place where it can be molded. At the same time, you are deciding who to let go and who to keep. This is no small task and will need to be done in phases. For example, you cannot replace your entire senior staff at once because you need certain things done. You will need to make priorities and decide in what order things will get done, but at the same time get it done quickly. You need to always remember that while you are replacing people, the company becomes dysfunctional as people wait to see if they are next.

Building trust in a dysfunctional company is important. Every president before you told the company how they would fix things, how they would make things better, and still the company degraded. They gave, or felt they gave, and the company took and still things are in a mess. They have no reason to believe you or to believe in you. This must change if you are going to sell them on your idea of the future.

I recall a meeting I had with the union early on when the union rep told me my story has been told so many times, he could tell it himself. Why should he or any of his members believe me when everyone else failed? This rep tends to embellish things quite a bit but the essence of what he was saying was true. How do they know that where others failed, you will succeed and, where others made promises they could not keep, if you say it, then it will happen? As I tell all my people in the company anyone is welcome to ask me anything they want, about any topic, and about any area of the company. This would also include my plans. I will answer any question as honestly as I can and will never intentionally lie to anyone. I also tell them to keep in mind that things do change and that the answer I give you today may not be the answer I may give 6 months from now.

Let's face it, everyone wants to keep promises that only glorify good times. You need to tell the company that hard decisions will need to be made and then you need to follow through with them. I fully understand you do not want to scare people because then people may leave, but you cannot use the same soft shoe every president before you used.

Most people try to minimize organizational upset by saying people are moved around to optimize the company and then, when the layoff begins, people walk around wondering how laying off their friends is optimizing the company. They now feel betrayed because what they heard is not what you thought you said. I am sure everyone has been told a hundred times it does not matter what you say. It only matters what was heard.

When you start with the company one of the first questions on everyone's mind, voiced or not, is will there be layoffs. Tell them straight up that you will be evaluating everyone in the company to ensure the company has the right people it needs to move things into the future. You feel they deserve to work with talented people who can turn this company around and make it profitable again. If there are people who cannot achieve this, then you are doing everyone a favor by replacing them with people who can.

You will find that the good people you do have will be happy someone is finally dealing with this and they will be your supporters. People who feel they are not very good at their job will worry they will not have it very much longer. In either case, no one will be surprised when the ax does fall, and very few will be surprised by who you eliminate.

The most important part of this is that you were clear on what was going to happen and how you would make the decision. You then need to execute the decision. You have begun to show your credibility at this point. When you are walking around the building and someone asks you a question, don't try to be cute and explain things in a manner they will not understand. Tell them the truth and say it so they understand without feeling condescended to.

I have seen people respond to a question by using business jargon no one, who had not been to business school, would understand. Are they doing this because they want to look smart or are they doing this because they want to make the person feel dumb? Intelligent people will speak to the level of the person they are talking with. Otherwise you are just bullshitting. Most people know when you are being condescending and will resent you for it. I tell people you might not like what I say but you will always know it is the truth. If you walk around the company today and ask if I tell the truth, the most common answer is never ask me anything you do not want to know because I will give you the truth, whether you like it or not. More important? This "If you don't want the answer don't ask the question" philosophy has to hold true up and down the food chain.

As you move from the authoritarian management style you will need people's support if you have decided to change the direction of the company. Being viewed as honest and trustworthy will become extremely important as you move in some direction. When you reviewed the company, its market, and decided what the future of the company needed to be, these people will become your greatest asset.

Assume that you will be doing more than just working on being a low-cost provider. Assume you plan to move into a different market or create value added products. Then you will need changes in the company. To accomplish this you may need different skill sets than those that currently work at the company. People need to understand why you are making this change and you will need their buy-in to succeed. You will be selling a vision to them — the direction you see the company going to. You need them to buy into your vision, so they are willing to devote energy to help get you where you need to be. You can clean up the company almost completely on your own, but you need the people behind you if you have any chance in fulfilling your vision of the future. This means you need to be able to articulate your vision in such a way that your employees can see what you see.

They need to be able to reach out and touch what you are selling, make it part of who they are, and embrace it as though it was their own. Since the biggest part of what you will be selling is hope, they need to see you as the one who is going to make this hope into a reality. The only way this can happen is if they believe in you and believe you can fulfill the promises, they hear you talking about. If you look at televangelists or talk show personalities people, follow them because they are filling a void that people have in their lives. You are doing exactly the same thing once you have decided on a direction for the company and present it to the organization. They want to believe, they have the need to believe, but have been lied to so often they are afraid to believe.

In the end they will first believe in you and, after some time, will believe in your vision, your future, and your dream. They need to see you as the person who is not afraid of the future, has a plan on how to get there, and every day they can see you are progressing towards this future. They need to see you win, small battles at first, and then larger ones so they know they have the alpha leader and you can make things happen.

Once they begin to believe, they will endorse your replacement of people since they can fully understand why it was needed. There will be very little resentment, and many will openly endorse the changes. They will see that you systematically went through the company and replaced everyone who was not contributing to the future of the company.

You will be looking at three very specific areas while reviewing the people you have. The first area will be to review who has contributed to the company, as a whole, over the years. Are they working on making the company better or were they only looking after themselves? I have found that most people in stressed companies are more interested in themselves than they are in the company. This is one of the reasons why the company failed to begin with. These people need to go.

The second thing you will be looking for are people capable of helping you move the company forward. To find them you must have a very clear vision of where the company is going. Are you going after cost reduction, expanding the existing market, or expanding into new markets? Each of these requires different talents so you need to make these decisions very early in your tenure in the company.

The third thing you are looking for is enthusiasm, and we covered this in great detail. If your more senior staff has no enthusiasm for the company and its future, then they must go. It does not matter how good or important they think they are. It is extremely important that you decide where the company is going very early because this will dictate who you need.

People who are very good at cutting costs will specialize in just-in-time manufacturing, finding waste, getting more output from both the equipment and people on staff. On the other end of the spectrum if you want to expand into a new market you need talent that knows how to break into new markets, how to market your product, how to position your product, and how to make an entry into the market in the shortest amount of time.

Clearly, these are not the same type of people. For example, if you choose someone who specializes in market entry when your plan is to reduce costs, it is a not only a waste of the company's money, but it is also a waste of time for you and the person you hired. Remember, the only thing you have less of than cash is time so making the right decisions are crucial.

I cannot stress this enough; you cannot turn a company around completely on your own. You must find the right people to help you move forward. To get to the right person for a specific position may require hiring a fire fighter first, then replacing that person with someone else. Firefighters never work out long term but can work wonders to make changes quickly and turn something around very quickly. You can always tell when you need to replace firefighter because they will begin looking at other departments and telling them how to do their job. Your other department managers will be in your office every day complaining about this fire fighter. This is your signal it is time to replace them.

The person they are replaced with, though, needs to be your long-term person. Replacing people creates dysfunction and trepidation in the company so you do not want to have a revolving door for the same position. Do not worry about the timing because it will be obvious to you when the time is right to make this move. They came to you with pride and dignity and they should leave the same way. Always remember the importance of this. Your job is not to break people but, rather, to use their talents. When and if the time comes to release them, let them go with the same pride and respect they came to you with.

Once you have the right people in the right places, you will begin to teach them how to make good decisions. This also means you must begin to get your ego in check and realize that just because their decision is not the same as yours does not make it a bad decision. This is why I have stressed not to focus on the final decision but to focus on how they reached this decision.

This is where most people go wrong. They only focus on the final decision and if they feel it was a good decision. If you focus on how that decision was made, then by default the final decision will be a good one. This will also ensure that you do not fall into the "only good decision is my decision," because once people realize that you will criticize any decision that is different than the one you would have made, they will stop thinking. Your goal is to teach them how to think, not to encourage them to stop thinking. This is also a good way for you to ensure that you are giving them the information they need to make a good decision. If not, then why?

You need your people to be making decisions in the company so you can slowly release control of the company and began relying on them to run the company. If you are fighting all the issues in the company every day, then you are not working on the bigger problem of direction and future of the company as a whole. People who say they can do both are crazy because no one can. You can either be strategically thinking about the future or you can be fighting all the fires in the company, not both.

Regardless of whether you plan on saving the company by becoming the low-cost provider or you plan to enter new markets, there is a great deal of strategic thinking to be done. What will it take to become the low-cost provider? Will you need to automate the factory, need new equipment, reduce scrap, or a million other issues. There will be piles of data that need to be reviewed so you can plot the course the company needs to take.

On the other hand, if you plan to move into new markets, then you must decide which one, why did you pick it, what will the entry point be, who will your competition be, and why do you think you can compete against them? The point is that no matter what direction you pick you need to keep looking at the big picture. This means you must rely on your people to take care of the details.

It should be obvious that your management style needs to shift where you are giving up control, delegating more, and supporting the decisions your people are making. The teams you started, and were active in, will be shifting as well. They are no longer trying to find ways to keep enough cash flowing into the company but are now looking at how to improve different areas of the company. They will be looking at how to improve the product you make or how to make the product you need to entire the new market.

This really is the point where you will need to ensure people are solving issues completely and taking responsibility. When things begin to turn around I often find people stop solving solutions completely. They seem to get the problem solved 80% of the way and then move on. I have never really understood this. Do they feel overwhelmed or just feel cocky? Unfortunately, it does happen, and you need to watch for it. It is easy to miss because, when you started, problems were being solved 100% and so it is easy to assume that this would continue to happen, but at some point, normally about the time you are on the upswing, this stops. This is one of the reasons you will have quality or yield teams running. All too often manufacturing quality improvements fix symptoms of failure rather than the root cause. This can be done by adding quality inspection steps or rework stations that make it more efficient to fix defects. Instead, a true understanding of root cause should be developed within the teams.

This book would not be complete if we did not talk about you and three things you need to answer:

1) Are you cut out to do this?
2) Are you prepared to stand alone while the company is evolving?
3) Once the company is profitable are you the right person to grow it?

If you already specialize in turning companies around then I hope you have found some new insights and thoughts you might be able to use to improve your skills. There are many books about management, manufacturing, sales, quality, etc. However, I have never seen a cookbook for turning a company around in which you can get answers for all these things needed to do so. It is also rare to find a book written by someone who has actually done the work rather than by someone who has written a book based on studies.

My environmental health and safety officer sent me link a few weeks ago to a YouTube presentation that an individual had put together. The video was not his entire presentation, he charged for that, but just 15 minutes on how to motivate people. The clip was interesting and obvious that he had a packed house. It seems everyone is looking for the next best thing to motivate their people.

I asked my EHS person to look him up and send me the list of companies he had worked at because I wanted to see what people he had worked with had to say. A few hours later I got an email telling me he could not find any company this person had ever worked for. So while the YouTube clip was interesting how much of what he was selling had ever been proven to work? How much did he just make up because it would sell out a room of people?

If turning a company around is something you have thought of doing, this book gives you a well-rounded picture of what it takes and the work that is involved. All presidents work long hours and have an incredible amount of stress but people who choose to turn a company around have even more. When people look at me with disbelief when I say this, I give them a simple scenario:

You have two motorcycles. One is brand new with all the parts you need laid out in front of you along with directions on how to put it together. Next to it is a 50-year-old beat up motorcycle with parts scattered everywhere. You have no idea if all the parts needed to build the bike are there. To make matters worse there are no directions and the make of the bike is unknown so you cannot go online and download a diagram. If the old bike is missing parts, where do you find replacement parts and how do you know which bolt goes where, other than it simply will not fit? How many parts will look just fine until you put them in a container of cleaner and you find out that, after the rust is removed, the part is defective and will never work? Given enough time both bikes can be assembled and will work, but which will be easier to assemble, and which will keep you up at night?

So now you have to ask yourself: are you ready to stand alone knowing many people in the company, along with the board, lack 100% faith in you and your ability? All of them have heard many promises from many people and all of them failed. You will need thick skin, be willing to take criticism, disbelief, and quite a bit of push back from both people in the company and the board. You will need to manage both groups, who will be struggling. The board wants things fixed, and as hard as it is to believe, change never entered their minds. When they think change they are thinking you will fix sales, thus fixing the company. The reason why I really do not bother much with how to fix sales is because that is exactly what everyone before you did. You know this failed and is why you are here. If things in the company do not work properly, then fixing sales is a waste of time.

There are some constants in business. Ask a salesperson how to increase sales and they will always say the same thing: improve quality, decrease price, keep plenty of stock, and then they can sell your product. I don't care what industry you are in. Sales will always make the same statement. When I was working for a high technology OEM our salespeople would say we were too expensive, quality was lacking, and our delivery was too long to enable them to close deals.

Now that I am in the food industry, my salespeople tell me our quality is below industry, our price is higher than anyone else, and we don't have the right product in stock. If any of this was true, then why are we selling to very large accounts who are not complaining? Why is it that I can pick an account, same price, same quality, and same lead time, but I can close it and the regular salesperson could not? I had always thought there must be a "Sales Excuse Manual" out there somewhere with three phrases in it, one per page. I have come to realize that salespeople in general are a dime a dozen, but good salespeople are rarer than gold.

Obviously, you will have to fix sales, but what is the point until you have the rest of the company working? This is what the board will struggle with because you are here to repair the company and make it functional again, not put a Band-Aid on things. The Band-Aid is why it is in the shape it is in to begin with. This is the very reason why this book is called "The Long Game" because, when you are done, this company will be healthy and ready to grow.

Most of your employees gave up long ago and will feel they just need to outlive you, just as they did the people before you. It will eventually dawn on them that you are serious when they begin to see your direct reports disappear, you are directly running most meetings, and you have taken over virtually every aspect of the company.

Sometimes you can make this happen quickly and sometimes it takes more time.

At one company I met with all of the VP's as a group so we could get to know each other. They went around the table but when one of the VP's told me I was not qualified to run the company I dismissed him on the spot. The rest of the team and then the entire company knew changes were coming. They did not know what, but they knew my approach would be unlike anything they had seen from the previous presidents. The faster you can send this message the easier it will be for you long term. It is one thing to say change is coming and quite another when they see it happen. To fire someone within 30 minutes of arriving at the company sends a clear unambiguous statement that you have arrived, and things will change.

Other companies took longer, and you just never know how long because, no matter how much you plan, there is always the unexpected that happens once in a while. Sometimes good, sometimes bad, but you need to be ready for it. I always think of the unexpected like cleaning the couch at home where you never know what you will find when you lift the cushions up. You could find anything from a few quarters to moldy broccoli. The question is not so much what you find but what you do next and how you view the moment. You can look at the moldy broccoli and be disgusted or you can smile, spray some disinfectant on the area and know you just got rid of both a bad smell and the potential for illness. In both cases, the moldy produce gets tossed out, but in one case you don't realize the good that came your way and in the other you do. As you work your way through the company you need to not only toss the bad people out, but you must also find ways to take what is left and make something good with it.

If you get rid of your CFO and half the finance team, you can either walk away thinking how much work it will be to rebuild this group or you can come to understand this now gives you the opportunity to really organize the P&L the way you want it to look. People need to see this positive attitude from you throughout the organization.

The final question to be answered is what comes next? You have now spent two to four years getting your company healthy, profitable and ready to grow, so what is next? Most people look at me with confusion when I discuss this topic. Their response is after I worked my ass off for the past several years and now I just need to grow the company and perform maintenance, why is there is any question of what is next?

There are two answers to this question since some people who are good at turning a company around are not always good at growing a company. The other reason is that many people who turn companies around grow bored when the work is done and will find things to break just so they have something to do.

This should sound familiar by now. Many people who turn companies around are the ultimate fire fighter on steroids, working on a grand scale. Don't get me wrong. There are many differences such as strategic thinking that good turn-around people have, and most basic firefighters do not. Basic fire fighters live in the moment and really don't think beyond getting the current issue resolved. Thinking two to four years down the road is simply beyond most firefighter's ability. There are many similarities between people who specialize in turnarounds and firefighters. We both like the adrenaline rush, we both like the hunt, and we both like the pressure of the moment.

You have trained your people to think, how to run a company without you, how to make good decisions, and have found a market that your company can grow. Now you wonder what your purpose is in the company and should you now leave it.

For those of you that have children you know this feeling. When your children started school you were going crazy taking them to soccer practice, track practice, swimming, and all the other activities they were involved in. They begin to drive and even though you are not taking them everywhere, you are now hosting their friends, going to games, and trying hard to stay part of their lives. Then they head for college and suddenly you have your entire evening for just you and your significant other. The first few days, maybe a week or two, both of you are delighted and talk about all the things you plan to do with this free time. You relax with a glass of wine and then somewhere during your second glass of wine it dawns on both of you that even with all things you can now do, things that were put on hold for the sake for the children, you are still going to have massive amounts of time with nothing to do. You shrug your shoulders thinking something will come along, but after a few weeks having completed your impressive list you look at each other and say "crap, now what?"

For years, you ran as fast as you could to stay ahead of everything, thinking two to four years ahead to ensure everything was in place so there were never any hiccups as the company moved forward. One day it dawns on you that your people really don't need you like they did, the company is running smoothly, like you planned, and everything you worked so hard to put into place is running like clockwork. Now the company needs someone to do the maintenance and start the next phase of the company.

The company needs a more traditional president who is concerned about plant efficiency, maximizing profits, and the best way to maneuver in the markets you moved the company into. This is a completely different skill set than what you have been doing for the past several years and you need to decide if you can make this transition or if you need to go find your next conquest.

There are some people who are capable of making this transition and they get to enjoy the fruits of their work, switching from the fixer to the grower. You have to decide if you are one of them because, if you tell yourself you are and in reality you are not, the company will suffer. Everything you worked to do will begin to fall apart right before your eyes. The first sign will be your best person will resign because they will feel that you are trying to take over their job because you are bored.

As I stated on the onset of this book, I called this The Long Game because this is not about a quick fix to maximize a company to be sold. This is about taking time, taking that old motorcycle and, with love and devotion, transforming it into something solid. You have to be willing to put in long hours and become proficient at many areas in the company but when you are done and look back at your work you know, beyond a shadow of a doubt, that this company, the company you just turned around, has had new life breathed into it and is ready for the future.

And you made it happen.

CHAPTER 14

Finale

I tried to write this book less like a book and more like we were sitting over coffee, talking about a job one of us just took. After reading the last chapter, I felt like I had gotten up to pay the bill and walked out on you so I wanted to try and sum up a few key thoughts.

So, what have we really learned about turning a company around? I think first and foremost it is not for everyone. You need to be willing to work very long hours and have very thick skin. You also need to understand that at the beginning of the endeavor you will stand alone, with virtually everyone against you. This means you need to be very self-confident about what you are doing and your ability to be successful.

You need to understand that turning a company around is quite a bit like getting your pool up and running in the spring. You need to shock it first and then slowly get into a routine. Companies are no different in that they have sat for years slowly going downhill with people who have accepted whatever fate lies in front of them. They are hoping for a Hail Mary but, when it comes, will fight it. This does not make sense, but it is true. Over the years I have given this a great deal of thought and have concluded that people might want the company, their job, to be saved, but never envisioned it would require change and commitment from them. Like so many things in life, everyone else is the problem, but not me....

We have also covered that when you start you will most likely rely on fear, but knowing this is very short-lived driver, and that you need to start working on plans on how to move from fear to a more sustainable emotion among employees from day one. You are not going to move from fear to respect in one step so do not bother trying. Respect is what you will work towards but, depending on the person, will most likely move from fear to indifference and finally to respect.

During the early phases of the project you will be evaluating everyone from director and above to determine who is salvageable and who needs to be replaced. You most likely will have three lists that everyone will go on and you must be brutally honest with yourself as to which list they are on. The "must go" and "stay" lists are easy. The one every person struggles with is the "maybe" list. The easiest way of answering this question is asking if this person worked directly for you would you be willing to put effort and energy into them. If you say yes then ask yourself would they bring enough to the party to have made the effort worth it? If the answer is no then put them on the must go list.

We talked about you needing to strategically think about the future of the company, virtually from the day you arrive. The reason for this is you need to ensure you hire the right people who can not only can help now but also have the right skill sets to help move the company into the future. It takes a completely different skill set to streamline a company than it does to reinvent a company so, depending on where you are going, you need to bring in the right skills.

We also discussed that as the company moves from a stressed company to a company that has a future your skill set will also need to change. You will go from being a dictator to a situational manger. This means you are what is needed at the time it is needed and will manage people in a way that gets the best out of. You have adjusted to them not the other way around.

Finally, why is this all worth it? Well, because you get to create something, something you and only you envisioned and then brought to fruition. Over time when you look back on the companies you ran and see they are still alive and well you can take pride that they are healthy because of the work you did and the effort you put forth.

For me, at the end of the day, gives me a sense of accomplishment I can find no other place. Therefore, I do it and I hope this is why you will take this on yourself.

Acknowledgments

The world is a better place thanks to people who take the time and energy it takes to turn a company around rather than just closing it. What makes it even better are spouses who put up with the long hours because they know their loved ones are helping other people. Not only has Linda, my wife, put up with the long hours but she was always there to listen when I came home frustrated. Linda, more than anyone, deserves credit for the success I have had over the years. She has always been there, providing a sounding board when needed and to offer advice when asked.

She spent days reading this book to ensure the editor got the best of what I could produce. Guys, this is true love. Even after 32 years of marriage your wife still wants her husband to look good and is willing to lose sleep helping him do just that. Thank you.

To Jerry Behne who felt I had a different way of leading people and felt this was something others could learn from. He talked me into writing this book and was always there with encouragement every time I felt like quitting. I used many colorful adjectives about him during the writing phase but want to thank him now that it is done.

I really need to thank Peter Scherb who I met in the late '80s and was beyond a doubt the worst manager I had ever had. Over time he worked on his skills and I can honestly say that when we parted in the late '90s he was the best manager I have ever worked for to this day. He not only worked on his skills but put an unbelievable amount of effort in me. To this day I have no idea why he believed in me but will be ever grateful he did.

I can honestly say writing this book was one of the hardest things I have ever done and owe my editor Nancy LaFever immense gratitude for being patient with me. (Aw, shucks, that's nice!) I am not a born writer so without her heavy lifting, this book would never have made it to a publisher. Thank you.

I would love to hear from all the readers who found this book helpful. Please contact me through LinkedIn and let me hear your thoughts.

Rod Moore

About the Author

Rod Moore is an Executive with proven international experience in the manufacturing industry. Over the past 20+ years he has helped many companies evolve from a position of failure to success. He has worked in the US, Europe and Asia which has provided a broad foundation in knowing what works to make companies profitable, regardless of where in the world they are.

His strength and competencies include leadership and management of both union / non-union shops. He has the ability to drive both performance and customer's market growth that, in turn, drives corporate growth. Using this mindset he has guided companies to substantially increase sales, improve profit, reduce delivery times and manufacturing costs.

Since results are a team effort, Rod takes care to ensure the entire organization is moving together with clear objectives and available resources. He motivates people, helping them see the bigger picture and their critical part of it. At the same time, by applying his strategic, operational and technical know-how to solve business problems he has helped companies focus on multi-pronged approaches to growth such as new products development, identification and penetration of new markets, cost reductions.

Over his career Rod has moved from R & D and an engineering background to senior level roles. His technical designs resulted in a number of patents over the years, while his hands-on approach has proven invaluable when identifying technical problems or the need to create a new out-of-the-box solution. Rod's 'if you don't want to hear the answer don't ask the question' management style is unusual in a world of political correctness, but it definitely achieves positive results for floundering companies.

www.ingramcontent.com/pod-product-compliance
Lightning Source LLC
Chambersburg PA
CBHW060329200326
41519CB00011BA/1876